Taking Kierkegaard Back to Church

Taking Kierkegaard Back to Church

The Ecclesial Implications of the Gospel

AARON P. EDWARDS

CASCADE *Books* · Eugene, Oregon

TAKING KIERKEGAARD BACK TO CHURCH
The Ecclesial Implications of the Gospel

Cascade Books
An Imprint of Wipf and Stock Publishers
199 W. 8th Ave., Suite 3
Eugene, OR 97401

www.wipfandstock.com

PAPERBACK ISBN: 987-1-7252-5958-4
HARDCOVER ISBN: 987-1-7252-5956-0
EBOOK ISBN: 978-1-7252-5957-7

Cataloguing-in-Publication data:

Names: Edwards, Aaron P. (author).

Title: Taking Kierkegaard back to church : the ecclesial implications of the gospel / Aaron P. Edwards.

Description: Eugene, OR: Cascade Books, 2022. | Includes bibliographical references and index.

Identifiers: ISBN: 987-1-7252-5958-4 (paperback). | ISBN: 987-1-7252-5956-0 (hardcover). | ISBN: 978-1-7252-5957-7 (ebook).

Subjects: LSCH: Kierkegaard, Søren, 1813–1855. | Theology. | Church. | Existentialism.

Classification: B4378 K5 E34 2022 (print). | B4378 (ebook).

Permission has been granted to reprint some material from parts of the following previously published articles:

- In chapter 2: Aaron Edwards, "Life in Kierkegaard's Imaginary Rural Parish: Preaching, Correctivity, and the Gospel," *Toronto Journal of Theology* 30.2 (2014) 235–46.

- In chapter 3: Aaron Edwards, "Waddling Geese in the Pulpit: Kierkegaard's Hermeneutics and Preaching," *Theology* 116.3 (2012) 80–89.

- In chapter 4: Aaron Edwards, "A Broken Engagement: Reassessing Barth's Relationship to Kierkegaard on the Grounds of Subjectivity and Preaching," *International Journal of Systematic Theology* 16.1 (2014) 56–78.

- In chapter 6: Aaron Edwards, "Kierkegaard as Socratic Street Preacher? Reimagining the Dialectic of Direct and Indirect Communication for Christian Proclamation," *Harvard Theological Review* 110.2 (2017) 280–300.

- In chapter 7: Aaron Edwards, "Thrill of the Chaste: The Pursuit of 'Love' as the Perpetual Dialectic between the 'Real' and the 'Ideal Image' in Kierkegaard's 'The Seducer's Diary,'" *Literature and Theology* 30.1 (2016) 15–32.

- In chapter 8: Aaron Edwards, "Taking the 'Single Individual' back to Church? The Possibility of a Kierkegaardian Ecclesiology," *Theology Today* 72.4 (2016) 431–46.

Contents

Preface

KIERKEGAARD WAS HEARTILY AMUSED by the modern fashion for writing prefaces before books. So much so, in fact, that he decided to write a satirical book composed entirely of prefaces to books that didn't actually exist. "Writing a preface," he said, "is like ringing someone's doorbell to trick him."[1] I think he means by this that, in writing a preface, one seems to be saying something important but is really saying nothing at all, and more than likely intends to distract the reader from doing something more important, like reading a book. I confess that I sometimes read prefaces hoping to find something more interesting than what the book-in-itself has to offer, hoping perhaps to stumble across something a little more off-guard, a little less functional, ideally attached to some intriguing time-bound date such as "Bonfire Night" or "Pentecost Sunday," even when such dates do not seem immediately relevant to anything in particular.

For all his satirical playfulness, Kierkegaard quite obviously valued prefaces. One of the reasons he enjoyed writing them (which also included the writing of prefaces *of* prefaces, naturally!) is that they enabled him to highlight to the cultured milieu of his time that the things we often think are the least important—the preliminary matters we wish to breeze past—are quite often the most important of all.[2] Indeed, in our hurried agitation to "get to the point," in our impatient refusal to stop along the way, we might miss the *real* point of our journey, as both the Priest and the Levite may testify. In the case of this particular preface, I'm not sure what wisdom it may have to offer to this end. But I'm glad if it offered you a brief respite before the supposed "proper" work begins. However, if

1. Kierkegaard, *Prefaces* and *Writing Sampler*, 5.
2. Kierkegaard, *Prefaces* and *Writing Sampler*, 73, 90.

you've begun to read this preface aright, then I hope you'll see that such work already *has* begun, as I'm sure Kierkegaard would agree.

I'm still not quite sure how I became a Kierkegaard scholar. It was something of a happy accident. But one of the primary reasons I remain interested in Kierkegaard is that he still seems to be saying things others have dared not to say, or if they tried to say them, they could not dream of saying them as arrestingly or as painstakingly as he seems to have done. His words, it seems, are particularly relevant to the contemporary situation of the individual, the Church, and the academy, for reasons this book hopes to have shown. Indeed, it sometimes seems as though Kierkegaard's words had dropped out of the sky for this very moment. Yet I suspect this is precisely how most generations of Kierkegaard readers have felt at various times.

I recall one of the first books on Kierkegaard I had ever read, my wife and I were typical newlyweds, struggling to make ends meet on our combined part-time wages from a coffee shop and a toy shop. Most of my early Kierkegaard reading—including some of the secondary literature I engage with in this book—was first read either on a lunch break at that coffee shop, or late into the evening in the company of a muffin or panini that was past its sell-by date. One evening, I was sat trying to read an essay in one of the excellent KRSRR volumes, on Kierkegaard's reading of how the birds and the lilies of Matthew 6 teach us not to be anxious. I recall that I kept circling around the same cluster of words for what seemed like an hour, barely taking in what I was reading. I was incessantly distracted because we had completely run out of money that week, and literally couldn't afford to buy any food. We had gotten used to relying on the "reduction" items at our local mini-supermarket, without which we couldn't afford to eat properly. However, in the preceding weeks these reductions—which had been our "manna"—seemed to have disappeared, either sold out whenever we happened to get there, or of little use to us when we did. We'd been back dozens of times in recent days to no avail, and there didn't seem to be any better strategy on the horizon.

With all this playing on my mind, I again tried to struggle along with the academic book before me, about this peculiar Danish theologian talking about birds and lilies. Then, of course, it struck me, and I don't mind saying that I fully believe that it was God speaking to me in that moment, essentially to say: "Have you tried my servant, Kierkegaard?" I realized that to listen to Kierkegaard at *that* moment actually meant to stop reading, and—despite the dubiously late hour of the night—to walk to the mini-supermarket "in faith." On arrival, it was difficult to contain the joy in my soul as I saw a reductions shelf absolutely brimming with all sorts of culinary treasures, all at an unprecedented 90 percent off! My basket, like that of the disciples, was literally overflowing. To top it all off, as I got to the checkout, I was told that it had just gone past a certain time of night and so all the items now needed to be *further* reduced to 97 percent off! It was very nearly the most literal fulfilment of Isaiah's promise: "And he who has no money, come, buy and eat! Come, buy wine and milk without money and without price" (Isa 55:1)! I believe that story, in its own way, has more than a little to do with what it means to read Kierkegaard, if we allow ourselves the ears to hear.

As for *this* academic book, thanks are especially due to those who made sacrifices so that it could be written. For the most part, this is my wife, Molly, now a full-time homemaker to our five young children, and no doubt feeling as though she still works in a toy shop most of the time. She has been an incalculable blessing to us all in more ways than I could ever express. As for the writing of this book, she has endured many late nights where I have been scribbling away at a book or tapping away at a laptop. Our ever-blooming bouquet of children, too, continue to be a relentless delight, and their considerable energies during daytime hours are at least part of the reason why much of this book has been written at such ungodly hours of the night.

I expect I would never have been able to get nearly as far with Kierkegaard had it not been for the generosity of the Hong Kierkegaard Library at St. Olaf College, Northfield, Minnesota, where I had a memorable summer fellowship back in 2012. This now seems like several lifetimes ago, but the memories of warm fellowship and enlivening conversation with many great minds—in person and in print—remain precious; much of what was planted during that time continues to bear fruit, especially in this book. I have also appreciated the opportunity to share various papers on Kierkegaard over the years at the annual conferences of The Society for the Study of Theology, The American Academy of Religion, and The Søren Kierkegaard Research Centre in Copenhagen, many of which were embryonic versions of the chapters of this book.

Kierkegaard's journals have probably been my friendliest companion in getting to know Kierkegaard's thought. They are significant because they offer a way into his thinking in a slightly less encumbered way to some of his more dense and/or ironical published works within the "proper" authorship. In Kierkegaard's journals we see him experimenting

with ideas and forms of texts which he was or wasn't planning to pub-
lish, and airing his views on all manner of curious topics, prefatory or
otherwise. Although the extensive *KJN* editions of the journals are now
available, I confess I have not yet migrated away from my first love of the
Hongs' *Journals and Papers*. I'm sure I will have to move house at some
point, and there is much more to be discovered in the comprehensiveness
of the *KJN*. However, at least for the purposes of this book, it seemed
more consistent to remain loyal to the editions which had already contributed to the research for the majority of the chapters.

Although many of the chapters of this book have emerged from
previously published papers and articles, most have been significantly
revised and expanded, as well as the addition of much completely new
material. Each paper I have written on Kierkegaard tends to have grown
out of a stray footnote from the previous one, and thus, in re-welding
these papers together, I do not see this as a disconnected collection of
essays conveniently bunched together under a catchall title. Each chapter,
though certainly addressing distinct topics rather than advancing a wholly systematic argument, has been remolded to fit the remit of the book:
to illuminate Kierkegaard's thought with regard to the role of the Gospel
in the life of the Church. It is not, then, a fully-fledged ecclesiology but
rather a cluster of unified engagements centering on Kierkegaard's kerygmatic contributions to the Church, in terms of what the Gospel appropriately *implies* for Church and individual before the world. I hope that
such spotlighting of Kierkegaard's thought on these important issues will
prove to contribute to ecclesiological reflection within—and hopefully
beyond—Kierkegaard scholarship.

Far from having no love for the Church, this book hopes to show
how Kierkegaard—who very nearly became a Church pastor himself—
had many incisive and insightful things to say about the use and abuse of
the Gospel within and from the Church. By imagining what a Kierkegaardian pastorate might have looked like, and by engaging Kierkegaard's
diagnoses of all that was going wrong with the Church of his own day, it
is hoped that readers are able to catch various glimpses of the radical-yet-
nuanced way he sought to apply the truth of the Gospel amid the various challenges introduced by the Danish instantiation of Christendom.
Indeed, as the latter chapters argue particularly, the "concept" of Christendom could resurface in different ways throughout the Church's life,
rendering Kierkegaard's caveated ecclesiological contributions directly

applicable to the "post-Christendom" Church, which might have otherwise believed itself to be "safe" from his gadfly attacks.

Aaron P. Edwards
The Seventh Day of Advent, 2020
(a little after two o'clock in the morning)

I

On Kierkegaard's Evangelical "Reputation"

A Kerygmatic Introduction

CHRISTIAN CHURCHGOERS COULD BE forgiven for wondering what on earth a thinker such as Søren Kierkegaard could ever have to do with them. The first time I ever heard the name "Kierkegaard" was, somewhat appropriately, in the context of absurdism. I was sitting in an undergraduate English literature seminar, listening to my tutor—a brilliant and polemical atheist—who was talking about this exotic-sounding Scandinavian as one of the great forebears of absurdist and existentialist thought. I might have taken no further notice but that I remember him casually adding that this exotic Scandinavian was "a profound Christian, albeit a very depressed one." The tutor then went on to talk about all these other famous atheists of the modern era—Sartre, Camus, Derrida, Foucault et al.—whose systems of thought were apparently unimaginable without the influence of the Melancholy Dane. I was somewhat intrigued that this enigmatic Christian thinker was somehow the intellectual grandfather for all their philosophical mischief which seemed so irreconcilable with the Christian faith. Naturally, I assumed that if Kierkegaard even was a Christian, he was likely a fairly uncommitted one. "Perhaps," I thought, "Kierkegaard was just one of those people who had grown up in a Christian culture, who appreciated the social stability of Christian rituals and services but who himself had experienced very little of what it meant to truly follow Christ in and against this world on a personal level." For those who know a little more about Kierkegaard than I did at the time, a wry smile can be the only suitable response to such an absurd conception of Kierkegaard's Christian faith given the fact that almost the precise opposite was the case.

Such an ironically mistaken judgment of Kierkegaard's Christian convictions, whether from Christians or atheists, is surprisingly common. Kierkegaard has always been a tricky thinker to deal with, refusing to sit neatly into any box into which he appears to have leapt, before sliding out the other side into another before you've realized where he is. James Collins, in the preface to the thirtieth-anniversary edition of his 1953 book, *The Mind of Kierkegaard*, referred to Kierkegaard's authorship as "this literary and religious Hobbitland" in which it was fascinating to delve, but not the most fashionable place to stay.[1] As Jacques Collette noted, in the postmodernist heyday of the 1960s, "Kierkegaard is neither Saint nor great theologian," but a somewhat "obstructive teacher."[2] Truly, it would seem, if Kierkegaard was ever going to be received as a substantial theological blessing to the Church, he could only be so with a fair amount of heavily qualified caveats. This opening chapter will introduce the primary themes of the book by discussing some of Kierkegaard's various reputational misdemeanors, working *backward* (as Kierkegaard sometimes liked to do) through the relativistic, postmodern, and post-evangelical interpretations, to the missionary and kerygmatic heart of Kierkegaard's thought which accentuates precisely how important Kierkegaard's voice remains for the Church.

Kierkegaard as Relativist, Postmodern, or Evangelical?

Because of the mystical elusiveness of Kierkegaard's authorship, particularly his use of multiple pseudonyms, it has often been easier for the anti-theist to claim him for their own deconstructive or existentialist purposes, and for the Evangelical Christian to claim Kierkegaard's liabilities for precisely the same reasons.

The "Relativist" Kierkegaard?

The most notable negative reading of this kind was Francis Schaeffer, who was possibly the most influential Evangelical voice of his generation,

1. Collins, *Mind of Kierkegaard*, vii. One imagines, of course, how delighted Kierkegaard would be to be classed as in some sense unfashionable. To be so, it seems, was the very epitome of his theological approach.

2. Collette, *Kierkegaard*, 24.

and who had at one time questioned whether or not Kierkegaard was even a "real" Christian at all.[3] Although Schaeffer later revised his view and came to see the value of Kierkegaard's devotional writings, he nonetheless saw Kierkegaard's thought as an essential separation between faith and reason. According to Schaeffer, the existentialist "turn" catalyzed by Kierkegaard's thought led directly to the many erosions to objective truth against which Schaeffer was himself contending in the mid- to late twentieth century.

In Schaeffer's own mission to respond to the great challenges facing the cause of the Gospel within his generation, he not only saw Kierkegaard's project as an unhelpful hindrance but as the actual cause of the whole mess. Schaeffer's interpretative schemas of thought were sometimes depicted through intriguing (if somewhat bizarre) arrowed diagrams depicting the trickle-down impact of particular thinkers upon the fissures within modern culture and society. Within one such diagram Kierkegaard sits, unmistakably and unforgettably, near the very "top" of the tree, complete with a set of dotted steps cascading down to the Sheol-lands of modern despair. There is no question that, for Schaeffer, Kierkegaard had inadvertently opened up a great pandora's box that terminated in what he called "the escape from reason,"[4] with all manner of terrible implications for the propagation and reception of Christianity in the modern world.

As much as Schaeffer later admitted that Kierkegaard would not have approved of this legacy, it was a deed that could not be undone. When making such an evaluation, however, it is difficult to know precisely how much of Kierkegaard's works Schaeffer had actually read firsthand, and how much was gleaned from secondary interpretations. For example, one of Schaeffer's key philosophical mentors, Cornelius Van Til, wrote a letter to Schaeffer in 1969 in which he noted, "None of the great modern philosophers, like Descartes, Kant, Hegel or Kierkegaard and others, have ever spoken of the God who is there. The systems of thought of these men represent a repression of the revelation of the God who is there."[5] Such a sweeping condemnation of Kierkegaard's theological value calls into question whether even Van Til had read all that much Kierkegaard, let alone Schaeffer. Kyle Roberts, in his aptly subtitled essay, "Francis Schaeffer: How not to Read Kierkegaard" (2012), even queried whether

---

3. Schaeffer, *God Who Is There*, 22.

4. Schaeffer, *Escape From Reason*.

5. Van Til, "Letter from Cornelius Van Til to Francis Schaeffer."

Schaeffer had read any Kierkegaard texts *at all*. This is especially because there are actually some substantive commonalities between Kierkegaard and Schaeffer in their approaches to the role of faith in accessing truth.[6]

Despite Schaeffer's latterly modified perspective on Kierkegaard's positive devotional Christian legacy, the negative headline on Kierkegaard's dubiously "Christian" value continued to be hugely influential upon a generation of Evangelicals. Kierkegaard was ultimately seen as "the key to modernity's self-destruction and to the undermining of a Christian world-view."[7] Even to this day, it is not uncommon to see eyebrows raised at the mention of Kierkegaard's name within Evangelical churches, denominations, and seminaries. Although many recognize the intensity of Kierkegaard's Christian piety, thanks in part to a consistent stream of theological appropriation of his thought over subsequent decades,[8] his philosophical musings on subjectivity continue to taint him as being somewhat untrustworthy vis-à-vis doctrinal orthodoxy, and of little help in counteracting the challenges of postmodernism to Christian thought and action today.

Schaeffer, of course, was not alone in his suspicion of Kierkegaard's less-than-ideal virtue as a thinker in and for the good of the Church. In the twentieth century, in which Kierkegaard ultimately made his proper "entrance" into the theological mainstream, most theologians and philosophers grappling with him still tended to hold him at arm's length. He was certainly not without his ardent admirers, particularly amid the massively influential German-speaking theologians like Karl Barth, Rudolf Bultmann, Emil Brunner, Helmut Thielicke, Paul Tillich, and Dietrich Bonhoeffer, each of whom were especially receptive to his theological contributions, at least initially. However, even when Kierkegaard seemed to form the central thrust to some of their theological endeavors, it was almost always piecemeal, and there were always plenty of Kierkegaardian bones to be spat out along the way.[9] Very rarely was Kierkegaard's authorship examined and appropriated in its entirety or according to its

---

6. Roberts, "Francis Schaeffer," 181–85.

7. Roberts, "Francis Schaeffer," 182.

8. Early examples of such positive theological appropriations include Gouwens, *Kierkegaard as a Religious Thinker*, and Walsh, *Thinking Christianly in an Existential Mode*.

9. For a representative example regarding Barth's reception of Kierkegaard, see chapter 4. On Kierkegaard's wider theological influence, see Barrett, "Kierkegaard's Theological Legacy," 159–74.

overarching theological vision. Kierkegaard was almost always used "to an extent" in light of some other pressing concern.

This somewhat half-measured approach to Kierkegaard's theological emphases was ironic in itself given Kierkegaard's critique of Christendom as only wanting relationship with God—and many other things—"to a certain degree."[10] Although the various partial readings of Kierkegaard are understandable given the stylistic range and scope of his authorship, they have contributed to various misunderstandings as to what he did or did not believe, and to the ambiguous reception he continues to receive in the Church to this day. Where, though, does the postmodern and/ or existentialist Kierkegaard come from? Does it not at least have *some* legitimacy?

The "Postmodern" Kierkegaard?

The most obvious justification for Kierkegaard as a "post"-modern thinker would seem to be his trenchant critiques of "modern" rationalism. This occurred particularly via the appropriated thought of the colossally significant G. W. F. Hegel, and his Danish followers such as Hans Latten Martensen, one of Kierkegaard's early theological tutors.[11] Indeed, one of the reasons Kierkegaard might come across to the likes of Francis Schaeffer as being quasi-relativistic, is because he was attempting to deal with the significant overreaches of reason enabled by the vast "system" of Danish Hegelianism. For Kierkegaard, this was a system which seemed too neat, too all-encompassing, too comprehensive in scope to account for the reality of the individual, or even the reality of reality. It was a complex framework of idealistic speculation which imposed itself upon the world, upon the individual, upon reality itself. Within this system, God's very being became inseparable from the world-historical process, and thus, the divine guarantor of the established sociopolitical order. Hegelianism, at least as Kierkegaard understood it,[12] literally functioned as the philosophical justification for the bourgeois culture of Danish Christendom. Within Hegel's system, everything—including God himself—was a merely objective reality which had no necessary

10. *Søren Kierkegaard's Journals and Papers*, 2:1405, 123.

11. See Thompson, "Hans Latten Martensen," 229–66.

12. For a complex discussion of the nuances on Kierkegaard's reading of Hegel(ianism), see Stewart, *Kierkegaard's Relation to Hegel Reconsidered*.

correspondence with individual subjects. Consequently, this system left no room for human subjectivity, nor paradoxical divine revelation, because such things interfered with the system.[13]

For Kierkegaard, this subsuming of the divine within a worldly system of immanence meant that the actual "practice" of Christianity had become virtually impossible.[14] The Hegelian system had, in a sense, annexed the Christian faith into a kind of hyper-objectivity, a matter of abstract academic speculation, as Kierkegaard notes in his *Concluding Unscientific Postscript*:

> Objective faith—it is indeed as if Christianity had also been proclaimed as a little system of sorts, although presumably not as good as the Hegelian system. It is as if Christ . . . had been a professor and as if the apostles had formed a little professional society of scholars. Truly, if at one time it was difficult to become a Christian, I believe now it becomes more difficult year by year, because it has now become so easy to become one.[15]

Since Hegelian speculative reason had become a kind of deified presence within the Christendom imagination, the possibility of subjective faith was diminished, if not abolished. The hyper-objectivity of the system, though saturated in the idolatry of speculation, led to "not thinking anything decisive about what is most decisive."[16]

This loss of the capability for individual decision left human society (and indeed, the Church) especially vulnerable to crowd-driven ideologies which could impose abstract systems upon reality in dangerous ways. Kierkegaard's intensive awareness of this vulnerability is certainly one of the key catalysts for his positive reception within postmodernity. As Stephen Backhouse notes, in his biography of Kierkegaard:

> A lot of the appeal to writers, poets, public intellectuals, artists, and idiosyncratic historians is Kierkegaard's approach to cultural movements that were defining "the modern age." He is heard to be saying something to the dehumanising nature of mass culture in all its forms, whether it be communism, fascism, or jingoistic patriotism.[17]

13. See especially Kierkegaard, *Concluding Unscientific Postscript*, 189–251.

14. Kierkegaard returns to this theme numerously and variously throughout his authorship. See especially Kierkegaard, *Practice in Christianity*.

15. Kierkegaard, *Concluding Unscientific Postscript*, 215.

16. Kierkegaard, *Concluding Unscientific Postscript*, 217.

17. Backhouse, *Kierkegaard: A Single Life*, 200–201.

That said, to critique heavily the concept of abstract systems and ideologies does not require a full-fledged "postmodern" approach to truth, nor ought such critiques—however vehemently expressed—necessitate the inspiration for methods such as Derridean deconstruction, so revered among postmodernists and so "feared" among Evangelical Christians.[18]

As this book will demonstrate (particularly chapter 4), it is very evident that Kierkegaard's critiques of systematic objectivity, and indeed his prominent emphasis on subjectivity, in no way abdicated the tenets of truth or reason, but are tethered more specifically to the content and practice of Christian proclamation. Indeed, as he reflected on the totality of his authorship, Kierkegaard believed that the suffering he endured throughout his life—particularly from the public—was a suffering "in the service of truth," as God's way of allowing him "to understand the truth."[19] The main difference between Kierkegaard's approach and the respective approaches of relativism and rationalism lies in his stress upon personal receptiveness to the *implications* of objective truth. This entails moving beyond mere objective speculation about abstract concepts— whether historical, doctrinal, philosophical or otherwise—toward allowing oneself to be subjectively shaped *by* the truth in existential decision and action. This is a far cry from absolute rejection of metanarratives, profound distrust of human power/knowledge structures, or radical deconstruction of propositional claims/truths.[20]

---

18. See Smith, *Who's Afraid of Postmodernism?*

19. Kierkegaard, *Point of View*, 25.

20. Many Kierkegaard scholars attempt to rescue the positive value of Derridean deconstruction as a partner to Kierkegaard's authorship, critiquing the usual theological critiques of postmodernism as caricatures, and attempting to place "deconstruction" into a qualitatively separate category to postmodernism. Mjaaland, "Postmodernism and Deconstruction," 96–97; and Shakespeare, "Kierkegaard and Postmodernism," 469–71. In Shakespeare's case, although he offers a nuanced and self-reflective approach with respect to the inbuilt ironies of postmodern (il)logic, his account of deconstruction still involves—precisely as one might expect—the inappropriate imposition of a lens for eliminating binary distinctions per se. Such dialectically non-subsumed binaries, of course, are central to how Kierkegaard thought theologically, particularly vis-à-vis the relationship between time and eternity, God and humanity, the Church and the world, etc. As I will argue in chapters 5 and 6, we ought not attempt to "out-nuance" Kierkegaard in our interpretation of him by re-blurring the lines between direct and indirect communication given Kierkegaard's extensive reflections on the reasons for using both methods in particular ways.

The "Evangelical" Kierkegaard?

There have been numerous attempts in recent years to rescue Kierkegaard from his aforementioned postmodern "reputation" and to reemphasize his affinity with Evangelical expressions of Christianity. Such an undertaking is not entirely straightforward, not only because it is difficult to categorize easily the ecclesial and/or theological concerns of Kierkegaard but because it is difficult to categorize easily the ecclesial and/or theological concerns of the term "evangelical."[21] What is meant by the term here simply refers to an orientation to the primacy of scriptural authority and Gospel proclamation and reception in the life of the Church. The point here is to highlight "Scripture" and "Gospel" (proclamation *and* reception) as the key delineators with their ensuing implications for the life of the individual and the Church,[22] thus avoiding any particular expression of contemporary Evangelical "culture" being mapped back onto Kierkegaard anachronistically.

As Roger Olson noted, Kierkegaard "was no 'evangelical' in the contemporary North American sense."[23] By this is meant the popular cultural trappings that often accompany the term "Evangelical" within its US context, such as Christian subculture, televangelism, megachurches, and various accompanying political entanglements. Olson's categorization of Kierkegaard as Evangelical refers instead to

> a Christian form of life that emphasizes personal conversion and relationship with God through Jesus Christ, the Bible as God's Word written, the cross as the center of Christian devotion, preaching and life and transformative action through missions and social change (but focusing primarily on individual transformation and social change only secondarily).[24]

---

21. The term "Evangelical" (particularly when capitalized) is notoriously difficult to define. This has been especially so in recent decades given that Evangelicalism has become increasingly splintered culturally, ecclesially, politically, and theologically. Even attempts such as David Bebbington's to define its very broad tenets (biblicism, conversionism, crucicentrism, and activism) are regularly critiqued as either overly limiting or no longer fit for purpose. See Bebbington, *Evangelicalism in Modern Britain*, 1–20. See also Noll et al., *Evangelicals*.

22. For discussions of Kierkegaard's understanding and expression of the Gospel and its wider implications, see chapters 2, 5, and 6.

23. Olson, "Was Kierkegaard an evangelical?"

24. Olson, "Was Kierkegaard an evangelical?"

As this book will explore, such elements were central to Kierkegaard's approach to Christian faith and are easily forgotten when those same elements find themselves bound up within the various sociopolitical entailments of contemporary Evangelicalism. Furthermore, the sheer pervasiveness of such elements within Kierkegaard's thought and practice point away from his postmodern and/or relativistic caricatures and situate him in far closer affinity with foundational Evangelical convictions than is usually supposed.

What Kind of "Evangelical" Is Kierkegaard?

To imagine the possibility of an "Evangelical Kierkegaard," as dubious as such a thought experiment might seem, is merely to highlight the centrality of the Gospel and its implications in the thought of a man who took Jesus Christ as seriously as any who have ever called themselves Christian.[25] Two contrasting examples of Evangelical appropriation of Kierkegaard include Kyle Roberts's *Emerging Prophet: Kierkegaard and the Postmodern People of God* (2013), and Mark Tietjen's *Kierkegaard: A Christian Missionary to Christians* (2016).[26] Both authors, in one way or another, represent "Evangelical" readings of Kierkegaard opposed to Schaeffer's critiques, yet both appear to sit on respectively different sides of the evangelical fence with regard to the appropriation of postmodernism. Their perspectives open up further ways to navigate our course as to whether Kierkegaard is better cast as a postmodern "emergent" (post) evangelical, or an alternative kind of "missionary" evangelical to the Church.

The "Emergent" Kierkegaard?

The notion of Kierkegaard as "Emergent" is an especially important version of Kierkegaard to critique, given that it represents a kind of hybrid

25. Indeed, so seriously does Kierkegaard take the claims of Christ in the Gospel that he holds the notion of "being" or "becoming" a Christian in extraordinarily high regard, casting doubt over the ease with which one often proclaims the piety of one's faith without truly understanding the implications.

26. It was only as I was midway through writing this chapter that I remembered that Roberts, Tietjen, and myself each gave papers as part of the panel on Kierkegaard and Evangelicalism for the annual meeting of the American Academy of Religion in Baltimore, 2013. My paper for that session formed the basis of chapter 2.

of both postmodern and Evangelical concerns, and thus forms a key focal point for discussing Kierkegaard's critique of the Church, and how this discussion might feed into more appropriate ways in which to situate his ecclesial and theological interests.

Kyle Roberts's *Emerging Prophet* (2013) attempts to situate Kierkegaard's ecclesial value not *away from* postmodernity, but *toward* it. For Roberts, "Kierkegaard offers a timely and prophetic voice for postmodern Christians, those who are seeking a fresh, deeply authentic way to practice the Christian faith in our complex, challenging world."[27] The "postmodern Christians" Roberts has in mind are those who, in one way or another, identified with what was called the "Emerging" or "Emergent" Church, representative of a short-lived collective of disenfranchised North American Evangelicals in the 1990s and 2000s, who were reacting against the hyper-marketized subculture of the modern Evangelical Church.[28] Emergent Christians saw some integral cracks in the hyperbolized forms of modern Evangelicalism, and were thinking and practicing how to move beyond their inherited Evangelicalism, both ecclesially and doctrinally. Roberts refers to it as "a postmodern-oriented renewal movement."[29] In practice, it was less a renewal movement within the Church and more an exodus of a large variety of creative-thinking innovators *from* the Church.[30] Emergent Christians were fed up with what they deemed to be the hypocrisy of the mundane and systemic forms of Evangelicalism in which they had been brought up. They yearned instead for the deconstruction of traditional modes of belief, more intimate and authentic community, more aesthetic forms of worship, deeper cultural engagement, and more blurred distinctions between Church and world.[31]

Although there are certainly some interesting initial connections with Kierkegaard's concerns, most points of genuine affinity between

27. Roberts, *Emerging Prophet*, 2–3.

28. This movement of thought also took hold in other Anglophone contexts such as the UK, Australia, and South Africa, but its reception was almost exclusively tied to Western post-Evangelical demographics.

29. Roberts, *Emerging Prophet*, 2.

30. There are, of course, dangers with assuming there was a clear "Emergent" umbrella, but despite the particular differences between various thinkers, leaders, and practitioners, the term still serves fairly accurately as a catchall term to sum up the post-Evangelical moves of that era to appropriate postmodern concerns to the Church by accentuating a cluster of values, such as deconstruction over system, community over individualism, conversation over dogma, and questions over answers.

31. For a representative example, see Gibbs, *Emerging Churches*.

Kierkegaard and Emergent Christianity are misleading because they overlook the more substantial points of difference. One such connection could be the propensity within Emergent Christianity to step outside of mainstream "established" churchgoing. The initial idea was for Emergent Christians to form new "authentic" communities that differed in form and style from the mainstream. However, just a few years after the many Emergent thought leaders were publishing numerous books and speaking at various high-profile conferences promoting the ideas of the movement, such leaders were not only no longer leading churches anymore, but were no longer attending church at all.[32] To some extent, this might seem to mirror Kierkegaard's infamous attack on the Danish Church whereby he also personally ceased attending church in protest, and even refused Communion from any Church officials on his deathbed.[33] However, there are stark differences in Kierkegaard's motivations and purposes compared with those of the Emergent Church. Kierkegaard's protestations were born primarily of the Church's failure to reject worldliness in light of the demands of the Gospel.[34] Although the Emergent Church tended to believe the Evangelical Church to be more indebted to modern cultural philosophical presuppositions (e.g., Cartesian epistemology) than the Gospel,[35] it did not tend to emphasize the *problem* of cultured "worldliness" (cf. 1 John 2:15) due to the focus on the importance of maintaining cultural relevance.

It would be true to say that the Emergent Church movement rightly questioned the worldliness of many of the modernist trappings

32. To many of the Evangelical critics of Emergent Christianity, such an "end" had always been somewhat inevitable. See, for example, Justin Taylor's analysis of Rob Bell, who at one time had led what was by far the largest "Emergent Church" in the world, but who ended up instead leading TV shows on general spirituality with Oprah Winfrey: "A lot of folks saw that he was on a certain trajectory and that he was now happy to leave evangelicalism in the rearview mirror. His decision to leave his church and literally sign on to the Oprahfication of spirituality has only solidified and deepened those concerns." Taylor, "Rob Bell Revisited." See also the case of Donald Miller, one of the most influential authors connected with the movement, who eventually decided that he could "connect" with God better by pursuing his own marketing business, without needing to belong to a church at all. See Tiemeyer, "Donald Miller."

33. See chapter 8.

34. See, for example: "In the proclaiming of Christianity they have left out and suppressed what does not please the secular and earthly mentality and thus have induced all this worldliness to imagine that it is Christian." Kierkegaard, *Judge for Yourself!*, 190.

35. See McLaren, *New Kind of Christianity*, 45–60.

in contemporary Evangelicalism, particularly the ways in which faith had become systematized and depersonalized. However, given that their critique was fundamentally indebted to postmodernist deconstruction rather than biblically consistent Gospel proclamation,[36] it failed to truly reform or renew the Church in any significant way, and could not sustain its own communities longer term. The culture-affirming nature of the movement led inevitably to the kinds of "aesthetic" worldliness for which Kierkegaard chastised the Danish Church,[37] including a lack of willingness to challenge the status quo within the wider culture as well as within the Church.[38] Danish Christendom believed itself to be entirely "Christian" whereas Emergent Christianity, despite existing largely within microcosmic forms of Christendom within parts of the United States and beyond, ultimately exists within a pervasively secular culture with which they must not only *converse* but also *contend*. The distinct lack of contention with "the world" proved to be one of its major downfalls and led to a kind of reverse of the caution in James 4:4, whereby their kinship with contemporary culture led to deconstructive enmity toward the Church.

Scot McKnight attempted to defend the Emergent Church from its deconstructive caricatures, quipping, "It is said that . . . they deny truth, meaning they've got a latte-soaked copy of Derrida in their smoke- and beer-stained backpacks."[39] However, it was precisely this indebtedness to Derridean deconstruction—whether garnered directly from Derrida or not—which proved to be the movement's eventual undoing. This is because its perpetually deconstructive vision could not lead to the growth and sustenance of missionally active ecclesial communities over the long haul. The apparent liberation offered by its ecclesial deconstruction did not lead to the full liberation offered by the Gospel. No doubt Kevin Vanhoozer had such deconstructive doctrinal-ecclesial trajectories in mind when, at what was perhaps the peak of the Emergent Church's influence, he said, "Postmodernity sets the captives free from certain aspects of modern thought, but not from the bondage of sin and death nor from meaninglessness and despair, nor does postmodernity set them free

---

36. See Kimball, *Emerging Church*, 21–100.

37. See chapter 8.

38. For further prominent Evangelical critiques of Emergent Christianity, see DeYoung and Kluck, *Why We're Not Emergent*, and Carson, *Becoming Conversant with the Emerging Church.*

39. McKnight, "Five Streams of the Emerging Church."

for others or the wholly other (God)."[40] As chapter 8 will demonstrate, Kierkegaard's deconstruction of the Danish Lutheran Church was even more caustic than the Emergent Church's deconstruction of Evangelicalism. Yet Kierkegaard believed his deconstruction emanated theologically without the handmaidens of secular philosophy having first laid the deconstructive foundation.

Kierkegaard's aforementioned critique of the modernist rationalism of the Church was, however, a form of systemic deconstruction that seems to harbor valid kinship with the Emergent critiques of Evangelicalism. As Roberts helpfully notes, "The connection of truth and knowledge with personal involvement is not a hindrance to progress, but an essential precondition of it."[41] There is, for sure, a sense in which modern Evangelical approaches to doctrine have often been so preoccupied with fighting for epistemological "certainty" that they have directly or indirectly undermined the existential necessity of faith. In response to this problem, Roberts opts for what he calls a "humble epistemology," whereby any theological claim must simultaneously acknowledge at any given moment that "God might be a fiction of our collective imaginations."[42] This is where I believe the case becomes drastically overstated. Quite simply, it is impossible to imagine Kierkegaard—let alone the Apostle Paul, who "wrote the book" on humility (cf. Phil 2:1–11)—declaring that God might well be a figment of their imaginations, not least because their ongoing proclamation came at immense personal cost. Roberts's supposed "humble epistemology," though critiquing a problematic understanding of modernist certainty, is in danger of becoming a functional glorification of doubt.[43]

Such an approach echoes Emergent authors such as Pete Rollins (with whom Roberts also interacts), whose "pyro-theology" epitomizes the deconstructive approach:

40. Vanhoozer, "Post/Modern Way," 81.

41. Roberts, *Emerging Prophet*, 43.

42. Roberts, *Emerging Prophet*, 47.

43. Roberts attempts to clarify this by citing "epistemological confidence" over "epistemological certainty" on the basis that "confidence" suggests: "But I could be wrong." This seems somewhat arbitrary, functionally. Ultimately, confidence (to act *con fides*, "with faith") remains a kind of functional certainty, even if not an Enlightenment kind of certainty, and is the kind of "certainty" Kierkegaard appeared to demonstrate in his own proclamation and in his critiques of those who did not practice what they preached. See chapters 2–4.

> [Pyrotheology] involves a deep critique of any religious/ideo-
> logical system that promises an escape from doubt and anxiety
> . . . It uncovers how faith helps us resolutely confront our bro-
> kenness, joyfully embrace unknowing, and courageously face
> the difficulties of life. While this journey into the dark might
> seem unappealing compared with those who sell the "Good
> News" of certainty and satisfaction, Pyrotheology exposes how
> this "Good News" is actually very bad news.[44]

In such a schema, the concept of "faith" is imagined to be the defiant
alternative to modernist certainty, but only by becoming subsumed into
its opposite, "doubt."[45] Kierkegaard's critique of ideologically rationalist
certainties was not intended to make faith indistinguishable from doubt,
nor to deconstruct the very notion of the Gospel. It was not that the
kerygmatic content of proclamation itself was inescapably and comprehensively ideological at its core, but that it was being abused *by* rationalism as an invasive force. In this light, it is not coincidental that in a recent
interview Rollins noted that, although he appreciates Kierkegaard's general existentialist tenor, "personally, I am drawn to Nietzsche more than
Kierkegaard,"[46] especially given Nietzsche's more overwhelmingly deconstructive approach to the core theological content of the Gospel itself.[47]

Contrary to Roberts, Rollins, and other Emergent perspectives,
faith is not simply the absence of certainty, but the existential acting-out
of one's convictions *as if* they are certain. When the writer to the Hebrews
says that "faith is to be sure of what we hope for and certain of what we do
not see" (Heb 11:1), they are clearly not advocating epistemological om-
niscience. The essence of Christian proclamation, the Gospel of Christ,
necessitates that faith requires conviction. To speak or act in faith is not to
voice an ambiguous "perhaps" to dampen down the significance of such
a truth claim *just in case* it might not be true after all. Rather, faith means
being prepared to bear witness *to* the proclaimed truth precisely because
the truth is held with functional certainty, a kind of active decisiveness.[48]
Following James, Kierkegaard's favorite biblical author, the one who asks
for wisdom must ask "in faith, with no doubting, for the one who doubts

---

44. Rollins, "Pyrotheology."

45. See Rollins, *Insurrection*.

46. Rollins, "Ripping the Curtain," 130.

47. See especially paragraphs 27–45 of Nietzsche, *Anti-Christ*, 139–61.

48. See chapter 5. See also Kierkegaard, *Christian Discourses*, 81–91.

is like a wave of the sea that is driven and tossed by the wind . . . a double-minded man, unstable in all his ways" (Jas 1:6–8).

It is evident that Kierkegaard did not express faith in a "double-minded" sense that could be implied by Roberts's and Rollins's approaches, vis à vis, for example, the clear proclamation of Christ as "the truth" (cf. John 14:6). Rather, Kierkegaard also critiqued the *problem* of doubt, particularly in light of modern skepticism: "The method of beginning with doubt in order to philosophize seems as appropriate as having a soldier slouch in order to get him to stand erect."[49] Indeed, for Kierkegaard, the ambiguous "perhaps" which sounds like humility to the postmodern ear could be equally employed by the rationalist *or* the postmodernist as a convenient ploy to avoid suffering for the truth—socially or otherwise.[50] After all, it would have been easy to avoid martyrdom by claiming a position of epistemological humility with regards to the supremacy (or not) of the Roman emperor (and/or of Christ). The elevation of doubt as a supreme virtue is a prime example of the oft-noted ironic one-sidedness of much postmodern reflection. Such an approach is indeed very sure of what it hopes to deconstruct, and very certain of what it cannot believe.

Kierkegaard might well agree with some of the deconstructive observations that emerged from postmodern approaches to modern Christianity, especially regarding the kerygmatic disruption of the bourgeois status quo.[51] However, such critiques can only work by emanating from the genuine conviction of an objective standard, like "New Testament Christianity," which the failing Church—hoodwinked by some ideological untruth—has not practiced. Where Kierkegaard might agree with many of the Emergent questions of the Evangelical Church within postmodernity, he is at least as likely to agree with Emergent critics too, such as D. A. Carson, who highlighted the absence of a consistent biblical perspective in their questioning: "My quarrel with Emergent is not that it is trying to read the times or that it thinks that postmodernism, properly defined, introduced serious challenges that need to be addressed; rather, its response is not as penetrating and biblically faithful as it needs to be."[52]

---

49. *Søren Kierkegaard's Journals and Papers*, 1:775, 359.

50. See chapters 5–6.

51. See Smith, *Who's Afraid of Postmodernism?*, 57–8.

52. Carson, *Becoming Conversant with the Emergent Church*, 87.

Whether Kierkegaard is communicating directly or indirectly, he is speaking from a place of significant biblical conviction.[53] He asks not whether we can prove that Christianity "might" be the truth, but given that Christianity *is* the truth, what should that *mean* for us? Kierkegaard is concerned with the fact that Christianity has unavoidable consequences for our lives which, if ignored, possibly mean that we have not believed what we profess to believe at all, however many cogent arguments for God's "official" existence we may be able to cite. For Kierkegaard, God is not interested in being merely "defended"—least of all by the established order—but in being proclaimed, believed, loved, and obeyed. Such activities require the confident conviction of faith, something which is especially needed at a time of significant worldly acclimatization and widespread decline within the Western Church. It is for this reason that it might be more appropriate to speak of Kierkegaard's potential ecclesial contribution to the "mission" of the Church in modernity.

The "Missionary" Kierkegaard?

Roberts's manifestly "postmodern Evangelical" appropriation of Kierkegaard is contrasted by Mark Tietjen, another Evangelical who asserts that "Kierkegaard is a voice that should be sought and heard for the edification of the church."[54] Tietjen, like Roberts, is keen to nuance Francis Schaeffer's casual dismissals, quoting C. Stephen Evans: "Poor Kierkegaard has suffered more than any author I know of from a generation of evangelical ignorance."[55] In attempting to redeem this problem, Tietjen notes the perennial difficulty of classifying Kierkegaard theologically, though adding that "it would be appropriate to describe Kierkegaard's as a practical theology."[56] In a sense, this rings true because Kierkegaard cared supremely about the existential outworking of Christian faith beyond doctrinal abstraction. Yet such a categorization could also be misleading depending on how one understands the discipline of "practical theology" within the modern academy. Kierkegaard would no doubt loath to be associated with the empirical and theoretical modes of discourse that

---

53. See chapter 3.

54. Tietjen, *Kierkegaard*, 25.

55. Tietjen, *Kierkegaard*, 46. See Evans, "Misunderstood Reformer."

56. Tietjen, *Kierkegaard*, 48.

tend to dominate this field today.[57] Ironically, the theoretical speculations which often appear within practical theology—often heavily informed by general religious, sociological, and anthropological categories—render much of the discipline of practical theology as being neither all that practical nor all that theological. This is precisely the kind of ironic state of academic affairs at which Kierkegaard loved to poke fun.

Kierkegaard could only really be called a practical theologian if it meant something more akin to "actualized theology." That is, not in the sense of theology needing to apply itself within modes of discourse currently approved by the academic guild, but in the sense of the enactment of Christian doctrine within one's life in the world. Indeed, elaborating on the specificity of Kierkegaard's unique contribution to the Church, Tietjen points to its explicitly missiological and prophetic dimension:

> Just as the prophets of God did not introduce new theology but simply repeated the same call and message God had given for generations and generations, so too Kierkegaard's message of Christianity to Christians is not conveying novel information. One might nevertheless think of Kierkegaard as he did himself, as a Christian missionary to Christians, insofar as the gospel his contemporaries have heard has not, in fact, been the gospel, but rather some familiar-sounding speculative, philosophy-infused religious pep talk.[58]

Kierkegaard was indeed a kind of "missionary," not because he came to preach the Gospel to those who had no access to Scripture, no knowledge of the doctrines of Christianity, or no awareness of Christian virtues and values. Rather, he came to restate—in creative, arresting, and often bizarre ways—precisely what this "Christian" society was supposed to have known all along and yet did not seem to know at all.

Yet even as a missionary *to* Christians, Kierkegaard is not easily categorizable. This is because a missionary calling within a nominally Christian religious culture might normally be called "revivalism," and yet this was a practice of which Kierkegaard was also dubious. For example, in his discourse "Against Cowardliness" Kierkegaard critiques the person who returns home from listening to a revivalistic sermon with uproarious enthusiasm and ideas for future change, only to spend their time remarking upon the passion and eloquence of the speaker and to

---

57. See, for example, Weyel, "Practical Theology," 150–59.
58. Tietjen, *Kierkegaard*, 52.

"sit there surrounded by lofty resolutions."[59] Kierkegaard knew that such abstract resolutions, however resolutely intended, may yet act as another subterfuge for the cowardly deliberation to *enact* them. Elsewhere, in *Concluding Unscientific Postscript*, he draws attention to the man whose personal revival, occurring in a fit of emotive existential excitement, leads him to "run around and proclaim Christianity," "and yet he demonstrates—the busier he is propagating and propagating—that he himself is not Christian."[60] As much as Kierkegaard stressed the importance of existential decision and proclamation, he recognized that even this could lead to the kind of response that lacked integrity or steadfastness.

Although it is still true to say that Kierkegaard's missionary efforts were indeed "outward" in the sense that he was actively propagating a return to the Gospel—and away from, in Tietjen's terms, "philosophy-infused religious pep talk"[61]—the point of Kierkegaard's message was not to achieve mere outward "conversion" but to inculcate what he called "inwardness." By this is meant the existential appropriation of decisive faith in one's life, irrespective of social, political, or ecclesial entrapments.[62] To do this within a context in which Christianity was so thoroughly integrated within the sociopolitical sphere, Kierkegaard's missionary task involved evoking true existential response to the Gospel through means of indirect communication. This was the primary purpose behind his pseudonymous authorship, which he referred to as "a godly satire."[63]

Echoing the contextual missionary approach of the Apostle Paul (albeit very differently), Kierkegaard's conscious missionary strategy was actually fairly straightforward: "to utilize everything, to get as many as possible, everyone if possible, to accept Christianity."[64] The fact that the context was Christendom, however, meant that this apparently straightforward task could not be a straightforward act of evangelism. Indeed,

---

59. Kierkegaard, *Eighteen Upbuilding Discourses*, 348.

60. Kierkegaard, *Concluding Unscientific Postscript*, 614.

61. Tietjen, *Kierkegaard*, 52.

62. For a discussion of the ecclesial implications of Kierkegaard's focus on "the single individual," see chapter 8.

63. Kierkegaard, *Point of View*, 17. For a discussion of Kierkegaard's complex use of both direct and indirect communication, see chapter 6. For a more particular example of what Kierkegaard might have meant by "Godly satire" within his indirect communication, see the discussion of the simultaneously "aesthetic" and "theological" purposes of *Either/Or* in chapter 7.

64. Kierkegaard, *Point of View*, 16.

as he says, "a missionary within Christendom will always look different from a missionary in paganism."[65] Christendom was unlike the paganism encountered by the earliest Christian missionaries because everybody thought they had already *been* evangelized. Yet Kierkegaard would also describe Christendom itself as "a pleasant, sentimental paganism," in which Christianity itself had become an idol, a human construction which was worshipped in place of the true God-man.[66] The phenomenal impact of Christian missionaries over the generations was now having the reverse effect upon Christian discipleship: "Now, since it has been demonstrated, and on an enormous scale, that Christianity is the truth, now there is no one, almost no one, who is willing to make any sacrifice for its sake."[67]

Because of the extreme condition of nominal faith within Christendom, Kierkegaard's missionary strategy meant, in practice, "to utilize everything to make clear what in truth Christianity's requirement is—even if not one single person would accept it."[68] This was, in fact, a paradoxical outworking of the aforementioned desire of his "to get as many as possible, everyone if possible, to accept Christianity." Kierkegaard knew that any mission to help people accept Christianity within Christendom actually meant making the reception of Christianity not easier—as might be attempted by the usual evangelist or revivalist—but making Christianity more difficult. In this light, it could be argued that Kierkegaard was something of an "anti-evangelist," but only to the extent that he believed this to be the most appropriate evangelistic *apologia* for the truth of Christianity in his time.

The "Kerygmatic" Kierkegaard

Kierkegaard's apparently indirect approach to Christian mission and his critical approach to revivalism might seem to lead to an ambivalent approach to the purpose and relevance of Christian preaching. Yet as many of the chapters in this book aim to demonstrate, nothing could be further from the truth.[69] Indeed, there is a particular relevance of preaching to

65. Kierkegaard, *Point of View*, 47.

66. Kierkegaard, *Practice in Christianity*, 143.

67. Kierkegaard, *Practice in Christianity*, 144.

68. Kierkegaard, *Point of View*, 16.

69. See especially chapters 2, 3, 5, and 6.

Kierkegaard's thought to the extent that it takes a distinctly kerygmatic shape. This is because preaching held, for Kierkegaard, the archetypal moment for the test of one's subjective appropriation of the truth. This is something that continues to be a problem for the Western Church today, Christendom or no Christendom.[70] Without the subjective integrity of the preacher in their proclamation, preaching truly does become something of a charade.

This is why, as I will argue in chapters 7 and 8, Christendom need not be seen as a mere "epoch," but can also be seen, Kierkegaardianly speaking, as a condition—a sickness—which afflicts the Church at all times. The Church is perennially tempted to be a subjectless Christianity in which the matter-of-factness of what is preached renders it impossible for individuals to wilfully act and suffer for such matter-of-fact truths. A Church without subjectivity—"Evangelical" or otherwise—is an essentially fictional Church because it would be a Church whose members do not live "subject" to the king. Such would be a kingdom in which there are no subjects at all, only "objects" to which people might point *en masse* from beyond the kingdom's borders by looking in over the wall or through a gap in the gates. In contrast, the preachers of this kingdom are to be those who live the truths of this kingdom by living "inside" its ramparts, not merely talking *about* the kingdom as an abstract thing but inhabiting its ways as living beings. To live within a kingdom necessarily entails a deference to whatever the king decrees, to live under the authority of the king's word as delivered by his heralds. Such preachers—seldom seen within much of the Western Church today—are to be those whose very lives are living sermons that keep on preaching beyond the gathered "religious" moments of congregational gatherings.

For preachers to truly heed the call of this king, Kierkegaard continually insists that this means they do not begin by preaching, but in the humility of silence. In one of his many dialogical reflections on Christ's call to contemplate the birds and the lilies, he imagines the way a person might respond to the call to seek the kingdom of God in a way that puts even preaching the kingdom before the kingdom itself: "Shall I then go out and proclaim this doctrine to the world? No, you shall first seek God's kingdom."[71] And how is a preacher to do this? By first learning to be silent: "In this silence is the beginning, which is to seek first God's

70. For a Kierkegaardian reflection on the contemporary Church within post-Christendom, see chapter 8.

71. Kierkegaard, *Without Authority*, 10.

kingdom."[72] Kierkegaard's reflections on silence, as with his reflections on indirect communication, have sometimes led to an anti-kerygmatic or exclusively apophatic interpretation of his concerns.[73] But as will be explored, Kierkegaard's disdain for the abuse of preaching was the direct consequence of the high regard he had for preaching, and how essential it was to the Christian faith. In a culture that was quite literally overcome by sermons, however, the value of silence as a prerequisite to proclamation became an important way of expressing how one cannot put anything, least of all preaching, above the pursuit of Christ's kingdom. Indeed, Kierkegaard saw that to preach sermons *about* the kingdom within a culture of incessant sermonizing (Christendom) could become a subtle way of avoiding the pursuit of that kingdom.[74]

Kierkegaard saw that the preacherly avoidance of the true demands of the kingdom led to a "socialized" or "public" conception of the pastorate, in which civic virtue or social affability alone was the prerequisite. Many of Kierkegaard's acerbic journal comments about pastors could easily have been written about contemporary equivalents:

> Pastors have finally ceased to be what they actually ought to be to the point that, in relation to what it really means to be a pastor, the factors by which they make a big hit and become honored, respected, and esteemed etc. are completely irrelevant—namely, that they are good mixers, people who can take part in anything, administer, deliver occasional addresses, in short, be a sort of more elegant edition of an undertaker.[75]

Kierkegaard had a curiously clear sense of "what it really means to be a pastor." This is partly because, as the next chapter will explain, he had intended to be one for a good deal of his life. Kierkegaard knew well the drastic contrast between the pastoral reality of Christendom and the pastoral ideal of the New Testament, and it is not coincidental that he should use the analogy of an undertaker here given the ways in which he would go on to describe the Church as literally putting Christians to death by its avoidance of the world-denying demands of Christianity.[76] This culture of social affability was repulsive to Kierkegaard, and was exacerbated by

72. Kierkegaard, *Without Authority*, 10–11.

73. See Kline, *Passion for Nothing: Kierkegaard's Apophatic Theology*.

74. See chapters 3, 6, and 8. See also Edwards, "Kierkegaard the Preacher."

75. *Søren Kierkegaard's Journals and Papers*, 3:3157, 446.

76. See especially the opening quotation to chapter 8.

the insipid sermons that seemed to undergird it.[77] But as this book will show, Kierkegaard's critique of Christian preaching is inseparable from the centrality of preaching to his thought and practice.

Taking Kierkegaard Back

The various reputational complications swarming in and around Kierkegaard's theological legacy may seem more hassle than they are worth. Given the need to "defend" Kierkegaard against the charges of relativism, postmodernism, post-Evangelicalism, etc., can Kierkegaard's thought really be brought to fruition in the contemporary Church? Ought we not leave him where he chose to leave himself, on the ecclesial outskirts, refusing to take Communion on his deathbed from any established minister of the Church? We may only do so if we are happy to make the same mistakes that Christendom itself made and makes. As has been seen, Kierkegaard's missional legacy is definitively *for* the Church, albeit in subversion to usual expectations. His kerygmatic approach calls the Church perpetually to reexamine its sermonizing, and everything else it says and does, in light of the One of whom it speaks.

It hardly needs to be said at this point that it's quite impossible to understand Kierkegaard without his Christianity. That first "version" of Søren Kierkegaard I heard about all those years ago in my absurdist seminar was indeed a caricature of somebody who was in actuality an embarrassingly overt Christian thinker—only, one who just so happened to be one of the great geniuses of modern thought per se at the same time. Although Kierkegaard's thought has proven to be a key voice in responding to the onset of the related trends of existentialism, relativism, postmodernism, and other bogeymen of the modern Church, his unequivocally Christian approach to the implications of truth ought to be seen as an ally rather than an enemy in responding to the complex challenges which continue to confront the Church today.

The remaining chapters in this book aim to flesh out how this is indeed the case—how Kierkegaard executed his call to be an author of ecclesial awakening—by engaging with the kinds of theological and ecclesial problems that most animated, inspired, and infuriated him. It is hoped that these will also animate, inspire, and infuriate us too as we navigate such theological issues in the choppy waters of the present religious and

---

77. See again chapters 2–4.

sociopolitical climate of our own time. Such problematizing was perhaps Kierkegaard's greatest theological contribution to the Church. It gestures toward why, in spite of his many reputational caveats, we must do all we can to take our friend Kierkegaard back to church.

2

Kierkegaard's Imaginary Rural Parish

The Pastoral Correctivity of the Gospel

As we saw in the opening chapter, Kierkegaard, perhaps more than most, is a thinker whose intellectual legacy is prone to misinterpretation. Indeed, over time he has been duly claimed by a host of varying schools within philosophy, theology, and literature, from the "Existentialist Kierkegaard" of Heidegger and Sartre, to the "Dialectical Kierkegaard" of Barth and Bultmann, the "Absurdist Kierkegaard" of Kafka and Camus, or even the "Literary Kierkegaard" of Auden and Updike. The breadth, depth, and literary allusiveness of Kierkegaard's writings certainly lend themselves to such a range of stylizations. Yet such range does not necessarily get at the heart of his authorship's main purpose: to invoke individuals to encounter the reality of Christianity. This meant not to undermine Christianity but to declare all that Christianity represents and requires. This is how he understood his task as a writer: "And what can I offer? I am a poet—alas, only a poet. But I can present Christianity in the glory of its ideality."[1] It is not an overstatement to say that Kierkegaard saw himself primarily, albeit unconventionally, as a preacher of the Gospel.

This chapter will begin to consider how he went about doing this, how he presented the glorious "ideality" of the central message of the Christian faith within his context. Indeed, it is only in relation to Christianity that Kierkegaard would ever be happy to call himself an "idealist." As we saw in the last chapter, it was virtually impossible for anyone

---

1. *Søren Kierkegaard's Journals and Papers*, 6:6727, 377.

in Kierkegaard's time to speak of "ideality" and *not* think of Hegelian ideal*ism*. Kierkegaard was a thinker who, above all else, sought for one's thought to be immersed in reality, beyond the trappings of idealistic speculation.[2] Perhaps the title of this chapter, then, might appear to him as highly inappropriate, by its speculations about an "imagined" situation that has no possibility whatever of becoming an actual situation:[3] imagining Søren Kierkegaard—the great anti-speculative realist—as a "real" pastor, and one whose relentless Gospel focus is of enduring use to the mission of Church proclamation today. Three further things immediately spring to mind that make this undertaking inappropriate: the first is that Kierkegaard was *not* a pastor. Although he trained as a theologian and preacher and was often inches away from applying for ordination, he remained very much a full-time thinker and writer. The second is that Kierkegaard is often known for his scathing attacks *upon* the established clergy; to imagine Kierkegaard as a *paid* clergy member, then, seems to be a contradiction that not even Kierkegaard could manage to hold! And the third and most prominent reason for the inappropriateness of this chapter is that Kierkegaard is, technically, no longer alive. Although his thought "lives on" in that well-worn metaphorical sense, there is now no likelihood that he will become a real, breathing pastor in a real, breathing congregation. He might well ask, why bother with such speculations? This is a question, of course, that all Kierkegaard scholarship must face, and indeed, occurs in the self-aware introductions to dozens of secondary academic works on his thought. Why are we busying ourselves talking about "Kierkegaard," we say, rather than busying ourselves with what Kierkegaard talked *about*; namely, living out the implications of the Gospel in actuality?

It would be tempting, of course to be bold enough to end the chapter here and dismiss the reader to "go and do likewise"! However, there is indeed a useful purpose in speculating upon Kierkegaard's ecclesial value *for* the Church a little further before seeking to imitate such urgency. We will do so by discussing the idea of Kierkegaard as a pastor based on his views on the pastorate and preachers, as well as what might be gleaned from some of Kierkegaard's pastoral interactions. We will then examine the primary tenets of Kierkegaard's corrective expression of the Gospel, noting that his message is essentially classically Lutheran. On this basis,

2. See chapter 7 for a fuller reflection on the "ideal" in relation to the "real."

3. On Kierkegaard's complex relationship to the category of imagination, see Gouwens, *Kierkegaard's Dialectic of the Imagination*.

we will see Kierkegaard's notion of correctivity with regard to Luther, where he argues that Luther might well have emphasized works more than grace if faced with the culture of Danish Christendom. Finally, we will evaluate the potential ecclesial impact of Kierkegaard's corrective expression of the Gospel upon a real (albeit "imaginary") congregation.

Kierkegaard the Rural Pastor

It is often forgotten, amid the gallons of secondary scholarship that pour freely from Søren Kierkegaard's legacy, that this great thinker often toyed with the idea of drifting away from the clamor of Copenhagen to become a rural pastor: "The wish to be a rural pastor has always appealed to me and been at the back of my mind."[4] The decision over whether to pursue the pastorate or the authorship has been described as a "long, intense struggle" throughout his life.[5] This struggle truly relented only with the "attack literature" of his later years whereby he closed off any hope of getting a job by repeatedly insulting his would-be employers. Indeed, one can only imagine the kinds of things Kierkegaard might have said in an ordination interview![6] His potent attacks upon the clergy largely centered upon their hypocrisy of not living out what they preached: "The pastors are like a person who stands on dry land and gives swimming lessons."[7] Similarly scathing analogies resound thunderously throughout his writings. Pastors are critiqued relentlessly for their comfortable living, respectable social status, and unwillingness to suffer for the truth. For Kierkegaard, these are "bread-and-butter" pastors,[8] "plump career-preachers,"[9] who preach not because they themselves have been stirred by their message, but because they are paid to do so. In one of Kierkegaard's satirical dialogues, a pastor declares to a new Christian,

"You must die to the world—that will be ten dollars."

---

4. *Søren Kierkegaard's Journals and Papers*, 5:5961, 358.

5. Benktson, "The Ministry," 224. "In spite of all his misgivings, SK knew that he had the 'vocatio interna'; he waited in vain for the 'vocatio externa.' To be a 'verbi divini minister' is what SK feels called to be and what he reaches towards, and—in eager pursuit of his ideals—he overreaches himself." Benktson, "The Ministry," 225.

6. See chapter 8 for a discussion of his attack literature.

7. *Søren Kierkegaard's Journals and Papers*, 1:668, 314.

8. *Søren Kierkegaard's Journals and Papers*, 3:3489, 593.

9. *Søren Kierkegaard's Journals and Papers*, 3:3522, 608.

The novice replies: "Well, if I must die to the world, renounce all the things of this world, I certainly understand that I will have to put out more than ten dollars for the sake of the cause, but there is just one question: Who gets the ten dollars?"

The pastor replies: "Of course I get it; it is my wages; after all, I and my family have to make a living out of proclaiming that one must die to the world. It is a very cheap price, and very soon much more will have to be charged. If you are fair, you yourself will understand that it takes a lot out of a man to proclaim that one must die to the world . . . Therefore it is very necessary for me and my family to spend the summer in the country in order to recuperate."[10]

Kierkegaard says that the careerist pastors of the State Church are more dangerous to Christianity than atheists.[11]

Given his many anti-clerical sentiments, can we really imagine Kierkegaard himself as one of them? Kierkegaard is often painted as the melancholic individualist in the splendid isolation of his Copenhagen apartment, thinking, scribbling, brooding, and pacing between his many stand-up writing desks. Such a depiction is not without truth, but it masks the fact that he was a pastorally interested thinker who saw his writing not as a means of speculative contemplation, but as a means of personal communication with individual people, such as those whom he addresses in his discourses as his "dear listeners." Indeed, Kierkegaard spent much time walking the streets of Copenhagen to meet, greet, hear, help, and observe people from all walks of life. Such excursions were not merely anthropological "research" but born of genuine love for neighbor, which he was committed to not only philosophically, but theologically.[12]

Reading his letters, we immediately become aware of this pastoral focus, as one who sought to enter in to the existential problems of those who sought his advice and counsel.[13] Kierkegaard's was not an existentialism devoid of sociality. Although he remained wary of "the busy, teeming crowd," in which "a person grows weary of society," he highlighted the perennial importance to return to humanity's "innate need for companionship."[14] We need not paint him as some heroic man of the

10. Kierkegaard, *Journal and Papers* 3:3169, 627.

11. Kierkegaard, *Journal and Papers* 3:3188, 462.

12. See Kierkegaard, *Works of Love*, 44–90.

13. See, for example, Kierkegaard, *Letters and Documents*, 107, 379–86.

14. Kierkegaard, *Works of Love*, 154.

people, of course, even if Bukdahl's point is apt that it was "the common man who constituted his hope for the future of Christianity."[15] Such people actually became the primary intended audience of Kierkegaard's later polemical writings against the State Church, precisely because he felt there was something in the more straightforward outlook of "the common man" which might receive the warnings about the abuses of Christianity at face value and perhaps lead to someone (actually) doing something about it.

Although Kierkegaard could be a withdrawn character, and certainly knew how to be blunt and sharp when needed, his social interactions often belied a natural pastoral interest, where he showed genuine concern for personal situations. As Hans Brøchner recollected, "I myself have learnt from experience how Kierkegaard understood that art of lifting one up when one felt bowed down; of comforting when one was worried—and this without your having to tell him what was weighing on you or upsetting you."[16] In the midst of a significant struggle with depression, Brøchner happened to meet Kierkegaard while out for a walk:

> Without my needing to say a word, he saw with his sharp glance that I longed to be lifted out of this despondent mood; and he knew, without seeming for a moment to refer to my trouble directly, how to set my heart at liberty. I left him happy and confident, and was for a long time freed from the power of depression.[17]

Kierkegaard's concern for those around him was not only a trait of his interested personality; it was an emanation of the theological conviction to appropriate the message of the Gospel within one's life and the lives of others.[18] It was also an application of what, in *Works of Love*, he calls "the duty to find in the world of actuality the people we can love

---

15. Bukdahl, *Kierkegaard and the Common Man*, 111.

16. Brøchner, "Recollections," 31.

17. Brøchner, "Recollections," 31.

18. Aside from ad hoc indirect counselling sessions in the street though, the fulfilment of Kierkegaard's pastoral calling was complex. Although his convictions about the desire to serve God and people seem evident from the way he lived his life, the particular desire to become a *rural* pastor was bound up with a mixture of escapism and personal guilt: "It appealed to me both idyllically as a wish in contrast to a strenuous life and also religiously as a kind of penitence to find the time and the quiet to grieve properly over that in which I personally may have offended." *Søren Kierkegaard's Journals and Papers*, 5:5961, 358.

in particular and in loving them to love the people we see."[19] Kierkegaard's pastoral concern for the individual is contrasted by Christendom's
preachers, whose sermons do *not* seem to have anything to say to the
direst needs of the individuals they "see" in the pews below them:

> Take any contemporary sermon you choose and hand it to
> someone who is really suffering, to someone suffering depres-
> sion bordering on insanity, to someone with an obsession, or
> someone suffering for the sake of the truth—it sounds like
> mockery of him; it does not dare to console him because it never
> dares to think of his suffering. That there are sorrow and adver-
> sity and hardship etc.[20]

Aside from what Kierkegaard saw as the economic hypocrisies of the
established pastors,[21] it was the sermonic assumption that the hearers
should be living "a cosy, pleasurable life"[22] that most frustrated Kierkegaard. Such assumptions came at the expense of the many who might be
in genuine need and would have felt little comfort from such sermons.

Given the pastorally deficient sermons he often observed, what
kind of sermons would Kierkegaard himself have attempted to preach in
his rural pastorate? Evidently, Kierkegaard had a lot to say both for *and*
against preaching, so it is especially difficult to imagine what week-to-
week sermons would have looked like. We are immediately confronted
with a plethora of speculative questions. Would he use his "maieutic"
indirect communication to lure his hearers into the truth of the Gospel,
or would he stick with the sharp-edged direct communication of his later
years?[23] Or perhaps he might favor the meandering expositional style of
some of his religious discourses? How seriously might we take the flippant comments in his journals, for example, that there should be preaching *every day*,[24] or that preaching should not happen in churches but on
the street?[25] And what about his curious notion that preachers should
not preach their own sermons at all but should simply read out a sermon

19. Kierkegaard, *Works of Love*, 159.

20. *Søren Kierkegaard's Journals and Papers*, 3:3501, 598.

21. See also Perez-Alvarez, *Vexing Gadfly*.

22. *Søren Kierkegaard's Journals and Papers*, 3:3501, 598.

23. On the paradox of Kierkegaard's direct and indirect communication, see chapter 6.

24. *Søren Kierkegaard's Journals and Papers*, 3:3521, 607.

25. *Søren Kierkegaard's Journals and Papers*, 1:653, 287. On Kierkegaard's intriguing comments on street preaching, see again chapter 6.

from Luther without telling the congregation, just to see if any suppos-edly "faithful Lutherans" might object to the challenging content?[26] Are these eccentric ideas merely frivolous, or might we have actually seen them borne out from time to time in his ministry? We can at least say that being a consistent congregant under Kierkegaard's preaching would not have been for the faint-hearted.

As a "bread-and-butter" Lutheran pastor, of course, Kierkegaard may have been expected to comply—in some sense, at least—with the homiletical guidelines that were normative for all Danish clergy at that time. According to Thulstrup, these guidelines included the rule that "sermons were not to contain anything too obscure or incomprehen-sible," that they should not sound overly "elevated," and that they "were not to exceed an hour in length as 'ordinary people' would find it boring." We also read that preachers must "keep to the text," and that they were "forbidden to allow addresses to be characterized by private emotions or to attack anyone for personal reasons."[27] The more one reads such parameters, in fact, the more it seems to make sense that Kierkegaard never received the official call from Bishop Mynster![28]

Yet from his discourses and his actual preached sermons,[29] we can certainly see a pattern in which one could imagine regular preaching tak-ing place with the explicit intention of edifying the believer.[30] Kierkeg-aard's discourses are often at pains to lift hearers *out* of the subjective fretfulness of their life and to renew them with the transformative power of the Gospel.[31] In addition, as will be seen in chapter 3, Kierkegaard's high view of Scripture—not just of a "doctrine" of Scripture, but of its efficacious use in the life of the believer—would have constrained many of his communicative ideals under the overarching need to deliver the appropriated content of Scripture to his congregation. This would not discount, of course, the use of various and highly imaginative types of

26. See *Søren Kierkegaard's Journals and Papers*, 3:2493, 72–3; 3:3496, 596.

27. Thulstrup, *Kierkegaard and the Church in Denmark*, 89.

28. For a discussion of Kierkegaard's critiques of Mynster's preaching and theol-ogy, see Tolstrup, "Kierkegaard's Critical Encounter with Bishop Mynster."

29. See chapter 4. See also Edwards, "Kierkegaard the Preacher."

30. For an example of recontextualized adaptations of some of Kierkegaard's dis-courses, which are dialogically applied to "real" situations, see Pattison and Jensen, *Kierkegaard's Pastoral Dialogues*.

31. See, for example, "Strengthening in the Inner Being," in Kierkegaard, *Eighteen Upbuilding Discourses*, 80–101.

biblical communication in order to achieve this goal. We can only specu-late, of course, over the extent to which the pressures of full-time minis-try would have curbed and shaped the ideals he himself speculated upon in the relative comfort of his Copenhagen apartment.[32]

Kierkegaard's Gospel

Leaving the various communicative possibilities to one side, what is the primary *kerygma* Kierkegaard might have preached in such a setting? As is well known, one of the many caricatures of Kierkegaard is that of the legalist. That is, that the Good News of what God has done for us is drowned out by an incessant and obsessive fixation upon what we ought to be doing for God. Many know the later opinion of Karl Barth, who referred to Kierkegaard's *Works of Love* as propagating, as he says, "the *un*lovely, inquisitorial and terribly judicial character which is so distinc-tive of Kierkegaard in general."[33] On certain readings, of course, Ki-erkegaard's persistent emphasis upon Christ-like imitation renders such a "legalistic" reading possible, if not probable. In *Practice in Christianity*, he says:

> We hear nothing but sermons that could more appropriately end with "Hurrah" than "Amen." No, Christ's life here on earth is the paradigm; I and every Christian are to strive to model our lives in likeness to it, and this is the primary subject of preaching . . . to keep me up to the mark when I want to dawdle, to fortify when one becomes disheartened.[34]

Kierkegaard is at such pains to remind us that being a Christian *requires* existential striving that it may seem that he rarely catches his breath for long enough to remind us of what such imitation is founded upon. However, if one peels back Kierkegaard's polemical front a little, it is not too difficult to identify the tenets of what he believed about the Gospel in a—dare I say it—"objective" sense.

In his dialectical wrestling over how to communicate Christianity in Christendom, Kierkegaard is still able to recognize the debilitating power

32. Ironically, of course, it is the idyllic peacefulness of the rural pastorate that Kierkegaard imagines would be far more comfortable than the dramas of Copenhagen life, however misguided such a notion may have actually been.

33. Barth, *Church Dogmatics*, IV/2, 781–82 (emphasis added).

34. Kierkegaard, *Practice in Christianity*, 107.

of legalism: "The brightness of the law is fatal, [but] that of the gospel infinitely salutary."[35] Such a classically Lutheran contrast between Law and Gospel is evident elsewhere throughout his writings. It has also been noted that Kierkegaard's conception of the implications of sin "exactly parallels Luther."[36] In *The Sickness unto Death*, Kierkegaard highlights the debilitating effects of sin as evoking an existential anguish that can be quenched only by the paradoxical forgiveness of the atonement. In a famous passage, he equates the astonishing impact of the proclamation of sin alongside the proclamation of redemption:

> The paradox is the implicit *consequence* of the doctrine of the Atonement. First of all, Christianity proceeds to establish sin so firmly as a position that the human understanding can never comprehend it; and then it is this *same* Christian teaching that again undertakes to eliminate this position in such a way that the human understanding can never comprehend it.[37]

To be brought to one's knees at the realization of our fall is essential to Kierkegaard's expression of the Gospel. To miss this crucial step and to jump straight to "grace" ultimately devalues grace, whereby the believer may never truly experience the need of forgiveness. Kierkegaard therefore emphasizes the importance of "the anguished conscience" first, lest the hearer of the Gospel feel no existential "hunger" for the atonement:

> Remove the anguished conscience, and you may as well close the churches and turn them into dance halls. The anguished conscience understands Christianity . . . If a person had the power to live without needing to eat, how could he understand the necessity of eating—something the hungry person easily understands. It is the same in the life of the spirit. A person can acquire the indifference that renders the Atonement superfluous.[38]

Such indifference to the atonement was, of course, a direct result of the skewed emphasis on grace, which became a kind of card-carrying doctrine under which all congregants felt settled to the point not only of indolence, but indifference. For Kierkegaard, there was a need for the appropriate existential "context" for hearing the Gospel, so that the atonement was truly received as the power of grace, rather than being

---

35. *Søren Kierkegaard's Journals and Papers*, 3:2533, 89.
36. Hinkson, "Luther and Kierkegaard," 39.
37. Kierkegaard, *Sickness unto Death*, 100 (emphasis added).
38. *Søren Kierkegaard's Journals and Papers*, 3:2461, 64.

assumed as an inalienable right which required no personal engagement whatsoever. This problem highlights the necessity of dialectical correctivity in one's Gospel proclamation, something Kierkegaard felt was especially needed in his day to correct the Lutheran legacy surrounding justification.

Kierkegaard's Lutheran Correctivity

It is important to note that Kierkegaard emphasized the importance of a Christian's action *not* because he ceased to believe in justification by grace through faith: "The error from which Luther turned was an exaggeration with regard to works. And he was entirely right; he did not make a mistake—a person is justified solely and only by faith."[39] Far from *dis*believing Luther's doctrine, then, Kierkegaard felt that justification could no longer be heard in his particular context. Rather, the context needed to be re-prepared to hear that truth's significance, because "times are different and different times have different requirements."[40] Kierkegaard emphasized that a true *reception* of grace in such a time necessitated outward striving. Indeed, Kierkegaard noted that Catholicism, for all its faults, rightly encouraged "imitation" of Christ, whereas Protestantism, in contrast, "has devised despairing humility, an invention of the secular mentality which once and for all declared imitation to be too exalted." The dubious result was that Christians could not only avoid the "strenuousness" of imitation but could even be honored for such avoidance under the false pretense of having been too humble to attempt it.[41]

Who, though, had really "devised" such a secular ploy? Surely not Luther himself? As is well noted, although Kierkegaard "never studied Luther in the proper sense of the word,"[42] his and Luther's thought shared a "deep affinity."[43] What Kierkegaard hoped to achieve was not a rejection of what Luther stressed but to bring back Luther's experience which

39. Kierkegaard, *Judge for Yourself!*, 193. Where Kierkegaard uses the term "faith," this is often a synonym for "justification by grace alone through faith alone," which he may also refer to variously as "grace," "the Lutheran conclusion," or "the Lutheran corrective."

40. Kierkegaard, *For Self-Examination*, 15.

41. See *Søren Kierkegaard's Journals and Papers*, 2:1923, 364.

42. Prenter, "Luther and Lutheranism," 125.

43. Hinkson, "Luther and Kierkegaard," 28, and Barrett, "Kierkegaard's Appropriation of Lutheran Doctrine."

preceded his epiphany over justification. Kierkegaard wants us to re-member that Luther first strove to justify himself for twenty years in a monastery before realizing his need for "a cure" for his "anguished conscience."[44] In Christendom, the anguished conscience was neither preached nor felt, thus the repetition of Luther's "cure" became a mere pantomime, totally missing the existential context of Luther's emphasis.[45] Kierkegaard's generation could not hear grace sufficiently because they had not *first* heard the Law and, consequently, had not experienced grace as a true "cure" for their failure to keep it.[46]

Kierkegaard's corrective was actually a corrective of a corrective which had become a normative.[47] Luther's corrective-turned-normative had become "confusing," producing "characteristics exactly the opposite of the original."[48] Kierkegaard's self-appointed task was to reorder the dialectic in order to be more contextually faithful to the Gospel:

> Not that the minor premise should now be made the major premise, not that faith and grace should be abolished or dispar-aged—God forbid—no, it is precisely for the sake of the major premise . . . [that] it certainly becomes most proper to pay more attention to the minor premise.[49]

In doing so, he was genuinely attempting to remain faithful to the "major premise" of grace as the essence of the Gospel.[50] Aside from the

44. *Søren Kierkegaard's Journals and Papers*, 3:2550, 100–101. Podmore's work on *Anfechtung* highlights the significance of spiritual trial for both Luther and Kierkeg-aard, particularly highlighting Kierkegaard's "Lutheran nostalgia" in the absence of this anguished conscience in Christendom. Podmore, "The Lightning and the Earth-quake," 574. See also Podmore, *Struggling with God*.

45. Kierkegaard likened this contextual contrast of presuppositions to a scholar, who, after twenty years of diligent scholarship, declares, "It is not scholarship that mat-ters!" Kierkegaard says that if an illiterate innkeeper overheard this scholar's declara-tion and agreeably declared, "It is not scholarship that matters!" this statement would not mean the same thing because of the variance in the preconditions of each person's statement. *Søren Kierkegaard's Journals and Papers*, 3:2543, 93–94.

46. *Søren Kierkegaard's Journals and Papers*, 3:2550, 101.

47. According to Tilley, a Kierkegaardian corrective contains three necessary te-nets: "It must aim at reforming the established order, be expertly one-sided, and it must not become normative." Tilley, "Corrective," 86.

48. *Søren Kierkegaard's Journals and Papers*, 1:711, 333. "We completely forget that Luther urged faith in contrast to a fantastically exaggerated asceticism." *Søren Kierkeg-aard's Journals and Papers*, 3:2484, 70.

49. Kierkegaard, *For Self-Examination*, 24.

50. Morgan somewhat misunderstands the theological ordering of Kierkegaard's

corrective measure, it is clear that Kierkegaard's "doctrine" of the Gospel was essentially Lutheran. On the theological reality of the Eucharist, Kierkegaard says—somewhat mirroring Luther—"Christ first sups with you, and only then do you sup with him. Grace is everything."[51] It is more than obvious that Kierkegaard is no Pelagian, but that he merely wanted to correct the skewed normative that had become "uncorrectable." For Kierkegaard, Lutheranism had become *un*Lutheran, undermining the Gospel that Luther had preached precisely by attempting to keep saying it just like Luther.[52]

Luther himself, however, does not entirely escape Kierkegaard's disapproval: "Luther turns Christianity upside down," he says, having preached the reassured conscience, because this is "completely opposite to the New Testament."[53] To preach "assurance" to the consciences of Christendom was futile because such people first needed their consciences aroused to existential restlessness. According to Kierkegaard, this predicament was Luther's own fault for not emphasizing this other aspect:

> Ah, but Luther was not a dialectician; he did not see the enormous danger involved in making something else supreme . . .

---

conception when he says, "There is no indication that Kierkegaard means to place justification before striving as Luther clearly does. Rather, it is only after a person strives and nearly despairs that Christ will raise her up . . . For Kierkegaard grace meets a person only as a person first strives toward the requirement." Morgan, "Grace and Christianity's Requirement," 923. It is not that Kierkegaard believes the anguished conscience is an essential prerequisite to God's gracious offer of justification. It is rather that, in Christendom, the proclamation of justification was bound up within the corrosive influence of Christendom's "idea" of grace, which proved to be a mere inoculation against the reality.

51. *Søren Kierkegaard's Journals and Papers*, 4:3936, 73. Regarding the believer's reception of justification Vainio places Kierkegaard closer to Luther: "But how is it that Communion enables forgiveness? The answer is amazingly classical—through substitutionary atonement." Vainio, "Kierkegaard's Eucharistic Spirituality," 19.

52. Unwittingly or otherwise, the Danish Lutherans had followed Hegel's own view of Luther, who saw him as having abolished the imitative elements of Christianity in order to create a fully enculturated Protestantism. See Hinkson, "Will the Real Martin Luther Please Stand Up!," 68–69. Hinkson also highlights J. G. Hamann's rejection of the "Enlightenment" appropriation of Luther, which had de-emphasized Luther's paradoxical and anti-rational emphases. In Hamann, Kierkegaard found a more faithful appropriation of Luther which captured Luther's true spirit, as opposed to the contextless repeating of Luther's dictums. "Will the Real Martin Luther Please Stand Up!," 71–76.

53. *Søren Kierkegaard's Journals and Papers*, 3:2550, 100–101.

He did not understand that he had provided the corrective and that he ought to turn off the tap with extreme caution lest people automatically make him into a paradigm.[54]

Such a criticism seems a little unfair to Luther for a few reasons. Kierkegaard's less-than-comprehensive engagement with Luther's writings meant that he was seemingly unaware that Luther actually demonstrates a clear understanding of works as "tributary" to faith in grace.[55] Indeed, Luther once even admonished his Wittenberg congregation "that he would stop preaching unless he saw more fruit of the gospel among them."[56] As Wood notes, Luther "never proclaimed God's great Yes, his acceptance of man in the gospel, without at the same time proclaiming his No, his rejection of all man's presumption and pretence."[57] Furthermore, Coe shows how Luther's sermons "regularly censure post-Gospel antinomianism with a dialectical rigour often missed by Luther's inheritors."[58]

Kierkegaard, then, appears to show a basic misunderstanding regarding Luther's dialectical awareness, claiming that "Luther struck too hard" in de-emphasizing works in the drive to attack self-righteousness.[59] However, even where Luther's sermons *do* speak one-sidedly,[60] it is not inappropriate to emphasize a singular truth in a particular context for a particular purpose, least of all in sermons. Indeed, why should it always be the corrector's responsibility to correct their own corrective? The necessarily polemical task of correctivity means that the corrector may be unable to see where future generations might misinterpret their thought. As already noted, of course, such divergent interpretations of Kierkegaard's own polemical emphases abound, so it is difficult to imagine how

54. *Søren Kierkegaard's Journals and Papers*, 3:2521, 83.

55. Luther, *Sermons* VIII, 225.

56. Meuser, "Luther as Preacher," 146.

57. Wood, *Captive to the Word*, 91.

58. Coe, "Kierkegaard's Forking for Extracts," 16.

59. *Søren Kierkegaard's Journals and Papers*, 3:2522, 84. Notably, Barth launched a very similar critique of Luther: "Out of his great knowledge Luther believed that he had to say again and again the one thing that motivated him. He ignored whole complexes of biblical concepts, e.g., that of law and reward, because he knew only too well what justification by faith is." Barth, *Homiletics*, 78.

60. See, for example: "Today, Papists, Anabaptists and other sects make outcry: 'What mean you by preaching so much about faith and Christ? Are the people thereby made better? Surely works are essential.' Arguments of this character have indeed a semblance of merit, but, when examined by the light of truth, are mere empty, worthless twaddle." Luther, *Sermons* III, 240.

Kierkegaard could *not* have seen the same problems applying to his own thought.

On a similar note, Kierkegaard emphasized that Luther's "undialectical" one-sidedness on the Gospel was due to Luther's over-responsiveness to his immediate context: "[Luther] constantly stood in the tension of combat, concentrated as a polemicist, stood in the smoke and steam of battle . . . which makes it impossible to find either the time or the quiet or the clarity to see whether what one has begun can be carried through."[61] Such a charge is certainly partially true of Luther, whose theological emphases and polemics were often responsive to the issues and opponents he faced at the time rather than "systematic" treatments. However, again, this may be even truer of Kierkegaard's own theology, which was so deeply embedded in the "combat" of his context that it is virtually impossible to understand his thought properly without reference to his unique cultural and ecclesiastical climate.[62] Kierkegaard laments, "O, Luther, who more than you has been used by adherents for the very opposite of what he intended?"[63] In light of all that has been said and done with Kierkegaard's own intellectual legacy in the twentieth century,[64] he need not have searched far to answer his rhetorical question!

To some extent this only further demonstrates the affinity of Luther and Kierkegaard. They both strove for the authentic expression of the Gospel in their own time which was both faithful to the New Testament and cognizant of the existential implications for their hearers. Yet their very expressions of the Gospel were, like the book of James itself, angulated for their respective moments.

Correctivity in Kierkegaard's Congregation

What impact, then, might such correctivity have had on Kierkegaard's imaginary flock? It is evident that Kierkegaard's primary mission in his writing was "to arouse *restlessness* oriented toward inward deepening."[65]

61. *Søren Kierkegaard's Journals and Papers*, 4:3617, 669.

62. In fact, Luther's awareness that his own task was dialectically corrective (by calling the Church to hear the Gospel in his time, instead of the Law) is similar to Kierkegaard's self-awareness of his own momentary emphasis upon Christian imitation. See Jung-Kim and Rasmussen, "Martin Luther," 206–7.

63. *Søren Kierkegaard's Journals and Papers*, 2:1923, 364.

64. See chapter 1.

65. Kierkegaard, *For Self-Examination*, 20.

This restlessness would also, undoubtedly, be evoked in his imaginary congregation, whether they would have liked it or not (!). However, Kierkegaard's intention in this method would not be to lay impossible burdens upon the shoulders of the faithful, but rather to evoke greater depth in the life of the believer through the prior deconstruction of idolatrous faith. Kierkegaard's discourses often lead us this way, in which the changeful dramas of our own lives are simultaneously challenged and soothed by the *dis*comfort that grace brings to both the broken and the proud.[66]

Kierkegaard's expression of the Gospel was adaptable in emphasis to the different ears he encountered, even if he presumed most of the ears in his generation were deaf, dull, and in need of a blunt awakening. It is for this reason that Kierkegaard is occasionally likened to a "revivalist preacher."[67] Although, as noted in the previous chapter, Kierkegaard was critical of revivalists per se,[68] at times Kierkegaard also shared their corrective approach to the self-protective malaise of the establishment. Ironically enough, it is in such moments of revivalist affinity that Kierkegaard becomes most aware of the normative limitations of the quiet country pastor he might otherwise have become:

> Revival preachers must be cunning. "The cultured" shrewdly stay away when they hear that there is to be such a preacher, or if they come they come mentally armed with a thousand prudential rules and evasions . . . The lie has been contrived that to be earnest about what is said is extremism. A quiet, modest, retiring country pastor probably cannot preach differently; there is no setting for the larger decisions. Nevertheless he can see to humbling himself and his listeners under eminence and greatness so that it all becomes a little more than a pleasant hour.[69]

Contrary to pietistic caricatures, Kierkegaard's attempt to "awaken" is anything but legalistic, not least because he never claims to have "arrived" himself. But primarily, Kierkegaard is not a legalist because his

---

66. As Vainio correctly observes, "While Kierkegaard sounds quite morbid in some of his *Discourses*, the overall tone is encouraging and positive." Vainio, "Kierkegaard's Eucharistic Spirituality," 22.

67. Kierkegaard's Christendomian contemporary, Hans Latten Martensen, referred to Kierkegaard in this way, with more than a hint of mocking condescension. See Backhouse, *Kierkegaard's Critique of Christian Nationalism*, 46.

68. See also Bukdahl, *Kierkegaard and the Common Man*, 116.

69. *Søren Kierkegaard's Journals and Papers*, 3:3481, 589.

task is precisely to counteract the outward legalism of Christendom, the sense of feeling the need to arm oneself with "a thousand rules and evasions" so as to avoid the unsettling challenge of the Gospel, in order that the "pleasant hour" of Sunday ritual may continue unencumbered by anything God might actually say. If legalism may be defined in the tenor of Jesus' rebuke to the Pharisees in Matthew 23, then legalism is the state in which outwardness gleams while inwardness rots: the very essence of a whitewashed tomb. Pastor Kierkegaard would no doubt insist that inward change is the only means by which outward expression can be genuine.

Of course, Kierkegaard's perpetual awareness of correctivity also leads us to imagine that his urgent emphasis upon works would *not* be "perpetual" after all. Just as he imagines that a reincarnated Luther in Denmark would immediately demand that his infamous Epistle of Straw be "drawn forward" again in an age that had closed its ears to discipleship,[70] so we might imagine that a more—dare I say it—"straightforward" proclamation of the Good News might resound from Kierkegaard's pulpit had his congregation bound themselves in functional works-righteousness. Indeed, far from remaining tethered to a single post, Kierkegaard's approach is at its most potent amid the perpetual tension of the life of faith itself.[71] So alert a dialectician is Kierkegaard that he can stringently emphasize the one thing needful for the sake of the moment without discarding the dialectical other, however "extreme" this may sound at the time.[72] Indeed, given Kierkegaard's overt attentiveness to the concept of correctivity, it is at least plausible to speculate that a more regular pastoral ministry involving the same people (albeit the same changeable people) would give him cause to exhibit this same sense of self-corrective correctivity, in which *each* moment could be spoken to with prophetic precision.

In this way, Kierkegaard may well appear in the guise of a "legalist" at times, but only from the perspective of the one whose particular existential situation renders Kierkegaard's emphasis no longer the

70. Kierkegaard, *For Self-Examination*, 24.

71. Hinkson notes that, for Kierkegaard, the dialectical striving of faith is welcomed as always "uncompleted." Hinkson, "Luther and Kierkegaard," 41. Similarly, Nowachek contends that one of Kierkegaard's main aims "is both to invite his readers to live within the tension of faith and to help them view this tension as itself something sacred." Nowachek, "Living within the Sacred Tension," 884.

72. For a further discussion of Kierkegaard's understanding of the Gospel in light of charges of "extremism," see chapter 5.

one-thing-needful. Although Kierkegaard may have been a tad harsh to expect Luther to "turn off the tap" of emphatic grace himself, we shall do well *not* to imitate Kierkegaard's strictness on this point and to do him the honor of adjusting his own tap for him as our own ecclesial situations allow. It is in this way that we may contribute to the Gospel's effective proclamation *and* hearing within each contingent moment. And in doing so, we may allow Kierkegaard (even if just for a moment) to become *our* imaginary pastor and we his imaginary flock.

3

Waddling Geese in the Pulpit

The Perils of Reading and Preaching the Bible

"To be alone with Holy Scripture! I dare not! If I open it—any passage—it traps me at once."[1] Kierkegaard's corrective expression of the Gospel, which we saw in the last chapter, was in part an attempt to be "a Luther to the Lutherans" of Danish Christendom. To a different extent to Luther, Kierkegaard also rediscovered the force of the Bible in his own time. He saw one of his chief tasks to be a prophetic voice by calling attention to the way the Bible was being (mis)read and (mis)preached by the Christendom Church:

> Just as Luther stepped forward with only the Bible at the Diet of Worms, so I would like to step forward with only the New Testament, take the simplest Christian maxim, and ask each individual: Have you fulfilled this even approximately—if not, do you then want to reform the Church?[2]

This chapter will discuss the way in which Kierkegaard's biblical "hermeneutics" strike at the heart of the lack of imitation in biblical engagement, not least in relation to those called to preach the Bible. I will first outline three core categories of Kierkegaard's hermeneutical approach: De-Familiarization, Appropriation, and Consequentiality. These categories will then be applied to preaching, with a particular emphasis on consequentiality. It will be seen that Kierkegaard's humorous parable,

1. Kierkegaard, *For Self-Examination*, 31.
2. *Søren Kierkegaard's Journals and Papers*, 6:6727, 377.

"The Tame Goose," aptly portrays both the problem Kierkegaard sees in Christendom preaching, and an exhortation to defamiliarize the message of the Bible for those who think they have heard it all before. Fred Craddock's "New Homiletic" will then be discussed as a modern example of a homiletical approach that attempts to apply a Kierkegaardian hermeneutic to narrative preaching. This may seem to harness some of Kierkegaard's concerns about indirect communication but it falls significantly short of exemplifying his concern for preacherly authority. Kierkegaard's ideal homiletic is one that exemplifies not a polished homiletical technique—narratival or otherwise—but an overt awareness of the preacher's existential engagement with the biblical truths being interpreted and proclaimed.

First, then, I will outline some of the key tenets of how Kierkegaard approached scriptural interpretation.

Kierkegaard's Biblical "Hermeneutics"

Kierkegaard's life and works were utterly dominated by his engagement with the Bible. As one of his pseudonyms says, no doubt evoking the reality for their author: "The Bible lies on my table at all times and is the book in which I read most."[3] Dalrymple has said that the Bible is "indisputably Kierkegaard's principal literary influence,"[4] while Pons notes that the Bible has a kind of "invisible omnipresence" throughout all his writings.[5] Yet because of his famed legacy as a philosopher, beyond the particular compartment of Kierkegaard scholarship he is rarely appreciated as a biblical reader or scholar. Rasmussen observes that "despite the depth, breadth, insight, and verve of Kierkegaard's biblical imagination, his reputation as an interpreter of Scripture remains obscured."[6] Richard Bauckham comments that Kierkegaard "is not an exegete, at least in the modern sense."[7] This statement—made in a biblical commentary which directly engages with Kierkegaard perhaps more than any other— is more a critique of historical criticism than a critique of Kierkegaard.

---

3. Kierkegaard, *Stages on Life's Way*, 230.

4. Dalrymple, "Abraham: Framing Fear and Trembling," 43–44.

5. Pons, *Stealing a Gift*, xv.

6. Rasmussen, "Kierkegaard's Biblical Hermeneutics," 249.

7. Bauckham, *James*, 161.

Bauckham is aptly highlighting the inherent problem of what it means to be a so-called modern exegete.

Kierkegaard's insights on Scripture are not usually deemed noteworthy to biblical studies because they do not conform to the historical-critical ideal for modern academic discourse. Kierkegaard himself was well aware of this problem and was dubious about the ways in which modern biblical scholarship was becoming an increasingly ironical mode of discourse vis-à-vis what it means to "interpret" Scripture:

> All this interpreting and interpreting and scholarly research and new scholarly research that is produced on the solemn and serious principle that it is in order to understand God's Word properly—look more closely and you will see that it is in order to defend oneself against God's Word.[8]

This is Kierkegaard's principal problem, that in the academy the Bible is often read critically rather than doxologically, that it has become a mere tool of the established mindset rather than an inspiration or a challenge leading to deeper imitation of Christ and his kingdom. Kierkegaard saw that the perpetual layers of academic scholarship on numerous facets of biblical texts and subtexts—even by the early to mid-nineteenth century—had gotten well out of control. It had led to a culture whereby genuine subjective encounter with the text—which is surely the primary "point" of a Christian wanting to interpret the Bible in the first place—had become impossible. For Kierkegaard, this culture is no accident but part of a sinister plot to avoid taking God at his Word: "Christian scholarship is the human race's prodigious invention to defend itself against the N.T., to ensure that one can continue to be a Christian without letting the N.T. get too close."[9] As long as the scholars can keep producing works of "further interpretation" in every new era, they may successfully avoid coming "face to face" with the inconvenient and/or dangerous implications of the text.

Kierkegaard's scathing view of this avoidant culture within biblical scholarship is one reason why Hannay is right to assert that, in a sense, "Kierkegaard's thought is antithetical to hermeneutics."[10] However, al-

---

8. Kierkegaard, *For Self-Examination*, 34.

9. *Søren Kierkegaard's Journals and Papers*, 3:2872, 270.

10. Hannay, "Something on Hermeneutics and Communication," 1. For a discussion of Kierkegaard and key themes within the discipline of hermeneutics more broadly, see Pons, *Stealing a Gift*, 16–49.

though Kierkegaard might have had little time for the merry-go-round of academic biblical hermeneutics, this is not because he did not think that biblical interpretation mattered, nor that it was somehow easy. He simply recognized that it was, ironically, far *easier* to speak of the endless complexities of scriptural interpretation when it resulted in one never needing to address its implications for oneself. Kierkegaard himself was in fact a voracious biblical "hermeneut." He not only included many profound scriptural expositions within his many published works, but in his journals and notebooks we see him constantly engaging with exegetical problems and concepts, evidencing robust interpretative engagement with the biblical text. Indeed, commenting on Kierkegaard's "marginalia"—the annotations made on one of Kierkegaard's personal copies of the New Testament—Dewey notes, "The delicate minuscule handwriting etched alongside the verses shows the touch of an exegetical virtuoso who can plumb the depths of meaning and capture it in word."[11] He adds that Kierkegaard's acute engagement with the Bible served as "a research tool and sounding board for his unfolding authorship."[12] But how did Kierkegaard's engagement with the Bible manifest in his own approach to understanding and communicating it for others?

Kierkegaard sought a "hermeneutical" approach that did not encapsulate reader and text in a ceaseless playground of interpretation like the biblical scholars but sought to enable the reader to engage in the world of the text itself, to let it inhabit their existence and speak to them with its own concerns. Although it has been noted that Kierkegaard's practical hermeneutical approach is very nuanced—"plurivocal" rather than systematic[13]—this does not mean it is mired in convoluted caveats regarding the meaning of language or contextual perspective. Kierkegaard's approach is indeed plurivocal in form but is underlain by a univocal understanding of the relationship between text and reader. This is more straightforward than is often supposed in the many academic tomes that exist on Kierkegaard's theories of communication. The key tenets of Kierkegaard's contextual hermeneutical approach can be summarized as *defamiliarization*, *appropriation*, and *consequentiality*.

---

11. Dewey, "Kierkegaard and the Blue Testament," 391.

12. Dewey, "Kierkegaard and the Blue Testament," 407.

13. Rasmussen, "Kierkegaard's Biblical Hermeneutics," 277.

Defamiliarization

Kierkegaard believed that the distance between reader and text which had arisen in the modern era must be bridged. But it was not a simple case of making the reader familiar with the content of the text. They already believed themselves to be familiar with it; it simply made no difference to them. Kierkegaard knew that to truly familiarize the Bible to people personally, the Bible must become *un*familiar again so as to challenge the reader afresh, every time it is read or preached. One way in which he sought to encourage this was through creative retellings of the biblical narratives, otherwise known as his "experimental hermeneutic," akin to Nathan's parable to David (cf. 2 Sam 12:1–12).[14] These attempts have been said to produce a deliberately "alienating distanciation" between text and reader,[15] for the purposes of eventual edification. Most famously, in *Fear and Trembling*, Kierkegaard rewrote the story of Abraham and Isaac from various perspectives in order to portray a kaleidoscopic range of perspectives emerging from Abraham's existential situation. This allows the reader to inhabit the world of the story itself and thus engage personally with its characters and consequences as though for the first time. What was most critical for Kierkegaard was that, when reading or hearing such a story, we never take Abraham's experience in vain. We cannot truly understand the text unless we take on the very same existential burdens and crises of faith as though they were our own.[16] It is most appropriate, Kierkegaard says, to be made "sleepless" by Abraham, even if one cannot comprehensively "understand" the challenge of faith.[17] This "sleeplessness," a kind of necessary anxiety for Abraham's paradoxical task—is only possible if the reader is able to shed their preconceptions and reimagine the narrative anew.

Appropriation

For Kierkegaard, textual *appropriation* is undoubtedly the most important aspect of his hermeneutical approach. This is the process of the

14. Engelke, "David and Solomon," 106.

15. Damgaard, "Kierkegaard's Rewriting of Biblical Narratives," 216.

16. "The rewritings seek to engage us in a dialogue with the biblical narrative by raising for us the questions with which the narrative characters struggle." Damgaard, "Kierkegaard's Rewriting of Biblical Narratives," 216.

17. Kierkegaard, *Fear and Trembling*, 28.

Bible being read subjectively, as though it were addressed to the present individual, not only to an ancient community. His most important
book on this topic is undoubtedly *For Self-Examination* (1851), where
he discusses the issue of scriptural appropriation at length, exhorting the
reader: "When you read God's Word, in everything you read, continually say to yourself: It is I to whom it is speaking, it is I *about whom* it is
speaking."[18] Kierkegaard is simultaneously aware of objective doctrinal
and historical themes in relation to Scripture,[19] but he is more concerned
that such truths are read with the overarching vision of Scripture as a
"love letter" from God,[20] not as a scholastic textbook. Despite his aforementioned issues with biblical scholarship, Kierkegaard did not reject it
entirely and was himself well trained academically.[21] But he did feel it was
grossly misplaced in its approach and led away from appropriation. This
was a problem which did not merely exist among scholars but filtered
down to pastors and congregants too. The primary objective was that the
Bible be read as the appropriated Word *from* God *to* us. For Kierkegaard,
this was essentially the primary purpose of Scripture, a communication
from God to his children, from lover to beloved. Thus, any attempt to
override or undermine this precept—however eloquent—undermines
the very ontology of Scripture itself: "If you are a scholar, remember that
if you do not read God's Word in another way, it will turn out that after a
lifetime of reading God's Word many hours every day, you nevertheless
have never read—God's Word."[22] Kierkegaard wanted to invert the way
in which the Bible is approached, so that it is not the reader who exegetes
the text but the text that exegetes the reader.[23]

---

18. Kierkegaard, *For Self-Examination*, 36 (emphasis added).

19. See chapter 4.

20. See Kierkegaard, *For Self-Examination*, 9–51. Brandt notes the impact of Pietists like Johann Gottfried Herder (1744–1803), who also believed the Bible should
be read as a divine "love letter." Brandt, "Paul," 193.

21. See Pattison, "Kierkegaard the Theology Student," 89–109.

22. Kierkegaard, *For Self-Examination*, 33.

23. See Polk's definition of Kierkegaardian appropriation as "a deeply personal
process of reading and knowing. It is the *how* of reading the New Testament which
accepts the fact that *you* are not exegeting the text but are being exegeted *by* the text;
that in it *you* are addressed by God and that *you* are being addressed with a call." Polk,
"Kierkegaard's Use of the New Testament," 244.

Consequentiality

Consequentiality refers to the inclination toward action as a result of reading the text. Kierkegaard leaned heavily upon the "hearing and doing" exhortation in James 1:22–25, emphasizing the fact that the reader's engagement with this "love letter from God" must consequently lead to existential and ethical transformation. As noted in the previous chapter, Kierkegaard especially valued James as "a theological corrective to what he perceived as a pervasive misunderstanding of and abuse of grace" within Danish Lutheranism,[24] whereby the imperative action advocated by James had been "shoved aside."[25] Following James, Kierkegaard emphasized the need for the reader to translate their appropriated hearing of the Word into transformative action. All hermeneutics, then, must ultimately lead to existential consequence. To this end, Kierkegaard loved the "unconditional obedience" of the birds and the lilies (cf. Matt 6:25–34), seeing them as the greatest possible teachers of the life of faith since, moment by moment, they peacefully submit to God's will alone.[26] To "serve two masters" in a hermeneutical sense is to try to read God's Word without allowing it to affect your life. Indeed, "embryonic theologians," he says, "ought to take care that, by beginning to preach too early, they do not talk themselves into rather than identify themselves with Christianity and take the consequences."[27] It is the avoidance of the true consequences of honest biblical exegesis that led to the prevalence of scholarly mediators that come between the reader and the text.[28] Biblical exegesis, it seems, is a perilous thing indeed. It requires the kind of courage that is rarely seen in the established Church: "Ah, how many have there been in Christianity's 1800 years who have had the courage to dare to be alone with the N.T. What dreadful consequences it could drive me to—this stubborn and domineering book—If I were to be alone with it this way!"[29]

24. Roberts, "James," 210.

25. Kierkegaard, *For Self-Examination*, 16.

26. See Stan, "The Lily in the Field," 59.

27. *Søren Kierkegaard's Journals and Papers*, 1:429, 172.

28. Kierkegaard explicitly urges believers to "read the N.T. without a commentary" because such mediation detracts from personal encounter with God through the text. Indeed, the one who reads Scripture through the lens of the commentaries of others "deals with the Scriptures contra naturam." *Søren Kierkegaard's Journals and Papers*, 1:210, 85.

29. *Søren Kierkegaard's Journals and Papers*, 3:2872, 272.

Biblical Interpretation and Authority

The three hermeneutical categories outlined above are essentially inter-linked. *Defamiliarization* enables the reader to actually hear and inhabit the text; *appropriation* encourages the reader to not only observe the truths within the text but to see such truths as being spoken to them personally as direct recipient; *consequentiality* urges the reader to not only apply scriptural truth to and for themselves but to be personally transformed by it, culminating in outward action, including a willingness to suffer for the truth. There are, however, potential questions which might be asked of Kierkegaard's hermeneutical approach. How do you guard against inappropriate and/or unorthodox subjective interpretations of Scripture? And how do Kierkegaard's hermeneutics relate to his view of biblical authority?

Defamiliarization and Subjective Exegesis

To think creatively about how we communicate Scripture for the sake of defamiliarization, distanciation, and ethical involvement is especially helpful for Christians who claim to hold biblical authority in high regard. This is because we may often find profound passages of Scripture (such as famous verses like John 3:16) to be utterly *un*profound purely because we may know them so well or have heard them so many times before. Such texts can lose their edge and become blunted by over-familiarity. This is what calls for such texts to be creatively "reintroduced" to the hearers so that the text is able to live again with the force and severity intended by its original inspiration. However, Kierkegaard's polyphonic rewriting of narratives such as Abraham's does open up the problem of relativistic readings that are more common in reader-response literary criticism. The subjective interpreter's own agenda could impose itself as a "new interpretation" of the text which appears irreconcilable with authorial intent, other parts of Scripture, or orthodox theology more broadly.

Kierkegaard's intent, however, is always to catalyze the subjective involvement of the hearer to the text itself, not merely to impose yet another "new interpretation." This, again, is why it remains debatable whether Kierkegaard actually cares about "hermeneutics" per se (in terms of how the academic discipline is normally understood).[30] As noted, Kierkegaard

---

30. Rasmussen defends Kierkegaard against potential criticism of his employment

wants the reader to fall into the world of the text, to feel its contours, and to experience what the authors and characters experience, that the reader may be inspired and challenged by the truth of that text for themselves. This strategy, though certainly open to eisegetical abuse, aims to create the subjective possibility for the power of the text to break away from the typed page and to infiltrate the reader's own context rather than merely remaining imprisoned within the author's original context.[31] This is also why Kierkegaard requested that his readers read his discourses (most of which are scriptural expositions) aloud, so that the biblical text may confront the reader audibly and personally, that this reading becomes a kind of "event."[32]

Kierkegaard's approach to the preeminence of the text (rather than its relativistic "interpretation") is further evidenced in an introductory aside on the nature of Scripture within one of the discourses:

> Since the importance of Holy Scripture is to be an interpreter of the divine to mankind, since its claim is to want to teach the believer everything from the beginning, it follows of itself that its language has shaped the discourse of the God-fearing about the divine, that its words and expressions resound again and again in the holy places, in every more solemn discourse about the divine, whether the speaker seeks to interpret the scriptural text by letting the text speak for itself or is using the scriptural expression in all its brevity as the clear and complete interpretation of the much he has said.[33]

---

of an inherited Pietistic lens for interpretation without "admitting" it: "[Kierkegaard's] aim is not to deny that we read in terms of interpretive horizons, but rather to insist that God's Word establishes a subjective relationship with the Divine Lover that reconfigures one's horizon and gives a new perspective on every other feature of life." Rasmussen, "Kierkegaard's Biblical Hermeneutics," 273. For Kierkegaard, his approach is not merely the employment of *his* hermeneutic, nor Luther's, nor Zinzendorf's; rather, he believes that it really is the case that such an approach is required by the Word of God itself, based on any honest engagement with the biblical text.

31. As Storer notes: "So long as a textual interpretation remains focused on the existential concern of the individual, and grounded in Christian concepts, Kierkegaard seems to think that the interpretation is appropriate." Storer, "Kierkegaard's Upbuilding Hermeneutic of Scripture," 195.

32. The eventedness of Scripture points forward to Kierkegaard's kerygmatic approach to biblical interpretation, given that the enlivening of the text of Scripture for subjective appropriation is essentially one of the primary purposes of the sermon. See Edwards, *Theology of Preaching and Dialectic*, 180–83.

33. Kierkegaard, *Eighteen Upbuilding Discourses*, 327.

Here we see a kind of rationale for Kierkegaard's use of the biblical text, to let the text both "speak for itself" and act as the hidden guarantor for the speech. This shows Kierkegaard's confidence in the clarity of Scripture rather than the usual obfuscation of much hermeneutical scholarship. The biblical text may undergird much else that the author of the sermonic discourse might say, even that which appears less overtly related. Indeed, many of Kierkegaard's discourses seem to be tangential, as though about something completely different to what was expected, and yet the reader is reminded that the whole speech, wherever it leads, may be genuinely governed by the "brevity" of the scriptural epigram which precedes, and "interprets," the discourse itself.[34]

How, though, does Kierkegaard's understanding of the authority and unity of the biblical text inform or chasten how Scripture might be interpreted?

Biblical Criticism and the Telos of Scripture

As noted, Kierkegaard's approach to biblical interpretation, though fundamentally animated by the initiative to defamiliarize, appropriate, and "consequentialize" the Word, is not monotonously applied within every instance. It is plurivocal in scope, using different scriptural voices in different ways. Within this varied approach one catches clear glimpses of Kierkegaard's understanding of the authority and coherence of Scripture by how he uses it. Indeed, Polk refers to

> Kierkegaard's habit of combining, juxtaposing, and paralleling passages from different parts of the biblical canon, interpreting one passage in the light of others, under the governing assumption that Scripture can function as a complex whole. He can scarcely think of one passage without thinking of another, then working them together in a perfectly coordinated harmony.[35]

For Kierkegaard, although the Bible is clearly understood as being a gift for—and to some extent, "about"—the one who reads or hears it, it has its own teleological coherence. That is, Scripture is not really about the reader; it is intended (by God) to draw the reader into its world and to encounter and challenge them, rather than vice versa. As such, for

---

34. For an excellent detailed study of Kierkegaard's discourses, see Pattison, *Kierkegaard's Religious Discourses*.

35. Polk, "Kierkegaard's Use of the New Testament," 238.

Kierkegaard Scripture is not a mere compendium of personal devotional applications; it is a theologically unified world into which the reader is invited.

Kierkegaard was not unaware of the critical issues surrounding various canonical books in terms of reliability, historicity, translation, and other such issues. Indeed, he regularly engaged with such problems in interesting and theologically rigorous ways.[36] Biblical criticism was not irrelevant but had lost its way via its dubiously curious interest in the peripheralities of Scripture, and the neglect of Scripture's core existential purpose and substance: "as if all this research and pondering and scrutinizing would draw God's Word very close to me; the truth is that this is the very way, this is the most cunning way, to remove God's Word as far as possible from me."[37] It is not, then, a question of ignorance to criticism on Kierkegaard's part, but one of emphasis: personal engagement must always supersede critical engagement; the latter must always serve the former:

> "But," you perhaps say, "there are so many obscure passages in the Bible, whole books that are practically riddles." To that I would answer: Before I have anything to do with this objection, it must be made by someone whose life manifests that he has scrupulously complied with all the passages that are easy to understand; is this the case with you?[38]

There are reminiscences here of Luther's critiques of Erasmus on the clarity of Scripture, whereby scriptural obscurity was used to negate the more glaringly obvious points of clarity which ought to dictate how the obscurity is interpreted within the context of the whole.[39]

For Kierkegaard, even the act of biblical translation, with all its semantic complexities, should be done in a spirit of near-desperation to hear and apply the words of the beloved. The difficult linguistic work involved in translation and interpretation must be viewed by the biblical reader as "scholarly preliminaries to a necessary evil so that he can come to the point—of reading the letter from his beloved."[40] The process of

---

36. For one of many theological reflections on history, see Kierkegaard, *For Self-Examination*, 27–31.

37. Kierkegaard, *For Self-Examination*, 35.

38. Kierkegaard, *For Self-Examination*, 29.

39. See Luther, *Bondage of the Will*, 72.

40. Kierkegaard, *For Self-Examination*, 27.

reading the love letter *as* a love letter must remain preeminent before, during, and after the work of biblical criticism or else biblical criticism is merely a "cunning" distraction. Without the theological telos for why Scripture matters in the first place, the scholar is not actually reading God's Word at all, however much work they seem to be doing with words.

One of the interesting ways Kierkegaard portrays the theological telos of Scripture is to critique how the overly specified ideal of Scripture's historical perfection is often equated with its inspiration and authority:

> Up until now we have done as follows: we have declared that Holy Scripture is divine revelation, inspired, etc.—ergo, there must then be perfect harmony between all the reports down to the least detail; it must be the most perfect Greek, etc. Let us now look at the matter from another side. God surely knows what it is "to believe," what it means to require faith . . . Now we are getting to the point! Precisely because God wants Holy Scripture to be the object of faith and an offense to any other point of view, for this reason there are carefully contrived discrepancies (which, after all, in eternity will readily be dissolved into harmonies); therefore it is written in bad Greek, etc.[41]

One might conclude from such a dialectical reflection that Kierkegaard believed Scripture to be unclear, or even erroneous. But the notion of "carefully contrived discrepancies" is actually a nuanced way of speaking of God's role in using Scripture to awaken faith in the recipient. The discrepancies point to the apparent disconnect between the world and God's Word. Hugh Pyper, in his *The Joy of Kierkegaard: Essays on Kierkegaard as a Biblical Reader* (2011), somewhat undersells Kierkegaard's view of biblical authority when he says, "What Kierkegaard wants to do at every turn is to recover the sense of the Bible as scandal. The very fact that its contents are disputed and disrupted is to him paradoxically part of its power."[42] Pyper is referring to the above passage regarding the necessary "offense" of Scripture as a kind of deconstructive trope for viewing the whole. This misses Kierkegaard's primary emphases upon the clarity and authority of Scripture. Kierkegaard saw Scripture as providentially roughshod in its aesthetic because this meant that Scripture disrupted the bourgeois certainties of Christendom and modern scientific rationalism. This required a kind of "faith leap" in order to receive it; though this was certainly no leap into the dark.

---

41. *Søren Kierkegaard's Journals and Papers*, 3:2877, 275.

42. Pyper, *Joy of Kierkegaard*, 22.

What Kierkegaard means by "discrepancies" is not that which is central to the core content of the Bible, nor even to any undermining of the authority of any of its parts. Highlighting linguistic or literary imperfection is a very different thing from challenging the clarity or theological unity of its content. The imperfections are significant because they mean that humanity cannot presume to possess God's Word on its own terms, in its own neat categories of perfection. Scripture is, in this sense, the supreme wisdom which arrives, as does the Gospel of Christ, in the guise of apparent "foolishness" (cf. 1 Cor 1:25). But Kierkegaard is not primarily interested in calling the Bible's authority a theological "scandal." Although God's Word is complexly bound up with the para-doxical revelation of Christ—the "sign of contradiction"[43]—it is not that Kierkegaard harbors complex notions of the "disrupted" system akin to postmodern philosophy. Nor is Kierkegaard primarily concerned with the "scandal" of scriptural uncertainty. Minor scriptural discrepancies serve the purpose of our lack of comprehensive control of God's Word in its *form*, allowing for the possibility of faith in its *content*. Kierkegaard re-mains exceptionally confident about the Bible's core meaning, not merely in the sense of its "headlines," but in both its whole and its parts. He demonstrated this by how he continued to use and lean upon Scripture's authority and coherence throughout his writings.

Kierkegaard's comments on biblical discrepancies, then, are not so much a commendation of higher biblical criticism as a critique of the scientific rationalism underpinning biblical criticism. In the hands of Christendom's modern scholars, the clearest and most challenging passages are treated as though they were either too confusing to truly understand or too poetically stimulating to simply obey. Indeed, "the pastors dispute about who can write most beautifully, while journals and periodicals with deep seriousness criticize the artistic aspects of the lan-guage, the construction, etc.," while forgetting that "God has not really given his word as material for a literary exercise."[44] For Kierkegaard, there is something in the telos of Scripture that is intentionally "offensive"—not against Scripture's theological unity and authority, but against those who would distract themselves from its imperative challenges to live an oth-erwise convenient life. This is the real "scandal," when Scripture's readers and preachers pretend to have imbibed its truths and yet find ways to

---

43. See Kierkegaard, *Practice in Christianity.*
44. *Søren Kierkegaard's Journals and Papers*, 3:2911, 296.

excuse themselves from living out such truths, existentially. And nowhere is this scandal more outrageous to Kierkegaard than in the perpetually unappropriated sermons of the Danish Christendom pulpit.

Kierkegaard's Hermeneutics and Preaching

For Kierkegaard, as we have seen, personal transformation is the primary goal of hermeneutics, taking the reader "from literary imitation to existential imitation."[45] It is upon this foundation that Kierkegaard's critique of preaching is best understood, explicitly linked to the third of the aforementioned hermeneutical categories: consequentiality. This gets to the heart of what sermons are for, and how sermons are meant to be conceived and received. Indeed, what on earth is the point of preaching if nothing happens? It is this precise concern which animates Kierkegaard's illustrative parable, "The Tame Goose," written in his journal in 1854.[46]

The Waddling Geese of Christendom

Kierkegaard imagines a church of geese gathering every Sunday to hear a sermon preached from a high pulpit, where an old gander exhorts the congregation that their creator intended a greater purpose for them, a "high destiny."[47] The gander proclaims that he and his fellow geese are aliens and strangers in this world and that their wings were so designed that they might fly away to distant lands and truly flourish. Every Sunday the geese hear the sermon enthusiastically, bowing and curtseying in response, before waddling on home. The following Sunday the same geese return to the same church and hear the same lofty sermon about their "high destiny" and the use of their wings, followed by the familiar waddling home. Every now and then the geese discuss among themselves why they never actually fly: "The geese had a shrewd mutual understanding about this. But of course they did not talk about it on Sunday; that, after all, was not appropriate."[48] The geese respond to such queries with nuanced arguments about the dangers of what happens to those who actually attempt to fly, pointing to those who are suffering and thin among

45. Rasmussen, "Kierkegaard's Biblical Hermeneutics," 253.

46. *Søren Kierkegaard's Journals and Papers*, 3:3067, 390–92.

47. *Søren Kierkegaard's Journals and Papers*, 3:3067, 391.

48. *Søren Kierkegaard's Journals and Papers*, 3:3067, 391.

them: "There you see what happens when you take seriously this business of wanting to fly."[49] They subsequently point to those who are plump and delicate among the congregation as those who demonstrate the favor and grace of God. The following Sunday the old gander again waddles up to the pulpit and the ironical cycle continues ad infinitum.

Kierkegaard, of course, wrote this parable as a direct attack upon the state of the Danish pulpit, where countless Christians partake of the same charade: "Man, too, has wings, he has imagination, intended to help him actually rise aloft. But we play, allow our imagination to amuse itself in a quiet hour of Sunday daydreaming, and otherwise stay right where we are."[50] Copenhagen's pulpits produced a seemingly endless stream of sermons which neglected the consequentiality which Kierkegaard deemed essential to any proclamation of Scripture:

> The trouble is not that Christianity is not voiced . . . but that it is voiced in such a way that the majority eventually think it utterly inconsequential . . . Thus the highest and the holiest things make no impact whatsoever, but they are given sound and are listened to as something that now, God knows why, has become routine and habit like so much else.[51]

Kierkegaard's critique of preaching is not against preaching itself, but rather against the lack of appropriation of the Word *in* the preacher. Since Kierkegaard's primary hermeneutical concern was inculcating existential response in the "hearer" of the Word, he argued that preachers must appropriate scriptural truth first to themselves, before attempting to proclaim it to others. The old gander in the parable is the perfect example of one who exhorts others to do what he refuses to do himself. The fact that the geese do not even seem to notice that the gander himself also waddles home each week demonstrates the pervasiveness of the condition. Sitting under such sermons, week after week, malforms the senses so that the hearers cannot even see the absurdity unfolding before them. The absurdity becomes the normality.

Elsewhere in his journal Kierkegaard writes about the perils of such a preaching culture, which becomes little more than rhetorical and performative entertainment:

---

49. *Søren Kierkegaard's Journals and Papers*, 3:3067, 391.

50. *Søren Kierkegaard's Journals and Papers*, 3:3067, 391.

51. Kierkegaard, *Sickness unto Death*, 102–3.

> If it is assumed that speaking is sufficient for the proclamation of Christianity, then we have transformed the church into a theater and can have an actor learn a sermon and splendidly, masterfully deliver it with facial expressions, gesticulations, modulation, tears, and everything a theater-going public might desire.[52]

The hearers have become distracted by the worldly aesthetics that have come to characterize the way preaching is imagined, devoid of theological substance or existential reality. People flock to the theater like the geese to their lofty sermon, and like the geese they go to great lengths to keep the charade precisely as it is, to "stay right where we are."[53] This is because their religious desires have been shaped not by the appropriation of God's Word but by the effervescent glitter of the theater-church and its pastor-actors.

Kierkegaard's parable is, in a sense, a prime example of a defamiliarization of New Testament teachings on suffering (cf. Matt 16:24–25; Col 1:24; 1 Pet 3:17–18). The use of such parabolic forms of writing—which also occur throughout Kierkegaard's discourses—highlights the key role of defamiliarization in the subjective and consequential appropriation of Scripture. The hearers know that suffering seems to be essential to Christian discipleship, yet they do not want to acknowledge that it is so lest they actually have to experience it. The parable, though not actually published in his lifetime, allows the reader of any era to see afresh the New Testament imperative and the absurd consequences that follow from ignoring its appropriation. Such use of indirect communication has often been seen as a Kierkegaardian catalyst for the use of storytelling as a replacement for the traditional biblical expository sermon, particularly within narrative homiletics.

Narrative Homiletics and Sermonic Authority

An attempt to redeem the preacher's personal connection with the preached material came via Fred Craddock's "New Homiletic." Originating in the United States in the 1970s, it has been extremely influential in shaping homiletical discussion for the postmodern era. Dissatisfied with the formulaic state of homiletics, Craddock wanted to bring "judgment against a church that gives recitations, lifeless words cut off from the

---

52. *Søren Kierkegaard's Journals and Papers*, 3:3519, 606.
53. *Søren Kierkegaard's Journals and Papers*, 3:3067, 391.

hearts and minds of those who speak and those who listen."[54] His attempt to counter this problem was the call to communicate the biblical text "inductively" rather than "deductively." This meant inviting hearers into the world of the text by telling its story rather than speaking to them about it from "outside" the text. In this, there is an obvious link with Kierkegaardian *defamiliarization*. Craddock was deeply influenced by Kierkegaard's concerns, finding many of them directly relevant to the religious culture of his own day. This was most evident in his book *Overhearing the Gospel: Preaching and Teaching the Faith to Those Who Have Heard It All Before* (1978), which was perhaps the first ever thoroughgoing homiletical engagement with Kierkegaard. In this book, he highlighted much of Kierkegaard's critique of the stale objectivity of the Christendom pulpit: "Kierkegaard did not, nor do we, seek to communicate timeless truths; the desire is for the proper word; the word that fits here, now."[55] Incorporating subjectivity into the new wave of postmodern homiletics, Craddock used Kierkegaard to assert that preaching need not concern itself with the proclamation of "objective" truth, but must leave space for the truth to be found wherever and whenever the listener may find it.

Craddock was responding to what he perceived to be an authoritarian approach to the pulpit in modernity, whereby approaches to preaching had not responded adequately to the shifting cultural expectations for communication in a postmodern era. Some of his critique remains valuable as a necessary corrective to the kinds of sermons which may be technically true (that is, "doctrinally" true) but which feel monotonous and lifeless, rendering them almost "untrue" to the living and active character of the Word of God (cf. Heb 4:12). However, Craddock's use of Kierkegaard to emphasize communicative uncertainty in preaching is highly problematic. Indeed, it has been said that "Craddock's emphasis on homiletic indirectness has been greatly influenced by Kierkegaard, one of the leading proponents of indirectness."[56] Kierkegaard was indeed a well-known proponent of indirect communication, though this is often misunderstood to be a method he favored at the expense of direct sermonic authority.[57] The way in which the New Homiletic moved toward open-ended narrative preaching may have rendered sermons more

54. Craddock, *As One Without Authority*, 159.

55. Craddock, *Overhearing the Gospel*, 86.

56. Bearden, "Theological Implications," 10.

57. For a discussion of Kierkegaard's complex use of both indirect and direct communication, see chapter 6.

entertaining, but it has not led to the kind of sermonic impact seen in other homiletical revolutions in church history. If anything, the main impact of the New Homiletic on the theory and practice of preaching has been the complexification of technique and the aestheticization of sermons. This can be seen in the slanted gravitation toward the priority of hermeneutical complexity and rhetorical technique within postmodern homiletics.[58] Even if unintentional, such gravitations ultimately led preaching closer to the "theater pulpit" which Kierkegaard despised.

As with Kierkegaard's superficial parallels with postmodern evangelicalism discussed in chapter 1, Craddock's approach ultimately negates Kierkegaard's ideal for what preaching is. His integration of defamiliarization and appropriation are evident in his desire to relate the text afresh to the individual, but what is lacking is the crucial tenet of consequentiality. Without this, the other two hermeneutical tenets become irrelevant, Christianly speaking. Craddock sought to catalyze active response from the congregation through the *non*-conclusiveness and deliberate ambiguity of narrative sermons. This attempt was intended to raise more questions than answers. The purpose was to inculcate subjective participation from the hearers, who are invited to think out the conclusions for themselves. There is no doubt a place for creative use of questions and ambiguity in preaching within a larger framework of scriptural authority. In reality, however, like the geese who admire the gander's sermon and continue to waddle home, such an approach as often leads to an absence of active response and negates the necessary heraldic authority required for Christian preaching.[59] In the narratival homiletical model, the authority of the Word of God becomes something alluded to but rarely proclaimed nor applied, lacking what Kierkegaard elsewhere calls "the power of conviction."[60]

As will be seen in the next chapter, Kierkegaard's critiques of the lack of subjectivity in preaching should not be taken to mean an abolition of pulpit authority per se. His critiques were almost entirely targeted at the preacher's lack of personal engagement with their message, not the mere fact that they were "preaching." In one case he even accuses the Danish clergy that they "do not know how to preach."[61] In condemnation

---

58. See Edwards, *Theology of Preaching and Dialectic*, 122–29.

59. See Edwards, *Theology of Preaching and Dialectic*, 110–15; 131–46.

60. Kierkegaard, *Upbuilding Discourses in Various Spirits*, 271. On Kierkegaard's use of the indirect mode *within* sermonic discourses, see chapter 4.

61. *Søren Kierkegaard's Journals and Papers*, 1:955, 417.

of their gander-like hypocrisy Kierkegaard declared that true preaching must happen despite damage to personal reputation. A true preacher may not merely wow the congregation with their narratival brilliance; they must be prepared to incur potential suffering and shame for the disapproval of the message; as Kierkegaard even says of himself: "I hope and believe that with the assistance of God I would be able to preach fearlessly even if someone spat in my face as I climbed the stairs to the pulpit."[62] His problem is obviously not with the act of preaching but with the fearfulness and timidity of the preachers, who fear their own social disgrace more than the judgment of God.

Craddock's use of Kierkegaard to evoke non-authoritative preaching is, in the end, deeply unsatisfactory because it only sees one side of the Kierkegaardian coin.[63] For Kierkegaard, the authority of the preacher is placed not in their own personality or their ecclesial office, but in the Word of God. Any attempt to downplay the authority of the divinely inspired message, then, potentially borders on blasphemy:

> If the person who is called by a revelation and to communicate a revelation wants to be silent about the fact of the revelation, then he offends God and reduces God's will to nothing. It is the very fact of the revelation which is decisive; it is this which gives him divine authority.[64]

Kierkegaard, of course, is thinking here of the kind of "prophetic" revelation afforded to an apostle. This was sparked by his interest in the case of Adolphe Peter Adler (1812–1869), the deposed Danish minister who believed he had received a new authoritative revelation from God, but later changed his mind.[65] The ongoing authority of apostolic revelation, however, is ultimately in Scripture itself. Thus, for Kierkegaard, the courage required of a contemporary preacher to interpret and proclaim Scripture is akin to the courage of a Paul or a Jeremiah to interpret and proclaim whatever God was inspiring them to say. Either way, the recipient of the revelation—whether directly prophetic or scripturally inherited—leans not on their own authority but on that of the one who inspired the revelation.

---

62. *Søren Kierkegaard's Journals and Papers*, 1:481, 190.

63. Again, see a further discussion of this paradox, and of Craddock, in chapter 6.

64. *Søren Kierkegaard's Journals and Papers*, 1:234, 98.

65. See Kierkegaard, *Book on Adler*.

In contrast to Kierkegaard's stress upon the significance of revelatory authority, Craddock's hermeneutical basis is majorly influenced by the postmodern suspicion of authority. This suspicion is ultimately the fundamental catalyst for the New Homiletic's critique of authoritative preaching, despite Craddock's own belief in the importance of the connection between Scripture and sermon. Craddock even made the startling critique that the traditional evangelical expository sermon was itself "unbiblical" because, by submerging the listener in the semantic details of the text, the sermon "fails to achieve what the text achieves."[66] In this, one can see his desire for the contours of sermons to be grounded in the contours and purposes of the scriptural text rather than some external ideology. For Craddock it was a kind of rationalist ideology which had led to the conservative expository approaches to Scripture which privileged the text's semantics over its intentions. In contrast, Craddock posited, "Preaching brings the Scriptures forward as a living voice in the congregation."[67]

Yet for those who followed after Craddock, in seeking to "bring Scripture forward" they had an ironic tendency to leave it behind, relegating it to the background.[68] This is because the New Homiletic, though informed by the variety of literary forms within Scripture, was ultimately underlain by the suspicion of preacherly authority which emerged from the sociopolitical and philosophical climate of the mid-twentieth century. Its critique of preacherly authority became an almost unquestionable ideology, one which ultimately held the greatest "authority" in terms of the function of Scripture within sermons. This deeper-lying postmodern suspicion limited the kinds of things that could be said from Scripture wherever the text seemed to go against the anti-authority mantra. Thus, although the New Homiletic assented to the *conceptual* authority of the text, the result was a gradual denigration of the *functional* authority of the text for both preacher and congregation.[69]

66. Craddock, *Preaching*, 28.

67. Craddock, *Preaching*, 27.

68. One could say that such textual "backgrounding" is precisely what Kierkegaard did in the aforementioned discourses which proceeded from a short biblical epigram. However, Kierkegaard combined such uses of Scripture with many more overt and direct expositions and proclamations throughout his writings. His readers could be in little doubt that his center of authoritative gravity was the need to hear and obey the biblical text.

69. For an illuminating discussion of this problem within postmodern homiletics, see Allen, "Homiletics and Biblical Authority," 489–515.

As for Kierkegaard, although he was also certainly influenced by contemporary philosophical movements, his reasons for challenging the scholars and preachers of Christendom were explicitly linked to his belief in the authority of Scripture. The cultured intellectuals of Kierkegaard's time, such as J. L. Heiberg (1791–1860), had seemed to imbibe Hegelian speculative philosophy so thoroughly that they could not think or speak for themselves beyond the Hegelian "script," almost as if Hegel himself had been invested with divine authority: "What they know they borrow from Hegel, and Hegel is indeed profound—ergo, what Professor Heiberg says is also profound."[70] What Kierkegaard then adds is intriguing: "In this way every theological student who limits his sermon to nothing but quotations from the Bible becomes the most profound of all, for the Bible certainly is the most profound book of all."[71] In this we see something like a Craddockian critique of the over-citation of Bible verses in sermons via the enslavement to a particular expository homiletic. Yet Kierkegaard's satirical comment is earnest when he refers to the Bible as "the most profound book of all." So too is his recommendation that Copenhagen's trainee preachers—who also drink deeply from the Hegelian well—would do better to merely cite Scripture and let it speak for itself rather than attempt to infuse Scripture with Hegelian abstraction.

The narrative homiletical emphases on sermonic ambiguity within postmodernity may seem to find kinship in Kierkegaard's indirect communication. However, the motivations driving such emphases often owe more to the epistemological uncertainty of worldly philosophical trends than the appropriated Word of God. Such motivations eventually become yet another way for Scripture to become co-opted for the service of other ends. Kierkegaard was no stranger to the theological incorporation of philosophical systems, though he undoubtedly sides with Tertullian—moreso than with any other Church father—in holding a sharp distinction between divine revelation and human reason.[72] If Kierkegaard's suspicion of Hegelianism was that it had become a fashionable philosophical gloss which blunted the force of scriptural truth, the same could be said of postmodern attempts to provide such a gloss, despite its radically different concerns and implications. As Polk notes, for Kierkegaard true Christian hermeneutics should assert that "scripture defines the

---

70. *Søren Kierkegaard's Journals and Papers*, 5:5697, 245.

71. *Søren Kierkegaard's Journals and Papers*, 5:5697, 245.

72. Mulder, "Kierkegaard's Reception of the Church Fathers," 162.

world, not the other way around."[73] Narrative forms of proclamation are certainly not alien to Kierkegaard's approach to scriptural interpretation and communication. However, his efforts to defamiliarize the Bible in Christendom were rooted not merely in creative retelling and ambiguous indirection but in the personal and consequential appropriation of the Word of God within the reader, hearer, and preacher.

A Homiletical Hermeneutic Unsuitable for Geese

For Kierkegaard, homiletics and hermeneutics are difficult to separate because his desire to interpret the Bible "existentially" is catalyzed by the same desire to think about how best to communicate that Word within one's context.[74] His critiques of Bible scholars and of preachers both stem from the same problem: avoiding the consequences of what is really there in the text in light of the ensuing inconveniences. Preachers must first face the consequences of what is in the text *personally*, and then face them *socially* when proclaiming that text to others. Neither Christendom's ganders nor their congregational geese wished to face the consequences of "flying." They could see what would happen if they did, and they had plenty of more appealing options either side of the bare-faced reality to really live according to what they had heard. They also had plenty of erudite scholars with nuanced "interpretations" of the text which might better suit their circumstances. Ultimately, they do not really want what the text has to say. They imagine that even if what is said really *is* in the text, it must be meant for somebody else, not them. This was the epitome of the Christendom condition.[75]

For Kierkegaard, the preacher must first allow the Bible to speak to them personally, to interpret it not as one looking for problems but as one who allows the Bible to find problems in oneself, and to act upon them. Only when the Bible has become de- and re-familiarized, appropriated and consequential in the lives of the preachers, can they truly proclaim that Word to others. A major problem for the practice of preaching in the modern West is that it has become technocratic, accentuating stylistic

73. Polk, *Biblical Kierkegaard*, 79.

74. The issue of contextual communication in light of the Gospel will be discussed in further depth in chapter 6.

75. For further reflection on the notion of Christendom as a "condition," see chapters 7–8.

form and communicative method over far more significant existential issues. Kierkegaard saw this in his own time: "It is absolutely unethical when one is so busy communicating that he forgets to *be* what he teaches."[76] Kierkegaard was aware that for the preacher to become existentially involved in their message, this meant more than simply acting in an impassioned manner in the pulpit. After all, the gander's sermon truly was a brilliant sermon, expertly delivered, speaking profound theological truth, inspiring his rapturous hearers, and evoking their hearty bows and curtseys. There was no problem of communication or rhetoric. The problem was what happened *after* the sermon. And the root of that problem is what did *not* happen *before* the sermon: the preacher's own consequential appropriation of the Word to be proclaimed.

The twin dynamic of personal engagement and impassioned proclamation is essential to Kierkegaard's homiletical hermeneutic. The defamiliarized text removes the initial existential barriers, allowing the preacher—and eventually their hearers—to receive the text as though for the first time, as a divine personal communication which catalyzes appropriative consequential change. This process cannot be short-circuited; it occurs when the preacher genuinely allows what they are reading and preaching to shape them. It is this deep-level existential immersion in the truth of the text that communicates to the hearers that this is something worth hearing, for it has already been heard—and done—by the one proclaiming it. As Kierkegaard asserted, "A preacher should be such that the listeners have to say: How can I get away from this man? His sermon catches up with me in every hiding place, and how can I get rid of him, since he is over me at every moment?"[77] In order for the preacher's sermon to remain "over" the hearer, the preacher cannot hide within the indirect mode for fear of appearing authoritarian. The authority of the sermon is an essential aspect of the Church's obedience to the authority of Scripture. But in maintaining this authority, the preacher must abandon the loftily inconsequential rhetoric of the theater-pulpit if they wish for their sermons to move their hearers beyond a Sunday churchgoing moment.

Kierkegaard highlighted better than any contemporary homiletician the perennial danger of fictionality in Christian preaching. If a hearer does not see the truth as true *in* the preacher, they may have cause

---

76. Kierkegaard, *Provocations*, 350.
77. Kierkegaard, *Book on Adler*, 105.

to assume that the truth might not be true at all. Kierkegaard said of the "at-a-distance" Hegelian preachers of Christendom:

> One immediately perceives in their discourse that they them-
> selves are not present in it, just as they also do not exist in it.
> Therefore, even if during the preaching the listeners do not sleep
> . . . yet they are absentminded, because in the discourse itself
> there is an in-between . . . the space of illusion. One perceives in
> the discourse that there is not this fresh influx from the richness
> of what has been experienced, which now in the moment of the
> discourse arises to a present life.[78]

More crucial than narratival skill is the palpable sense that the preacher truly believes what they are saying, not only by how they say it but by how they live it. This is the only way to avoid "the space of illusion" whereby sermons become absurd fictions of the reality. Indeed, preachers will only make flying geese of their congregations if they have first learned to fly themselves. They cannot merely speak about it but must demonstrate the "fresh influx" based upon both the glorious and the adverse "effects" of such flying in their own lives. To a large extent this was precisely Paul's defence of his preacherly authority before his Corinthian "geese," who had severely doubted his preaching abilities, yet could not doubt his willingness to suffer for what he preached (cf. 2 Cor 11:1–12:10).

As delightful as Kierkegaard's parable is as an illustration of the hermeneutical and homiletical issues discussed thus far, he is aware that even the parable itself could become a sly surrogate for the old gander's lofty sermon: aesthetically appreciated but existentially ignored. For us contemporary readers, Kierkegaard left a sharp sting in the tail of his tale:

> And if someone reads this, he will say: This is delightful—and
> that's the end of it. He will waddle home to his family, will re-
> main or will strive with all his might to become plump, delicate,
> fat—but on Sunday the pastor will preach and he will listen—
> just exactly like the geese.[79]

To truly appreciate what you have just read, you must not allow it to re-main a mere quotation on the page of a book that you and I may soon forget. You and I must do something about it—right now, even—if we are to ensure that this will not be "the end of it," lest the ghosts of those geese come back to haunt our churches too! Does such a homiletical

---

78. Kierkegaard, *Book on Adler*, 106.
79. *Søren Kierkegaard's Journals and Papers*, 3:3067, 392.

imperative trouble you within an academic book? Shouldn't we save such personal exhortations for sermons? Scholarship, after all, is meant for critical reflection, not for encouraging people to change their life. Quite so, Kierkegaard might add, smiling as he watches us waddling home.

4

What Barth Got Wrong about Kierkegaard

Subjectivity, Objectivity, and Preaching

ON MAY 18, 1851, in the church of a Copenhagen army barracks, Søren Kierkegaard preached a sermon. The very fact that Kierkegaard preached sermons at all—not least in church pulpits—counteracts many of the aforementioned "subjectivist" caricatures of him which still exist today, in part due to his focus on subjective appropriation, as we saw in the previous chapter, as well as the noted mixed reception he received within twentieth-century philosophy and theology, as we saw in the first chapter.[1] Indeed, the theme of his sermon that day, "The Changelessness of God," is especially difficult to reconcile with the notion that Kierkegaard was more concerned with existentialist or anthropocentric psychology than "objective" theological doctrine. This chapter will offer a more in-depth example of one of Kierkegaard's most important twentieth-century interpreters, Karl Barth.

Undoubtedly the most influential theologian of the twentieth century, Barth was one of the many aforementioned critics of Kierkegaard's general "anthropocentric" theological legacy. However, it is perhaps noteworthy that during his time as a burgeoning preacher in Safenwil, a time in which many of his major theological foundations were undergoing radical transformation, a younger Barth once sat in his armchair for an entire evening reading a translation of Kierkegaard's *The Moment*, the book in which Kierkegaard's 1851 sermon was later published. Due to

---

1. See also Matulštík and Westphal, *Kierkegaard and Postmodernity*.

the heavily edited edition, however, Barth never found that sermon.[2] This "Kierkegaard" seemed more the nonconformist revolutionary than the outright Christian preacher. In a letter to his theological sparring partner, Eduard Thurneysen, Barth noted that he awoke that night at 3 a.m. from a turbulent dream in which he was being fired at by bourgeois soldiers of the established order and wondered whether this was a coincidence of his evening's reading.[3] Indeed, Barth's perpetual gravitation toward the immediacy of his context at this time tended to filter into his own preaching, often more concerned with the subjective clamor of contemporary events than the objective truths of Christian doctrine.[4] Barth's eventual transition away from Kierkegaard was, in part, an attempt to leave behind this perceived doctrinal captivity to all things *momentary*, not least in himself. It may be, however, that Barth's view of Kierkegaard could well have benefited from reconsidering the doctrinal implications of that sermon he never read.

It is well-documented, of course, that the thought of Barth and Kierkegaard shares something of a tarnished kinship.[5] On the one hand, the early Barth's indebtedness to Kierkegaard is obvious; and on the other, the mature Barth's growing suspicion of Kierkegaard becomes more emphatic with each volume of the *Church Dogmatics*. As is well known, it was Kierkegaard's repeated emphasis on "subjectivity" that most troubled Barth. Yet it seems that for the little he actually read of him, Barth rarely considered Kierkegaard's preaching as being of any particular importance. This chapter will assess two ways in which we might see Barth and Kierkegaard closer together by analyzing their conceptions and practices of preaching. Firstly we will see, in Kierkegaard's attitude to preachers and in his own preaching, a greater sense of theological objectivity which better frames his thinking on the role of subjectivity. Secondly, in Barth's preaching, we will see greater elements of a subjective focus through

2. Christophe Schrempf, the anti-ecclesial translator of this text, conveniently omitted Kierkegaard's overtly Christian sermon from the German edition (*Der Augenblick*), preferring instead to emphasize Kierkegaard's incendiary attacks upon the established Church.

3. Barth, "Barth, 24. Juni 1920," 400.

4. See Barth, *Homiletics*, 118; Barth, "On the Sinking of the Titanic," 31–42.

5. See, among others, Barrett, "Karl Barth," 1–42; Gouwens, *Kierkegaard as Religious Thinker*, 20; McCormack, *Barth's Critically Realistic Dialectical Theology*, 217, 237; McKinnon, "Barth's Relation to Kierkegaard," 31–41; Oakes, *Reading Karl Barth*, 28; Wells, *Influence of Kierkegaard*, 262; Ziegler, "Barth's Criticisms of Kierkegaard," 434–51.

which we find a similar dialectic of objectivity-and-subjectivity. In both, it is the proclamation of the Gospel itself that grounds their contrasting emphases, whereby the objectivity of the *preached* word is dialectically inseparable from its subjective hearing. However, in order to situate the significance of their similarity here, it will first be necessary to provide an extensive account of Barth's "subjective" reception of Kierkegaard, and—prior to this—to highlight how the terms "subjectivity" and "objectivity" feature in the context of this debate.

A Note on Subjectivity and Objectivity

These two decidedly "modern" concepts have been used conjunctively and dualistically in various ways in theology, philosophy, and literary theory, especially in the nineteenth and twentieth centuries. Although certain key thinkers such as Kant and Hegel have had a considerable impact upon the widespread use of such terminology (especially for both Kierkegaard and Barth), it is notoriously difficult to track their etymologies with exact precision. James Brown, in his 1953 *Croall Lectures* at the University of Edinburgh, undertook an extensive study of these terms in relation to modern theology, with particular reference to both Barth and Kierkegaard. He noted the inherited complexity and ambiguity in meanings that had led—even by that time—to a profound difficulty in using these terms without heavy qualification.[6] He did, of course, note the shades of interpretation that exist at general levels before illustrating their uses in particular thinkers. One such general presupposition he found is a tendency to favor "objectivity" as the more preferable proponent of "truth" within the pair: "The modern world has arrived at a distinction between subjective and objective thinking, which in its popular version at least tends to identify truth with objectivity and error with subjectivity."[7] Such a perception, though certainly hyper-generalized, does remind us of the difficulties of extracting the meaning of "subjectivity," particularly if our intention is to redeem its use within theological speech, as Kierkegaard had attempted to do.

Regarding the actual definition of subjectivity, of course, an exhaustive treatment of its usage and multifarious interpretation—even in

---

6. Brown, *Subjectivity and Objectivity in Existentialist Thought*, 30 (first published as *Subject and Object in Modern Theology*, 1955).

7. Brown, *Subjectivity and Objectivity in Existentialist Thought*, 12.

modern theology alone—is not explored here beyond its relevance for Barth and Kierkegaard. Brown notes three clusters of the general meaning of subjectivity as "that which pertains to the mere individual act of presentation," "anything and everything which a feeling and a thinking creature experiences in itself" and "all convictions extending beyond the immediate evidence of the facts."[8] Subjectivity, then, may connote a number of different emphases but usually gravitates toward the individual, the personal, the self, and the particular, rather than, say, the universal or abstracted principle beyond the confines of the self. This juxtapositional definition, more importantly, is how Barth seemed to conceive of "subjectivity" as a category in his reading of Kierkegaard. That is, subjectivity was that which had a propensity or fixation for the human self or the existential elements of feeling rather than that which is primarily oriented toward an exterior object.

Without wanting to oversimplify Barth here, it should be noted that his use of objectivity and subjectivity, following Kant, was often somewhat dualistic in its appearance. That is not to say he *was* dualistic in his conception, but simply that he had a tendency to express the two terms as though they were completely antithetical and non-correlative. An interesting example of such an antithetical expression is in his little book on Mozart (who was, incidentally, both his and Kierkegaard's favorite composer). Barth spoke of

> the great, free "objectivity" with which Mozart went through life
> ... The subjective is never his theme. He never used music to express himself, his situation, his moods. I do not know of a single instance where one can with any certainty explain the character of a work from a corresponding episode in his life, so that from the succession of his works one might trace something like a biographical line.[9]

The same could certainly not be said for Kierkegaard! Many within Kierkegaard scholarship today are at pains to move beyond an overly "biographical" reading of his works in the wake of much exaggerated psychoanalytical interpretation.[10] However, as noted in the previous chapter, so frequent and overt are many of the parallels with Kierkegaard's life-events that it is virtually impossible to separate his life from his

8. Brown, *Subjectivity and Objectivity in Existentialist Thought*, 23.

9. Barth, "Mozart's Freedom," 48.

10. See, for example, Thompson, *Kierkegaard* (1974), and Garff, *Søren Kierkegaard* (2005).

authorship. Barth was no doubt aware of this. The most telling revelation from the passage in Barth's Mozart book, however, is the rhetorical antithesis through which Barth would present objectivity in stark contrast to subjectivity. Objectivity is portrayed not in its own right, but—ironically enough—by reference *to* "the subjective," by being *un*concerned with the anthropological, the existential, the emotional, or the biographical. To Barth's mind, Mozart was admirable because he was able to prevent his own existential crises from penetrating his works, thus affirming a sense of truth which lay beyond his own experience. This, for Barth, is the virtue of "objective" thinking.

On overt doctrinal matters, Barth often deployed this same distinction between the subjective and the objective, relating to human existence and divine being. Although in many cases Barth presents an antithesis, he evidently *did* portray a dialectical relationship between subjectivity and objectivity when he spoke of the objective and the subjective within God's being and acts.[11] However, when using the terms to portray the distinction between God and humanity, the dialectic is altered to that of a hierarchy, necessitating a submissive reciprocation on the part of the human subject: "What we have said about the objective content of truth of the reality of Jesus Christ, which includes our own reality, presses in upon us, from its objectivity to our subjectivity, in order that there should be in us a correspondence."[12] It is evident that Barth wants to uphold both the distinction and the correct ordering between the two (*from* the objective, *to* the subjective), while highlighting their complementarity.[13] The sharp distinction between them, as we will see, feeds his gradual suspicions of Kierkegaard, who is imagined by Barth to be solely committed to subjectivity at the expense of objectivity.

It is certainly true that Kierkegaard's use of subjectivity played *the* crucial role in his entire theological framework. His *Concluding Unscientific Postscript* (1846)[14] is perhaps his best-known work in this regard,

11. See, for example: "The inalienable subjectivity of God conceals itself in the hard objectivity of revelation"; "the objectivity in which God himself remains hidden in his subjectivity." Barth, *Göttingen Dogmatics*, 1:193, 332.

12. Barth, *Church Dogmatics*, IV/2, 303.

13. See also Barth, *Church Dogmatics*, I/1, 172 and II/1, 14.

14. Although written under Kierkegaard's pseudonym Johannes Climacus (who is *not* a Christian as such, but trying to "become" one), it would be incorrect to separate him *entirely* from Kierkegaard's own thought, since Kierkegaard saw himself as dialectically placed in between both Johannes Climacus and Anti-Climacus (the "ideal" Christian). See *Søren Kierkegaard's Journals and Papers*, 6:6433, 174. It should be noted

in which we find many uses of the famous phrase "Truth is subjectivity." Needless to say, this aphorism could be (and has been) interpreted simplistically as if Kierkegaard, therefore, did not value "objective" truth. What Kierkegaard has in mind, however, is the subjective appropriation of objective truth to the individual. In fact, when he derides "objective truth" here, he is deriding the *merely* objective attitude toward truth rather than a wholehearted engagement with it; as Ziegler states, "To claim that 'truth is subjectivity' is to claim that we know the truth of faith in a more-than-merely cognitive manner. Note well—*not* a non-cognitive manner, but a more-than-merely cognitive manner."[15]

A pertinent section of the *Postscript* equates "subjectivity" with "inwardness."[16] Inwardness, here, means the personal response to the objective truth, as grasped by the individual rather than a dispassionately perceived piece of information. Indeed, another famous phrase demonstrates the corrective nature of this thought-pattern: "In a Christian country it is not information that is lacking; something else is lacking."[17] For Kierkegaard, Christendom was in no need of "objective" theological emphases. There was, in his mind, an absurd overabundance of objectively-described theology on display already—and almost none of it made any significant difference to those who spoke or heard such truths, as exemplified by the waddling geese and ganders in the previous chapter. Effectually speaking, then, such objective truths may as well not be "truths" at all. This is not to say that Kierkegaard was relativistic (in the sense of one's reception of an object *necessitating* its existence) but he did believe that to speak *of* the object of, say, the Gospel, is to respond to it in some way, and that to neglect this response is to neglect something of that object's ontology. If an objective truth is not appropriated, Kierkegaard does not think that it therefore ceases to exist, but rather that this truth has not been *truly* spoken and heard unless it has been either appropriated or outright rejected. Indeed, as Gouwens notes, "The question is whether, and if so to what degree, the thinking person 'lives within' the idea entertained or the belief that is held."[18]

that Barth rarely read Kierkegaard with the pseudonymous distinctions in mind.

15. Ziegler, "Barth's Criticisms of Kierkegaard," 440.

16. Kierkegaard, *Concluding Unscientific Postscript*, 187–251.

17. Kierkegaard, *Concluding Unscientific Postscript*, 614.

18. Gouwens, *Kierkegaard as Religious Thinker*, 51.

The category of "subjectivity" for Kierkegaard, then, is not the grounding of truth *within* the individual, but in the inward application *of* the objective truth, which he believed to be essential if one is to speak of objective truth at all. This is particularly important when that "object" is a theological doctrine, or indeed, God himself. Kierkegaard is overtly committed to subjectivity, but only as a category for rightly situating one's approach to objectivity, rather than treating subjectivity in isolation. Come highlights this dialectic well when he says that, for Kierkegaard, "there is both an objective source and a subjective source of Christian theological formulation, and neither one works without the other."[19] We will see this demonstrated more acutely when we come to analyze Kierkegaard's own preaching and homiletical practice. Before this, however, we will chart Barth's reception of Kierkegaard and his negative perception of Kierkegaard's subjectivity.

Barth's "Broken Engagement" with Kierkegaard

Barth is often seen as one of the primary catalysts for the Kierkegaardian "renaissance" in early twentieth-century Germany.[20] It is true that Kierkegaard was very much en vogue in theological circles of that time and had a significant impact on the up-and-coming dialectical school of theology. Kierkegaard's project is frequently mentioned as though it were a kind of "grammar" for the trajectory of their thinking at that time: "[Our theology] whether we wished it or not, has been taken not as a gloss but as a text, a *new* theology. This was the case even with that most venturesome of the knights of the chessboard, Kierkegaard himself."[21] Kierkegaard is even mentioned in the same vein as "Luther, Calvin, Paul, and Jeremiah" as a proponent of "a clear and direct apprehension of the truth that man is made to serve *God* and not God to serve man"[22] Barth's initial Kierkegaardian influence was especially evident in his second edition to *Der Römerbrief* (1922), in which we see Kierkegaard quotations and allusions sprinkled around freely, as well as the oft-quoted comments in the preface in which Barth says he had paid "more attention" to Kierkegaard for use in interpreting the New Testament, as well as the "infinite

19. Come, *Kierkegaard as Theologian*, 44.
20. Søe, "Karl Barth," 224–37.
21. Barth, *The Word of God and the Word of Man*, 98.
22. Barth, *The Word of God and the Word of Man*, 196.

qualitative distinction."[23] Barth's sense of Kierkegaard here is not simply as a depository of a few interesting concepts or turns of phrase, but rather to Kierkegaard's general "spirit," as someone in whose lineage Barth hopes to stand. It is clear that the early Barth saw Kierkegaard as something of a comrade-in-arms—perhaps, even, a distant mentor. For *this* Barth, Kierkegaard was the romanticized prophet of radical Christianity, who had refused to succumb to the anthropocentric idolatry of his age. It is one of the most curious footnotes of modern theological history that Barth would eventually come to see Kierkegaard in exactly the opposite light.

Kierkegaard's infamous broken engagement to Regine Olson, which many have interpreted as playing itself out in some of his writings, demonstrates precisely the opposite of that for which Barth had praised Mozart's "objectivity." It was because of this growing awareness of Kierkegaard's perpetually "subjective" focus (in the broad sense in which Barth understood the term) that he eventually felt the need to part company with the Melancholy Dane. It is difficult to pin down any precise "moment" when Barth's thinking changed, though it certainly crystallized over time. Retrospectively, he would even come to say: "not even in *Romans* was I a real friend of Kierkegaard, let alone a Kierkegaard enthusiast."[24] Although Barth would reflect that his theological development came through Kierkegaard's "school," his final assessment was that Kierkegaard's theology was ultimately "groundless and without object."[25]

To some extent, a milder form of this critique was present even in the *Römerbrief* period, where Barth expresses the concern that "there proceeds . . . from Kierkegaard the poison of a too intense pietism."[26] But this earlier measured awareness of Kierkegaard's "extremities" gradually became more negative and emphatic. By the latter sections of the *Church Dogmatics*, Kierkegaard is labeled outright as "anthropocentric" and the primary influence behind "the modern theological existentialism."[27] Barth's gradual change of heart is perhaps understandable when we remember that he was so regularly engaged in theological polemics in which the name "Kierkegaard" was being invoked by his adversaries as a chief influence. Barth equates this increasing Kierkegaardian influence

23. Barth, *Romans*, 4, 10.

24. Barth, "To Dr. Martin Rumscheidt," 273.

25. Barth, "Thank You," 100–101.

26. Barth, *Romans*, 276.

27. Barth, *Church Dogmatics*, IV/3, 498.

upon some of his contemporaries with the nineteenth-century obsession for "the individual experience of grace" through which "the great concepts of justification and sanctification came more and more to be understood and filled out psychologically and biographically."[28] He concludes, "We will do well not to allow ourselves to be crowded again into the same *cul de sac* on the detour via Kierkegaard."[29]

Oddly, as late as 1964, Barth was still considered by many outside of theological circles as a Kierkegaard "expert" and was invited to speak on the contemporary relevance of Kierkegaard at a UNESCO symposium in Paris alongside such noted "existentialist" thinkers as Karl Jaspers, Martin Heidegger, and Jean-Paul Sartre, each of whom were due to give papers.[30] It is an invitation Barth politely declined, though one imagines Barth's presence at such a conference would have made for a rather fascinating exchange. The conference lineup can only have added to Barth's concerns over the anthropocentric impact and applicability of Kierkegaard's thought, cementing an opinion he had voiced a year earlier in Copenhagen: "The fact that the existential philosophy of Heidegger, Jaspers, and Sartre could grow out of and be based on [Kierkegaard's] work is understandable and legitimate."[31] Further comments relating to Kierkegaard's "existentialist philosophy" also highlight that Barth had, by the 1960s, stricken Kierkegaard from the theological "canon." For Barth, "existential" thought could not be considered "theological" in itself. It had been imported *into* theology—an importing for which he admits a partial "unwitting responsibility" in his earlier Kierkegaardian enthusiasm—as an "instrument" rather than a necessary component.[32] To Barth's mind, Kierkegaard too became an "instrument" for existential thought rather than a genuinely "theological" voice. By this time, of course, Barth's view of Kierkegaardian subjectivity is barely coming from his own reading of Kierkegaard at all. It is apparent that Barth cannot separate Kierkegaard from his existentialist legacy, regrettable though it may be for Kierkegaard's subsequent reputation within many theological circles.

Indeed, included with the posthumous publication of Barth's 1923–24 Göttingen lectures on Schleiermacher is a fascinating epilogue,

28. Barth, *Church Dogmatics*, IV/1, 150.

29. Barth, *Church Dogmatics*, IV/1, 150.

30. Barth, "To Hermann Diem," 154. On the conference itself, see McBride, "Sartre's Debts to Kierkegaard," 39n1.

31. Barth, "Thank You," 99–100.

32. Barth, *Church Dogmatics*, III/4, xii.

entitled "Concluding Unscientific Postscript on Schleiermacher." The allusion to Kierkegaard, of course, is obvious. Throughout this short piece, he mentions the Dane not only as the "forerunner" to Bultmannian existentialism,[33] but as one "in conformity with the spirit of the middle of the nineteenth century." This is a striking comment given that "conformity" to the zeitgeist is rarely associated with Kierkegaard, of all people! Barth even places Kierkegaard in the lineage of the great "father of liberalism" himself:

> In short, despite the fact that the vocabulary of [Kierkegaard's] recent theology included concepts which Schleiermacher certainly would not have cherished—such as Word, encounter, occurrence, cross, decision, limit, judgment, etc.—I could not allow myself to be deceived that within their own context they did not break with the narrowness of Schleiermacher's anthropological horizon.[34]

Clearly, Barth saw a covert connection between Schleiermacher's general theological trajectory and that of Kierkegaard's, regardless of whether Kierkegaard knew it or not. Given the theological "battles" in Barth's own context, the lens through which he came to see Kierkegaard became increasingly narrow and inherently negative by association. As we noted in chapter 2, Barth referred to *Works of Love* with that rather swiping comment about "the unlovely, inquisitorial and terribly judicial character which is so distinctive of Kierkegaard in general."[35] Indeed, in both his early affirmations and latter defamations of Kierkegaard, it is often only "in general" that Barth wishes to see him, disregarding both the complex nature of Kierkegaard's authorship and his theological nuances. Perhaps because at one stage many had conflated Barth's own theological project a little too closely with Kierkegaard's, Barth was keen to disassociate himself from all or most things Kierkegaardian.[36]

---

33. "And as to Kierkegaard, I must confess that the appeal of the existentialist theologians to him as their great and direct forerunner has made me a little reserved toward him." Barth, *Theology of Schleiermacher*, 271.

34. Barth, *Theology of Schleiermacher*, 271.

35. Barth, *Church Dogmatics*, IV/2, 781–82.

36. Barrett comments that in the mid-twentieth century, as Barth's fame "skyrocketed," this "paralleled a rise in interest in Kierkegaard, who was frequently lumped together with Barth in the ill-defined category of 'neo-orthodoxy.'" Barrett, "Karl Barth," 6.

In reassessing Barth's relationship to Kierkegaard it is important to note that his later criticisms must be viewed in light of what he read of him. As discussed in chapter 1, there is a common theme here with many of Kierkegaard's interpreters. The task of mapping Barth's reception of Kierkegaard is notoriously tricky given that we cannot be sure precisely which of his texts Barth read and when he read them.[37] Another problem lies with Christoph Schrempf's German translations in the editions Barth had read. These were heavily abridged, distorting, and largely ignorant of Kierkegaard's Danish context and theology.[38] Suffice to say, we are to take due caution when we assume that Barth even knew the Kierkegaard he thought he was rejecting: "Barth's familiarity with Kierkegaard may have been so inadequate that he failed to appreciate many of the basic dynamics of Kierkegaard's authorial project, and he may have been more in agreement with Kierkegaard than he realized."[39] When it comes to Kierkegaard's view of preaching, of course, separating him from his contemporary context proves particularly problematic, since it was the preachers of his day who catalyzed so much of his homiletical—and "anti"-homiletical—thought.[40]

Barth's rejection of Kierkegaard seems to have stemmed from a fundamental misunderstanding not only of Kierkegaard's emphasis upon subjectivity, but of Kierkegaard's applicability into realms of theology and philosophy deemed dangerous for genuine faith and ecclesial edification, not least for the task of preaching. One of his earlier (notably less anxious) critiques of Kierkegaard evidences this in highlighting the importance of ecclesial consciousness: "The venture of Christian preaching is the venture of the Christian church. Christian preachers are not just individuals, as Kierkegaard depicted them."[41] This seems to demonstrate that Barth did not consider that Kierkegaard himself had any significant positive concern for preaching. Kierkegaard, he thinks, merely refers to "them" as

---

37. See McCormack, *Barth's Critically Realistic Dialectical Theology*, 234; Barrett, "Karl Barth," 7.

38. Schreiber, "Christoph Schrempf," 305–8. Ziegler notes that this malnourishment of the "true" Kierkegaard was something all had to endure: "Skewed as they were in particular by the anticlericalism of the translators, these editions were nonetheless *the* source through which Barth's theological generation came to know Kierkegaard." Ziegler, "Barth's Criticisms of Kierkegaard," 436.

39. Barrett, "Karl Barth," 19.

40. See Tolstrup, "Jakob Peter Mynster," 282.

41. Barth, *Göttingen Dogmatics*, 1:53.

though attacking the (im)piety of "the preacher" in general, rather than the particular problem of pulpit hypocrisy within Danish Christendom. Barth thus sees Kierkegaard as a deconstructive voice to preaching but not as a preacher in his own right who could be equally constructive.[42] It is, however, in the area of preaching that one of the clearest bridges can be seen between Barth and Kierkegaard. Here we may see in both thinkers a complementary dialectic—rather than an antithesis—between subjectivity and objectivity.

Kierkegaard as Preacher and Homiletician

It is my contention that preaching was one of the most important emanations of Kierkegaard's theology. Although Kierkegaard's readers have often been distracted from studying it by the many other exciting elements in his writings, preaching is without doubt one of the most frequently recurring concerns in his entire authorship. Due to the relatively scarce attention paid to Kierkegaard's positive approach preaching, it is worth giving a brief account here before progressing onto his connection with Barth's preaching. Imagining Kierkegaard in his context as a preacher (of sorts) shows Barth's interpretation of Kierkegaard's "subjectivism" in a different light. After all, Barth was primarily concerned with—as he says himself—"the situation of the parson in the pulpit."[43]

Burgess has said that "Kierkegaard's lifelong concern for the theory of Christian preaching is one of the least known aspects of his thought . . . If Kierkegaard himself had been able to select the field in which he would be remembered he might have picked homiletics."[44] Of course, his emphases on indirect communication, on the need for action over mere speech, and his incessant critiques of contemporary preachers such as Mynster and Martensen, often make him appear as if he vigorously opposed preaching. He would even say that "what we call the sermon (that is, a speech, a rhetorical oration) is a completely incongruous form of

42. Notably, Busch does speak of Barth's "discovery of Kierkegaard's scandalous preaching" in between Romans 1 and 2. Busch, *Barth & the Pietists*, 93. However, this would most likely refer to the "attack literature" in *The Moment*, not to Kierkegaard's sermons or discourses.

43. Barth, *Church Dogmatics*, I/1, 254.

44. Burgess, "Kierkegaard on Homiletics," 17. He even argues that *Concluding Unscientific Postscript* (1846) was, in fact, intended to be a kind of "'sermon manual' for listeners." Burgess, "Kierkegaard on Homiletics," 25.

communication for Christianity."[45] But as we have already seen in the previous two chapters, such critiques are not aimed at the act of preaching itself but rather at the absurdity of the preacher: "A handsome court preacher, the cultured public's chosen one, steps forward in the magnificent castle church, faces a chosen group of distinguished and cultured people, and preaches movingly on the apostle's words: God chose the lowly and the despised—And no one laughs."[46] It was precisely because Kierkegaard cared so much about preaching that he felt so indignant about the way the preaching of the Gospel was so abused in Christendom by the "preacher-squawking"[47] and "preacher-prattle" of false "blubbering preachers."[48] These were men who were content with the aesthetically emotive performance of preaching rather than the congruence of their preaching with the lives of themselves and their congregations.[49]

In the context of Kierkegaard's entire authorship it could be seen, as Collette has said, that Kierkegaard was more of a dialectical rhetorician or playful ironist than religious preacher; that he was "neither preacher nor pastor."[50] But this does not take into account the extent of Kierkegaard's thoughts on the subject, nor his extensive practice. Lowrie notes the significance of the fact that Kierkegaard was, in his everyday life, "a constant hearer of sermons."[51] He was profoundly affected by sermons, would travel to various churches in Copenhagen to hear them, and would also read and comment upon printed sermons from various preachers on a regular basis.[52] Søltoft notes that "his reflections on the nature of preaching are many and varied," and that "Kierkegaard had a lively interest in the sermons of his time" as "an avid reader of the edifying literature of his day."[53] We see not only focused discussions of preaching in his works, but also notable ad hoc references to preaching situations in pseudonymous texts such as "The Seducer's Diary" (a text we will discuss in more detail in chapter 7). Reflecting on Cordelia going to confession, Johannes makes

45. *Søren Kierkegaard's Journals and Papers*, 3:3499, 597.

46. *Søren Kierkegaard's Journals and Papers*, 3:3491, 594.

47. *Søren Kierkegaard's Journals and Papers*, 4:3958, 86.

48. Kierkegaard, *Practice in Christianity*, 62.

49. See again chapters 2–3.

50. Collette, *Kierkegaard*, 14–18.

51. Lowrie, *Kierkegaard*, 275.

52. See Coe, *Preaching a Sigh*.

53. Søltoft, "Power of Eloquence," 241–42.

the offhand comment that "there is nothing to prevent one's imagining the church in which all this takes place being so spacious that several very different preachers could all preach here simultaneously."[54] There are different ways one could imagine and articulate churchly spaciousness, but for Kierkegaard, it is preaching that comes to mind. Such casual references even from his "aesthetic" pseudonyms are significant in that they show how much the practice of preaching dominated Kierkegaard's theological, philosophical, and literary imagination.

There are also, of course, some eighty "discourses" that Kierkegaard published separately from the pseudonymous works, comprising over half of his entire authorship. Interestingly, Kierkegaard refrains from calling them "sermons" because he says he does not have "authority" to preach.[55] However, one wonders whether there is more indirectness in this distinction than is often seen, possibly relating to Kierkegaard's complex category of "authority," which as often means living a life in tandem with one's message as it does church ordination or commissioning.[56] In any sense, these discourses are certainly sermonic in form, usually with a prayer beforehand, an assumed congregation of "listeners," a quoted biblical text, and an expositional exhortation of the text's theme. Lowrie, perhaps over-simplistically, refers to them as "the eighty sermons which he modestly called discourses."[57] We may certainly say, with Pattison, that the discourses "are not so far removed from sermons as first seems

---

54. Kierkegaard, *Seducer's Diary*, 128.

55. This distinction appears in the preface to each mini-collection of discourses, eventually published as one volume. Kierkegaard, *Eighteen Upbuilding Discourses*, 5, 53, 107, 179, 201, 295. It should also be noted, however, that Kierkegaard's draft for the preface to his first two "discourses" calls them "sermons" outright, perhaps before he had considered the distinction. See *Eighteen Upbuilding Discourses*, 430–31. At the very least, such overlap shows that these discourses do bear the same content as sermons regarding their overt uses of Scripture and their theological orientation for the edification of "listening" believers. For a more detailed discussion of the sermon/discourse tension, see Edwards, "Kierkegaard the Preacher," 147–51.

56. See also Kierkegaard's additional distinction found in the journals where he notes, not only the prerequisite for ordination, but also the caveat that discourses may deal with "doubt" whereas sermons cannot. *Søren Kierkegaard's Journals and Papers*, 1:638, 262. Kierkegaard, however, is far from consistent with these genre distinctions. See *Søren Kierkegaard's Journals and Papers*, 4:234, 646. To add to the confusion, the "sermon" he preached in Citadelskirken in 1851 was later published in *The Moment* as a "discourse"! The residual ambiguity could well have been intentional on Kierkegaard's part.

57. Lowrie, *Kierkegaard*, 276.

to be suggested."[58] However we interpret their official "genre," most of the discourses certainly reflect the theological content of the sermons which Kierkegaard certainly *would* have preached had he found himself ministering in the rural parish we imagined in chapter 2.

In addition to the discourses, of course, we have the sermons we know Kierkegaard *did* preach, not only in his homiletical training at the Royal Pastoral Seminary,[59] but also at the Friday communion services, as well as occasional Sunday services too.[60] In the *Letters and Documents* we see feedback given for Kierkegaard's seminary sermons and regular sermons.[61] One listener wrote to him, saying, "If only you would preach more often . . . It is your clear duty," while another (a deaf lady) thanks him for his "written" preaching (the discourses) because, she says, "I cannot hear your homilies, and you do say something that fortifies me."[62] This shows evidence that at one time he may have preached more frequently. In any case, it is worth noting Plekon's comment in an article on Kierkegaard's Citadelskirken sermon: "In mid-19th century Copenhagen, those not ordained but with the degree *cand. theol.* were nevertheless regularly called on to preach."[63] Kierkegaard could well have been called upon more frequently within this ecclesiastical pattern, especially in the years preceding his more overt attacks on the established Church.

Alongside his preaching, there is also regular correspondence between Kierkegaard and other preachers who were struggling with various aspects of their own preaching. Clearly he was seen by those he knew as

58. Pattison, "'Who' Is the Discourse?," 29. See also Pattison, *Kierkegaard's Upbuilding Discourses.*

59. For an analysis of Kierkegaard's time as a homiletical student, see Edwards, "Kierkegaard the Preacher," 145–47.

60. It is not known for sure how many Sunday sermons he preached. Most tend to assume he preached only four or five times in his life, an estimate I believe may be too low. Slemmons asserts that the sermon of 18 May 1851 was "the one and only discourse he ever preached in a Sunday service." Slemmons, *Toward a Penitential Homiletic,* 299–300. There may well have been more Sunday preaching occasions, especially since this event does seem odd as an isolated occasion. He seems to have had the future option to preach at his own choosing. See *Søren Kierkegaard's Journals and Papers,* 6:6769, 416. Hong suggests the sermon was "an attempt on his part to clarify whether it was his future task to preach." *Søren Kierkegaard's Journals and Papers,* 3:880.

61. Kierkegaard, *Letters and Documents,* 16–22, 379–84.

62. Kierkegaard, *Letters and Documents,* 384, 107.

63. Plekon, "Kierkegaard at the End," 69.

a reliable source of homiletical advice.[64] Holmer notes that Kierkegaard "reflected long and fruitfully on the purpose, form, style, and limits of the sermon."[65] In fact, at one point, there was even a possibility of Bishop Mynster giving Kierkegaard a job at a homiletical seminary, and perhaps even running his own.[66] On this, Burgess rightly speculates that "Kierkegaard might have made a brilliant if eccentric professor of preaching" (though he aptly wonders about the administrative nightmares that might have ensued!).[67]

What can be in no doubt is that Kierkegaard held the analysis and practice of preaching in incredibly high esteem. This leads us to conclude that we must view his theological emphases upon subjectivity in an altogether different light to those, like Barth, who found such emphases as an ultimate blemish on his theological record. Against Barth's view, we might see Kierkegaard as both a deconstructive *and* constructive voice for preaching. We could not expect Barth to have known too much of Kierkegaard's overt homiletical leanings or practices. But Kierkegaard's preoccupation with proclamation, even in his typically unconventional manner, shows there is far more to his fundamental doctrinal trajectory than the aphorism, "Truth is subjectivity."

The Subjective-Objective Dialectic in Kierkegaard's Preaching

It is especially in Kierkegaard's approach to preaching that we see just how much he valued the objective content of the Gospel. As we have seen in the previous two chapters, the proclaimed Gospel must go beyond mere speaking and listening, it must shape the way the preachers and hearers live. Breuninger notes that Kierkegaard's model of communication "encompasses the objective nature of truth, but extends to the subjective appropriation of that truth."[68] Seeing Kierkegaard as he saw himself—as a "corrective"—helps us to see why he did not go out

---

64. See, for example, one letter in which a German preacher appears to be dissatisfied with his own Danish sermons and asks Kierkegaard if he can "solve the riddle" for him. Kierkegaard, *Letters and Documents*, 384–6.

65. Holmer, "Kierkegaard and the Sermon," 1.

66. See Thulstrup, *Kierkegaard and the Church in Denmark*, 110–11.

67. Burgess, "Kierkegaard on Homiletics," 17.

68. Breuninger, "Søren Kierkegaard's Reformation of Expository Preaching," 33.

of his way to stress the Gospel's objective content as publicly as he did its subjective appropriation.[69] As we have seen many times already, the sermons of Danish Christendom had become impersonal observations which undermined the truth's "trueness":

> In Christendom, sermons, lectures, and speeches are heard often enough about what is required of an imitator of Christ, about the implications of being an imitator of Christ, what it means to follow Christ, etc. What is heard is generally very correct and true; only by listening more closely does one discover a deeply hidden, un-Christian, basic confusion and dubiousness. The Christian sermon today has become mainly "observations": Let us in this hour consider; I invite my listener to observations on; the subject for our consideration is, etc. But "to observe" . . . signifies keeping very distant, infinitely distant, that is, personally [distant].[70]

Such observational distanciation in sermons shows why Kierkegaard's subjective corrective was so important, locating the essence of the Gospel beyond the merely spoken word, in existential actuality. This does not divorce the Gospel from the spoken word, of course; it rather becomes the outworking of a true hearing of the word (cf. Jas 1:22–25). There is a dialectical relatedness to the objective and the subjective which cannot be separated, even as one is emphasized over the other: "For Kierkegaard the objective truth of a teaching or proclamation was not a major issue, since he presupposed it."[71] It is this underlying presupposition that is often overlooked, with the objective content ultimately remaining, for Kierkegaard, the "true" foundation for preacherly subjectivity. There can be no "subjectivity is Truth" without the objective truth in which subjectivity can be evoked. The subjective appropriation of this truth is seen as intrinsically connected to its effectual "trueness."

We turn now to the aforementioned sermon, "The Changelessness of God," which Kierkegaard preached on May 18, 1851. On the face of it, it appears like many of his discourses, opening with a thematic prayer and the quoted biblical text: James 1:17–21. His first move is one of juxtaposition with our human situation:

---

69. *Søren Kierkegaard's Journals and Papers*, 6:6693, 358.

70. Kierkegaard, *Practice in Christianity*, 233.

71. Thulstrup, *Kierkegaard and the Church in Denmark*, 145–46.

My listener, you have heard the text read. How natural now to think of the opposite: the temporal, the changefulness of earthly things, and the changefulness of human beings! How depressing, how exhausting, that all is corruptibility . . . How sorrowful that so often change is for the worse! What poor human consolation.[72]

With such an opening we may feel Barth was right to identify Kierkegaard as "anthropocentric" since he seems to have bypassed God and delved straight into the despair of human existence. But this is just a preacherly ploy. His very point is that if we were to remain in this "spirit of gloom," contemplating the subjective human realm of changefulness, "we not only would not stick to the text, no, we would abandon it, indeed, we would *change* it."[73] Unlike our human situation, this text speaks, he says, "from the mountain peaks . . . lifted above all the changefulness of earthly life."[74] If the "existential" or "subjective" is that which marks our changeful, earthly lives, then that which is above and speaks *into* such changefulness can only be an evocation of objectivity.

Indeed, the "mountain peak" is a profound metaphor not only for God's transcendence but, more specifically, for the "transcendence" of his Word and the "objective" theological truth of the text. This is the very reason it may speak *into* our own subjectivity with authority, because it comes from an objective and divinely authoritative location. The listeners of this sermon—always addressed directly—are urged to "listen upward" to this mountain peak "because from above there is always only good news."[75] Kierkegaard continues to move through the text with expository precision, unpacking it phrase by phrase and exhorting the listeners with the joy and gladness contained within it: namely, the Gospel message that God does not change, that he offers peace, that he keeps his promises, and that he loves us. Kierkegaard continues to juxtapose these doctrinal truths with the subjective human situation, but always as a springboard back to the overwhelming emphasis of his main point: "But God is changeless."

The sermon itself is essentially an impassioned affirmation of the orthodox Christian doctrines of God's immutability, omnipotence, and benevolence. Of course, in contemplating Kierkegaard's theology we

72. Kierkegaard, *"The Moment" and Late Writings*, 269.

73. Kierkegaard, *"The Moment,"* 269 (emphasis added).

74. Kierkegaard, *"The Moment,"* 269.

75. Kierkegaard, *"The Moment,"* 269.

would be foolish to ignore Kierkegaard's trenchant criticisms of dogmatic theologians or his criticisms of "Hegelian" objectivity, which remain lifelong polemics. For Kierkegaard, systematic thinkers must take themselves into account lest they articulate a system in which they themselves cease to exist.[76] Kierkegaard is no "systematic" theologian, but he was certainly an expounder of doctrinal truth. As Slemmons comments, in this sermon, "[Kierkegaard's] overriding concern is not to compare human experience with human experience, but human experience with the divine revelation."[77] Objective doctrine and experiential encounter are woven together in the act of preaching in a complementary dialectic.

We see many subjective emphases in this sermon too, including a constant addressing of the listeners' personal situations. Kierkegaard does not want his congregation to get away with merely "observing" this sermon; he wants to trap them in it, to ingrain it into the realm of "actuality." This extends to a point he makes about the anxiety that God's changelessness ought to provoke in us. When we think God is unwatchful or unconcerned, he remains the changeless one, eternally interested in the "trivialities of your life" even when he seems most absent: "For us light-minded and unstable human beings there is sheer fear and trembling in this thought of God's changelessness. Oh, do consider this well, whether he shows any signs of noticing or not—he is eternally changeless!"[78] This is a message of both judgment and grace, since understanding who God is—and who we are in light of his changelessness—urges us to submit our changeful wills to his changeless will in the call to obedience. But just as we think this sermon is verging on Law, just as the preacher admonishes us that God's changelessness "must plunge a person into anxiety and unrest to the point of despair,"[79] there is a sudden volta which drags us back to the Gospel:

> When you, weary from all this human, all this temporal and earthly changefulness and alteration, wary of your own instability, could wish for a place where you could rest your weary head, your weary thoughts, your weary mind, in order to rest, to have a good rest—ah, in God's changelessness there is rest![80]

76. See Kierkegaard, *Concluding Unscientific Postscript*, 205–9.

77. Slemmons, *Toward a Penitential Homiletic*, 305.

78. Kierkegaard, "The Moment," 276.

79. Kierkegaard, "The Moment," 278.

80. Kierkegaard, "The Moment," 278.

Here Kierkegaard demonstrates the "cure" for the "anguished conscience" discussed in chapter 2, where the hearer has been appropriately prepared for the moment of reassurance.

As the sermon begins to close, we are forcefully prodded again, just like his conclusion to the waddling geese parable,[81] lest we forget the truth's urgency and become too comfortable with its hearing: "My listener, this hour is soon over, and the discourse. If you yourself do not want it otherwise, this hour will soon also be forgotten, and the discourse . . . [and] this thought about the changelessness of God will also soon be forgotten in changefulness."[82] Yet almost as soon as this warning is uttered, the Gospel proclamation resounds back again as he concludes with a prayerful flourish proclaiming God's "overwhelming security," the one from whom "no one strays so far that he cannot find his way back."[83] Yet it becomes even more reassuring than that, as God is the "spring that even searches for the thirsting [and] the straying."[84] Sponheim rightly observes the "law-gospel dialectic" at play in this discourse.[85] It is one in which the proclaimed Gospel of who God is and who he is *for us* triumphs over our impulse to ascend toward him. And yet, for Kierkegaard this subjective notion of human response is not divorced from its objective Gospel element. The content of Christian proclamation, for Kierkegaard, is fundamentally God-oriented at precisely the same time as it is existentially directed.

Here it is worth noting that two of the reasons Barth highlights for leaving Kierkegaard's "school" were that "the Gospel is the glad news of God's 'yes' to man"—unlike, he assumes, Kierkegaard's negativity—and that the Gospel "is the news from on high"—unlike, he assumes, Kierkegaard's subjectivity.[86] However, as we have seen, for Kierkegaard the Gospel comes not from *Existenz* but from "the mountain peaks" of God's transcendence *to* the human subject. Furthermore, this Gospel does not consist of a dialectical uncertainty but brings the good news of wonderful assurance and rest in divinely-wrought salvation. Surely Kierkegaard's preaching passes Barth's "test" on these two counts, at least? Yet we can

81. See chapter 3.

82. Kierkegaard, "*The Moment*," 279 (emphasis added).

83. Kierkegaard, "*The Moment*," 280.

84. Kierkegaard, "*The Moment*," 281.

85. Sponheim, "God's Changelessness," 103.

86. Barth, "Thank You," 101.

even see that a similar dialectic of objectivity and subjectivity can also be found in Barth's own preaching.

The Objective-Subjective Dialectic in Barth's Preaching

Barth, of course, though appearing to some as the austere dogmatic theologian with his magisterial *Church Dogmatics*, was first and foremost a preacher, concerned indeed with "the situation of the parson in the pulpit."[87] It was the "situation" of preaching, in fact, which had sparked what became known as the dialectical school of theology in the 1920s.[88] Preaching, for Barth, is always bound up with the essence of dogmatic theology, to the extent that the primary purpose of theology is to assist and examine church proclamation.[89] Willimon even goes so far as to say, "I do not think that anyone should venture to interpret Barth who is not a preacher."[90] This is not only because one often detects the sound of the preacher in Barth's great rhetorical flourishes but also because Barth's whole approach to theology is governed by his primary understanding of Christ as the content of Christian proclamation.

Notably, Bultmann criticized Barth's actual sermons for their formulaic nature and lack of existential verve, highlighting Barth's *un*relatedness to Kierkegaard on the point of "true" exegesis in preaching:

> I am of the opinion that Paul spoke to the existence of his hearers very differently from the way you and Thurneysen do, namely, by lighting up their existence under the Word . . . I might also say that the Kierkegaardian element that once influenced you and Thurneysen so strongly has now disappeared. And Kierkegaard did indeed understand exegesis.[91]

Kierkegaard is cited here as the "truer" exegete because, for Bultmann, Kierkegaard understood that it is through "existential" knowledge that *true* knowledge of the object arises. To miss this critical element in the name of "objective" doctrinal formulae, for Bultmann, was to miss the kernel of exegesis and preaching itself. We might not only defend Kierkegaard from Barth's criticisms but perhaps also defend Barth from

87. Barth, *Church Dogmatics*, I/1, 254.
88. Barth, *The Word of God and the Word of Man*, 100.
89. Barth, *Church Dogmatics*, I/1, 3–4.
90. Willimon, *Conversations with Barth on Preaching*, 4.
91. Bultmann, "Bultmann: Marburg, 10 December 1935," 83.

Bultmann's criticisms, by which we may see more of a subjective emphasis in Barth than Bultmann could see. In both cases, the connections between Barth's and Kierkegaard's preaching are illuminating in bringing them both closer together than Barth himself had imagined. It is not incidental that preaching is the avenue through which this comparison takes place. Preaching was, after all, the theological activity of which both spoke such a great deal and was of critical importance within the scope of their wider theological endeavors.

Barth's preaching, particularly after his "rediscovery" of the significance of the Reformation, was overtly scriptural and expository in style. This was thoroughly intentional in that, similarly to Calvin's practice, it was the preacher's role to call the congregation from the subjective complexities of their lives *to* the objective truths of Scripture: "If preachers are content to make their sermons expositions of scripture, that is enough."[92] This approach correlates to his emphasis on theocentric rather than anthropocentric preaching, as Willimon says: "Barth keeps reminding us of what a joy it is to talk about this God rather than to speak only of ourselves and our idols."[93] Consistent with Barth's thought as a whole, we see here how objectivity is the first marker in the dialectic. Whereas Kierkegaard tends to approach the objective by first emphasizing the subjective, Barth usually attempts to speak *from* the place of objectivity, as it were, in order for that objectivity to take root in the subjective person. It is in this way that their endeavors may be seen alike, even if articulated differently. However, it will also be seen that in their preaching there is a commonality in their overall vision for what preaching seeks to accomplish (subjective appropriation of objective truth) as well as in some of their sermonic expression.

It would be easier, perhaps, to find Kierkegaardian emphases in some of Barth's Safenwil sermons. But to truly demonstrate the preacherly kinship these two shared, it will be more illuminating to see similarities in some of Barth's later sermons, a period in which Barth was evidently more settled in his dismissals of Kierkegaard. In the 1950s and 1960s Barth preached once or twice a year to the inmates at Basel prison, Switzerland. In these sermons we find very similar emphases to Kierkegaard's. It is to be expected, of course, that Barth wants to stress the

92. Barth, *Homiletics*, 76.
93. Willimon, "Preaching with Karl Barth," 10.

objective nature of doctrinal truth and the triumph of grace in the Gospel over against immediate anthropological or existential concerns:

> From its first to its last word, preaching follows a movement . . . [which] does not so much consist in going towards men as in coming from Christ to meet them. Preaching therefore proceeds downwards; it should never attempt to reach up to a summit. Has not everything been done already?[94]

Such emphases upon the objective basis for the preached Word are well-known aspects of Barth's theological endeavor, so it is unsurprising that they are present in almost all his Basel prison sermons. Yet we also see interesting "points of contact" between his sermons and his congregation's existential situations. There are recurrent references to "your [prison] cells" and "this chapel of ours" where he makes tangible personal connections between the content of the sermon and the places these prisoners will return to once the preaching moment is over.[95] In opening one sermon, he asks a barrage of questions, empathizing with the prisoners' confusions: "Who is God? What is he like, where is he, what is he? One or other of you may be wondering at this moment. What is meant by the word, what does it say to me, what am I supposed to do about it?"[96] Barth really *is* invested in the personal responses of his hearers. Although, for Barth, the Gospel will always be triumphant and God has always done everything there is to "do about it," he clearly does not see this as mutually exclusive to what his hearers will do in response to the sermon. This attitude extended not only to the sermon itself but to his general posture of compassion toward the prisoners' everyday lives and stories, as Busch's biography notes:

> Barth did not want merely to preach to his audience. In order to preach to them properly he also wanted to get to know them personally, and so he often went to visit them in their cells. For instance, he once reported that "this morning I listened at length to three murderers, two confidence tricksters and one adulterer, added the odd remark here and there and gave each a fat cigar."[97]

---

94. Barth, *Prayer and Preaching*, 71.

95. Barth, "Lord Who Has Mercy on You," 10.

96. Barth, "Lord Who Has Mercy on You," 10.

97. Busch, *Karl Barth*, 415.

There is an important connection here between personal interaction and preaching which might be otherwise missed when reading of Barth's anti-subjectivist approaches to Kierkegaard.

We also see Barth emphasizing his listeners' anxieties as well as a point of empathetic vulnerability where he openly voices his own recurrent nervousness in the days leading up to the sermon: "There is a well justified anxiety about heavy responsibilities which can be placed upon us: I need not hide from you the fact that for as long as I can remember, every time when I am to preach, and so too yesterday and today, I have felt anxious."[98] He wants to show them that he, the preacher, is *with* them in what they suffer, that feelings of isolation and anxiety are faced not only by prisoners in cells but by preachers in pulpits, too. In the same sermon he asks a very piercing and—one might say—"subjective" question: "Does not the thought sometimes force itself on us that we might be living in one great mad-house—and is that not a thought that arises anxiety?"[99] Barth, like Kierkegaard, is pointing to the situational anxieties that afflict human life before launching into the triumphant consolation offered in the Gospel, which ultimately dispels *all* anxieties. This juxtaposition of human anxiety with objective truth—which we see so frequently in Kierkegaard's Citadelskirke sermon—is distinctive of much of Barth's preaching, even in his Safenwil years. See, for example, Barth's Easter sermon of April 8, 1917:

> While we human beings ran our own ways with our hard, thick heads; while we with our little hostilities and foolishness soured life for ourselves and others; while we worshipped Mammon and waged war and suffered distress in this dark world, a world full of questions, enigmas and difficulties. This is Easter: that in the midst of all that, on the third day Jesus Christ rose from the dead![100]

This type of preaching is more than just a juxtapositional "technique," it is an attempt to propel the congregation, initially, further *into* their difficulties in order to lift them out via the comfort of God's Word. For Barth, of course, it is God who is doing all the lifting, not the preacher. Nonetheless, he continues to make this particular move—from the human situation to divine consolation—with a distinct and subjectively-oriented purpose.

98. Barth, "But Take Heart," 108.
99. Barth, "But Take Heart," 109.
100. Barth, "April 8, 1917," 15.

This is remarkably similar to Kierkegaard's entire homiletical approach, and perhaps even his authorship as a whole.[101]

In these prison sermons Barth is not content with a mere textual exposition with some gracious and high-sounding rhetoric, safe in the knowledge that he has "proclaimed the unchanging Gospel." He truly wants his sermons to make an existential impact on his hearers. This is not limited to the immediate preaching moment itself. He, like Kierkegaard, wants his hearers to remember the substance of the message long after he has gone: "It is, by the way, my most important concern, each time I am permitted to be here, that the word from the Bible should stick in your minds and stay with you afterwards rather than my sermon."[102] As we have seen, Kierkegaard's problem in Christendom was that the message of the Bible had become obscured and unappropriated by the aestheticized sermons that were apparently representing it. Such sermons, so greatly admired and so poorly followed, were pharisaic stumbling blocks to the Gospel. This, too, is Barth's concern for the Basel inmates. He wants the Word of God to speak louder than his own words, and to be remembered and heeded as the prisoners return to their cells. This is an almost identical concern to the conclusion of Kierkegaard's sermon where he exhorts his hearers not to forget God's "changelessness" once the sermon ends. In one of Barth's closing prayers to his sermons, he offers perhaps the most overtly Kierkegaardian motif of subjectivity when he prays, "Speak your word to all of us . . . Tell it to each one so that he is not only called a Christian but may again and again become one afresh."[103] This was perhaps Kierkegaard's greatest message to Christendom, to introduce the notion of "becoming a Christian" to those who thought they already were.

A Tale of Two Subjective Preachers

It is evident, from Barth's sermons and overall homiletical outlook, that if Kierkegaard is to be labeled a "subjectivist" then Barth himself can be no less deserving of the same label. Ideally, of course, neither thinker would be tarred with such a brush. In their preaching, both declared the

101. Such an approach is especially evident in Kierkegaard's three "stages" of existence and in Kierkegaard's pseudonymous literature as highlighting the *cul de sac* of the "aesthetic" life, ultimately attempting to propel his readers through the "ethical" toward an embrace of the latter "religious" stage. See Kierkegaard, *Point of View*.

102. Barth, "What Is Enough—31 December 1962," 78.

103. Barth, "But Take Heart," 114.

objective truths of Christian doctrine and sought to make these truths temporally significant in the hearts, minds, and lives of their occasional congregations. The subjective dimension may well have been down-played in Barth's theology, but in his sermons we see a latent emphasis on subjective concerns as the necessary outworking of the objective content. In the last completed section of the *Church Dogmatics*, Barth said, "The object and theme of theology and the content of the Christian message is neither a subjective nor an objective element in isolation."[104] For Kierkegaard this is an almost identical burden. In their very different contexts each sought to emphasize different forms of communication for the same Gospel in which the subjective and the objective are dialecti-cally related. Although there may well be an appropriate ordering within such a dialectic, the subjective and objective elements within preaching are inseparable, even as Kierkegaard and Barth were articulating different avenues *into* it.

Barth and Kierkegaard were two very different kinds of preacher who both considered, in great depth, the implications of what it means to proclaim the Word of a changeless God to eminently changeable human-ity. Kierkegaard himself was ever aware of the implications of God's over-arching gaze over all his preaching, as he said in *Practice in Christianity*:

> It is a risk to preach, for as I go up into that holy place—whether the church is packed or as good as empty, whether I myself am aware of it or not, I have one listener more than can be seen, an invisible listener, God in heaven, whom I certainly cannot see but who truly can see me.[105]

Such a passage could equally have come from Barth's pen *or* pulpit. It is also a paragraph he possibly *did* read. Yet his ignorance of Kierkegaard's wider preacherly concerns remains something of a "subjective" blind spot.

As has been said, what is especially notable in evaluating Barth's reading of Kierkegaard is the fluctuation between his earlier and later opinions. In the *Göttingen Dogmatics*, Barth could say, "Kierkegaard is only too right. No matter how we look at it, one of his most profound insights is that the subjective is the objective."[106] And yet Barth could later say, "Because I cannot regard subjectivity as being the truth, after

104. Barth, *Church Dogmatics*, IV/3, 498.

105. Kierkegaard, *Practice in Christianity*, 234.

106. Barth, *Göttingen Dogmatics*, 1:137.

a brief encounter I have had to move away from Kierkegaard again."[107] Barth may not have been able to say with Johannes Climacus that "truth is subjectivity," but as we have seen, particularly in his preaching, Barth exhibited the dialectical relationship between subjectivity and objectivity in a similar way to Kierkegaard. For Kierkegaard, preaching was the arena in which his theology of subjective appropriation is mediated and finds its greatest relevance. He simply did not know of an ultimately subjective existentialism. The only "existentialism"—for want of a better phrase— which makes any sense to Kierkegaard is that of the subjective reception of, and obedience to, the proclaimed Gospel of Christ. Had Barth known this a little more clearly, he might have felt a longer-lasting kinship with the Danish gadfly. For us, we might consider them as firm allies in the subjective proclamation of the objective Gospel of Jesus Christ.

Indeed, as will be seen in the next chapter, it is not at all surprising that Kierkegaard's expressions of the Gospel in his time placed him in Luther's "prophetic" lineage and served to lay the groundwork for Barth's own recovery of the Gospel in his radical break with anthropocentric liberalism. Nor is it surprising that all three of these theological giants were fundamentally shaped by their encounters with the Apostle Paul's "radical" Gospel.

107. Barth, "Selbstdarstellung," quoted in Busch, *Karl Barth*, 173.

5

Is Kierkegaard an Extremist?

The Nuanced Radicality of the Gospel

ONE OF THE ANIMATING interests in this book so far has been the navigation through the many "Kierkegaards" that have been known to appear over the past two centuries, particularly surrounding the hermeneutical multiplicity that has arisen over Kierkegaard's complex authorship. However, as I have begun to argue, it can become all too easy to settle for an ambivalence as to what Kierkegaard's convictions actually were, particularly those theological convictions which were most fundamental. Where we have so far discussed Kierkegaard's relationship to both Luther (chapter 2) and Barth (chapter 4), this chapter will continue to bring Kierkegaard into dialogue with these theological giants, among other interpreters, as one who sits somewhat in between them as the influenced and the influencer. Where the previous chapters have considered the correctivity, subjectivity, and objectivity of the Gospel, this chapter—and the next—considers the radical implications of the Gospel.

Such implications, however, are easily obscured by those who are interested in separating them from the core of Kierkegaard's thinking, as though they were extremist aberrations from the supposed "center" of Kierkegaard's thought. Perhaps the most prominent theological interpreter of Kierkegaard's authorship in recent decades in this regard has been George Pattison, whose work has often taken the stance of blurring the lines between Kierkegaard's theological, philosophical, and literary intentions. This chapter is not an attempt to respond to George Pattison's work in any comprehensive sense, but to engage with him critically on the particular point of Kierkegaard's conviction about the Gospel, and its implications for sin, redemption, and the wider homiletical tone of Kierkegaard's theology. Contrary to Pattison, I will argue that Kierkegaard's theology of sin and redemption is indeed "radical." One might even be tempted to call it "unnuanced," however odd that might sound of one of the most complex and reflective thinkers of the modern era. To see Kierkegaard in this way, however, would be to misunderstand the inherent nuance of polemical simplicity that characterized much of his directly theological work.

Notwithstanding the ongoing interaction between the direct and indirect aspects of his authorship (including the mystique of the pseudonymous characters) it is the second authorship—in light of his journals and his subsequent reflections—which yields the possibility of a confident reading of Kierkegaard's "view." It will be affirmed, in distinction to Pattison's immanentist hermeneutic, that for Kierkegaard, the effects of both sin and the Gospel are radically transformative. Sin is no mere inconvenience or blot on an otherwise beautiful canvas, but a pure corruption of the human self. Furthermore, the effects of sin cannot be undone without the radical redemption of the Gospel. It is this Gospel which is seen to be apocalyptically invasive rather than naturally immanent in the world. In light of Kierkegaard's radically emphatic understanding of the Gospel, some interesting conclusions emerge regarding how academic "nuance" is often an abuse of complexity by excluding the possibility of a radical emphasis.

We will first address this issue by reintroducing the problem of hermeneutical ambiguity regarding Kierkegaard's kerygmatic thought (first noted in chapter 1) by which the truly paradoxical force of his approach is often missed.

Between Ambiguity and Extremity

One feature of Pattison's reading of Kierkegaard's project is that Kierkegaard's view of sin and the implications of the Gospel—accentuated most overtly in his so-called later period—is a significant departure from his distinctively Christian position, and from evangelical orthodoxy as a whole. Pattison asserts that Kierkegaard's theological position "darkened" with the attack literature,[1] implying that such darkening provides us with a hermeneutical trajectory for the inherent untrustworthiness of Kierkegaard's radical kerygmatic emphases in general. There is no question that there were more moments of pronounced negativity during Kierkegaard's "attack" period, especially vis-à-vis his echoes of Schopenhauer, who begins to creep into the journals more frequently in the 1850s. In one 1854 journal entry—where Kierkegaard is actually critiquing Luther—Kierkegaard cites Schopenhauer before going on to state that "the world is immersed in evil."[2] Such comments, at a time when Kierkegaard was becoming increasingly withdrawn from ecclesial and public life, no doubt contribute to his reputation as the "Melancholy Dane."

However, it is perhaps too convenient to tar "the late Kierkegaard" with the brush of Schopenhauerian pessimism as though this colored his other supposedly extreme views about the seriousness of humanity's sinful state *coram Deo*.[3] For one thing, Kierkegaard himself regularly showed a sense of frustrated self-awareness at the idea that he was somehow a "mad" Christian.[4] Indeed, he often contrasts this with the problem of the perpetual middle way:

> In the world of mediocrity in which we live it is assumed—and this is one of the ways used to safeguard mediocrity—that only crackpot boldness, etc. should be deplored as offensive, as inspired by Satan, and that the middle way, however, is secure against any such charge. Christ and Christianity are of another mind: mediocrity itself is the offense, the most dangerous kind of demon possession, farthest removed from the possibility of being cured.[5]

---

1. See Pattison, *Kierkegaard and the Theology of the Nineteenth Century*, 125.

2. *Søren Kierkegaard's Journals and Papers*, 3:3044, 376.

3. Indeed, where there is affinity with Schopenhauer, it is as much influenced by the fact that Schopenhauer's own views on humanity—though ultimately irreconcilable with orthodox Christianity—were continually informed and ultimately shaped by his interactions with Christian theology. As William Mackintire Salter noted over a century ago, even in Schopenhauer's "pessimism" we can recognize the kind of radical attitude to the world that characterized the earliest Christians: "If we call him pessimist, let us admit more in common with those who condemned this world and looked for another some two thousand years ago in Palestine than with those who are ordinarily spoken of as pessimists." Salter, "Schopenhauer's Contact with Theology," 310.

4. *Søren Kierkegaard's Journals and Papers*, 6:6257, 57.

5. *Søren Kierkegaard's Journals and Papers*, 4:4494, 320.

This journal entry was written on July 5, 1855, in the year of his death, and just two days before his infamous "Medical Diagnosis" in *The Moment*, whereby he compared the Danish Church to a disease-ridden hospital deceptively poisoning its patients to death.[6] One can sense Kierkegaard's frustration at how impossible it was for those within the Christendom system to see the system's inherent madness precisely in its mediocre failure to embody its central Christian message. Such an approach, though, is not exclusive to the attack period. Five years earlier, we see a critique along similar lines regarding devotion to Christ: "He who does not involve himself with God in the mode of absolute devotion does not become involved with God. In relationship to God one cannot involve himself to a certain degree, for God is precisely the contradiction to all that which is to a certain degree."[7] For Kierkegaard, to speak of and relate to *this* God cannot be done on "mediocre" or "ambiguous" terms; it can only be one-sided and all-encompassing.

Such "unambiguous" expressions cannot be conveniently excised from the authorship as though they were a regrettable aberration, the crazed ramblings of an unhinged penitent winding himself up before the impending doom of death row.[8] Where Roger Poole warns against "blunt" readings of Kierkegaard which interpret his religious consistency with all too much certainty,[9] it is perhaps even more important to counteract those "incisive" readings of Kierkegaard which blunt his homiletical Gospel emphasis. It was, after all, Kierkegaard's commitment *to* the Gospel's radical existential implications that undergirded the great doctrinal experiment that was his authorship.

6. See chapter 8, cf. Kierkegaard, *Attack upon "Christendom,"* 139–41.

7. *Søren Kierkegaard's Journals and Papers*, 2:1405, 123. Indeed, Kierkegaard's critique of holiness "to a certain extent" goes hand in hand with his theology of suffering as the mark of devotion which was so overtly missing in Christendom: "One who in truth has become involved with God is instantaneously recognizable by his limp." *Søren Kierkegaard's Journals and Papers*, 2:1405, 123. For Kierkegaard, the Danish Church, in its comfortable assimilation and social religious guise, existed very much *without* a limp. This context dominated his expression of the Gospel throughout the second authorship.

8. What is more, we might ask, why ought Kierkegaard's "central period" be privileged as his most trustworthy or reasonable? Although he certainly thought much about death, it cannot be the case that he had succumbed to some kind of death-row morosity in his later theological stances, as though he *knew* that he was, in fact, *in* his "latter period" at the time rather than an ongoingly "present" period.

9. Poole, "Unknown Kierkegaard," 48–75.

Pattison offers an account of Kierkegaard's journey in and through the fog of ambiguity in such a way that his final convictions (theological or otherwise) merely reflect one of the many oscillating moments in a dominantly ambiguous existence: "'Kierkegaard' is not to be identified with one or other unambiguous gesture, poetic or political, but is rather found in the complex movements he traced in the contested and ambiguous elliptical space."[10] This is why, for Pattison, Kierkegaard's "unambiguity" is seen as a "quest," that which teems with mystery and without necessary conclusiveness.[11] Although he is right to stress the importance of the ambiguous elliptical space, it might be more appropriate to call Kierkegaard a "post-ambiguitarian." This is where we might retain the nuance in his more acerbic expressions of thought. To be post-ambiguous is not to reject ambiguity entirely but to see that even though one recognizes the role of ambiguity, it does not dictate one's outlook, nor—more importantly—one's quest. What, though, is the problem at the heart of the Kierkegaardian quest—and how much of a "problem" is it? That is, how much does humanity truly *need* the revelation of the Gospel, and *why* do we need it?

Between Religiousness and Reformation

Kierkegaard's view of the Gospel is undoubtedly shaped by his Reformational inheritance. This was key to his pervasive impact upon twentieth-century Protestant theology, even with its many variations.[12] Central to this inheritance is a necessarily "low" view of natural humanity prior to divine revelatory encounter. Such a foundation underlies his view of what is accomplished in the work of redemption, as will be seen. However, Pattison counters this: "Kierkegaard's actual position is considerably more nuanced than this rather standard account of what is going on in his theology . . . his position involves both a theology of redemption and a theology of creation."[13] It is certainly the case that Kierkegaard did not *merely* hold a view of total depravity which ignored the ongoing

10. Pattison, *Kierkegaard and the Quest for Unambiguous Life*, 28.

11. On this, note a somewhat jarring contrast with Kierkegaard's negative reference to "the knight errant" who embarks upon a quest in inconclusive doubt about what may befall him. Kierkegaard, *Gospel of Sufferings*, 92.

12. See Stewart, *Kierkegaard's Influence on Theology* I.

13. Pattison, *Kierkegaard and the Theology of the Nineteenth Century*, 81.

redemptive work of God, but neither can his position on the necessity of the divine rescue of fallen humanity be masked by God's subsequent sanctifying work. We see this radical position most overtly in the distinction between the two "types" of religiousness.

At the apex of Kierkegaard's three stages of existence (aesthetic; ethical; religious) is the distinction between Religiousness A and B. Where Religiousness A tends to refer to the natural religiosity of the human spirit, Religiousness B is the recipient of radical divine revelation.[14] At the heart of the endeavor to interpret Kierkegaard theologically is to work out what to do with this distinction and how it might apply more widely across his soteriological thought. It appears that a clear dialectical taxonomy exists between the two. Religiousness A and B are precisely and necessarily a binary distinction. Within this, the radicality of Religiousness B cannot be a mere "option" of equal weighting, but is *always* "the ideal" and "essence" of true Christianity—and indeed, true religion. This does not mean that there is no interaction or movement between the two, but merely that at all points, the great taxonomical headline remains in place: that faith comes by hearing, that revelation from without is *required* in order to rescue and liberate us into true freedom.

To hold to a theology more inclined to Religiousness A, as Pattison appears to—with all the implications of human possibility therein—is not the primary issue here. The more pertinent question is why he would choose Kierkegaard (of all people) for this task, when doing so inevitably invokes so much pushback from Religiousness B *against* the notion of divine immanence? After all, there are plenty of more suitable suitors within the history of theology for that particular marriage of divinity and contingency. Kierkegaard—though perhaps far more interesting to read than a Schleiermacher or a Tillich—is far too committed to the radicality of the Gospel to allow for any notion of individual freedom that might compete with the radical impact of Christ's unique revelation *upon* the individual.[15] Indeed, it was this christological fixation, coupled with the time/eternity dialectic, that was—unsurprisingly—the very thing that so captivated those dialectical revolutionaries of the *Zwischen den Zeiten* journal in 1920s Weimar Germany.

Perhaps one could even say that the famous debate between Karl Barth and Emil Brunner over natural theology (including Barth's radical

14. See Kierkegaard, *Concluding Unscientific Postscript*, 555–85.

15. See Kierkegaard, *For Self-Examination*, 145–209; Kierkegaard, *Practice in Christianity*, 124–44.

"Nein!" to Brunner's entire "eristic" project) centered precisely on the same kind of problem of the impasse between Religiousness A and B.[16] The idea of a point of contact (*Anknüpfungspunkt*) in humanity, to which Barth was so hostile, was an issue of dialectical taxonomy. For Barth, one cannot somehow have and eat one's revelational cake. In Pattison's reading, however, Religiousness A offers a "privileged position" vis-à-vis faith, which might somehow avoid what he calls "the 'crater' left by the exploding shells of revelation à la Barth."[17] This notion of A as "privileged" is another way in which Pattison is attempting to add "nuance" to what might otherwise appear an uncouth rendering of human religiosity. However, it seems to summon the image of a "first class" compartment in the reception of divine revelation as though it comes "closer" to it than others. This seems oddly out of sync with Kierkegaard's ear for identifying and satirizing hypocrisy.

In many respects, Barth's *Römerbrief*—that famous "bombshell"— was Barth's own Diet of Worms with nineteenth-century theology (or, Religiousness A). And like Luther, whom Barth would go on to love and hate in appropriately tumultuous measure,[18] he wanted to stress the "one thing needful," that God is in heaven and you are on earth.[19] It was that and precisely that—as ludicrously crude as it sounds to the so-called "privileged" ears of Religiousness A—that required Barth's radical break, one made with the overt help of Kierkegaard.[20] It was this same kind of radical expression that Kierkegaard articulated in the time-eternity disjunction,[21] the double-paradox of the atonement,[22] and the infinite qualitative distinction.[23]

In Pattison's case against the radical Kierkegaard there is an apparent ease with which the doctrinal substance of the Gospel, which Kierkegaard so vigorously proclaimed, is simplistically categorized under rubrics like "the Augustinian-Lutheran view" or "the Reformation doctrine."[24]

16. See Kierkegaard's influence on Brunner in Brown, *Believing Thinking, Bounded Theology*, 141–81.

17. Pattison, "Kierkegaard, Freedom, Love," 6.

18. See Brian, *Covering Up Luther*.

19. Barth, *Epistle to the Romans*, 310–11.

20. Barth, *Epistle to the Romans*, 10, 99.

21. Kierkegaard, *Concept of Anxiety*, 87–9.

22. Kierkegaard, *Sickness unto Death*, 100. See chapter 2.

23. Kierkegaard, *Practice in Christianity*, 28–9.

24. See Pattison, *Kierkegaard and the Theology of the Nineteenth Century*, 8, 93,

One does not, of course, want to exude naïveté or ignorance by bypassing the hermeneutical reality that singular figures or traditions have always held doctrinal truth claims which exhibit contextual particularity. Yet this is a different thing to the obvious implication of a condescending use of a phrase like "the Augustinian-Lutheran view," which suggests not just particularity, but idiosyncrasy. This would even seem to be the very kind of bourgeois strategy Kierkegaard might have mocked in his day, to deflect attention from the substance of the doctrine itself by calling it "the X view" as a sly ruse to deny its potential existential implications.

For all the wealth of caveats surrounding Luther's legacy, it is abundantly clear that he had that unique ability to see through the mire and to take a courageous stand for that which was being quietly but violently neglected in his time.[25] Although arguably Kierkegaard's "stand" actually seems virtually the opposite of Luther's, by accentuating striving rather than mere grace, he always maintained that his emphasis is precisely what Luther himself would have preached in nineteenth-century Copenhagen.[26] Thomas Carlyle, in his famous 1840 lectures on the "heroic" motif in human history, called Luther the great "Prophet Idol-breaker; a bringer-back of men to reality."[27] It can become all too easy, with a half-millennium of hindsight, to assert that the intensity of Luther's experience negates the possibility that his imperatives can speak meaningfully beyond his time.[28] But this would surely be to miss the entire point of the Reformation: "The Reformation age, amid grievous destruction, swept away the clutter, pursued simplicity of vision, and directed the gaze of the

---

158, 160; *Kierkegaard and the Quest for Unambiguous Life*, 216.

25. "His greatest intellectual gift was his ability to simplify, to cut to the heart of an issue—but this also made it difficult for him to compromise or see nuance." Roper, *Martin Luther*, 422. However, this does seem to underplay Luther's dialectical nuance, particularly in his varied homiletical expression, alert to various diversities of congregation and context. See Kolb, *Martin Luther and the Enduring Word of God*, 174–208.

26. Kierkegaard, *For Self-Examination*, 24. For a revised view of Kierkegaard's reading of Luther vis-à-vis their respective kerygmatic emphases, see Coe, "Kierkegaard's Forking for Extracts from Extracts of Luther's Sermons," 3–18.

27. Carlyle, *On Great Men*, 58. The heroic motif also evokes the potential idolatry inherent in Religiousness A, and the problem at the heart of theological immanence whereby the eternal is infused with the temporal indiscriminately, whereby God's revelatory activity is minimized under a false ideality.

28. The opposite case is made by Ryrie, who argues that Luther's "shattering spiritual experiences" continue to speak today not for their theological import but for their resonance within the culture of modern individualism they helped create. Ryrie, *Protestants*, 19–20.

worshipper towards that which truly mattered."[29] Indeed, Luther's reformation was of a most *existential* kind. At heart it was primarily about his own condition before God, and only secondarily—perhaps even "accidentally"—did it happen to affect the rest of world history. The doctrinal revolt was inseparable from its existential import.[30]

Kierkegaard might also be called an existential reformer, notwithstanding his own caveats that he could never be a reformer because he could not live up to Luther's heroism,[31] and was dubious about those who followed in the Reformer's wake without the same existential involvement.[32] However, if Luther *was* right, then the truth to which he bore witness, and the truth to which the Reformation as a whole bore witness, cannot be swept away under a neat category as though we could somehow move *beyond* it, like a Hegelian sublimation en masse. Indeed, it would simply be too convenient—and perhaps too suspiciously Christendomian—to separate Luther's view of the Gospel into a "perspective" of the past as we continue on at a safe distance from his aggravating light. Rather, "contemporaneity with Luther," to borrow a concept (albeit somewhat blasphemously!) from *Practice in Christianity*—is Christianly essential, at least in regards to the condition Luther was proclaiming. If Luther is right on the diagnosis and cure of sin—as Kierkegaard believed he was—we no longer have the diversionist luxury of assuming that his condition was *only* his. Even if his thunderous experience was idiosyncratic of the anguished conscience ad absurdum, this does not remove *us* from facing the potential implications of our sinful state before a holy God, nor for how we interpret Kierkegaard's appropriation of it.

What Hugh Pyper says of Kierkegaard could also be said of Luther: "What he burns to communicate is good news, while knowing that the majority of his hearers cannot tell good news from bad and have a

29. Chadwick, *Reformation*, 443–44.

30. "Luther's inner certainty depended on identifying his cause with Christ's." Roper, *Martin Luther*, 189.

31. Kierkegaard, *Judge for Yourself!*, 211–13.

32. "It has often been said that a reformation should begin with each man reforming himself. That, however, is not what actually happened, for the Reformation produced a hero who paid God dearly enough for his position as hero. By joining up with him directly people buy cheap, indeed at bargain prices, what he had paid for so dearly." Kierkegaard, *Present Age*, 63.

tendency to mistake the disease for the cure and the cure for the disease."[33] As Pattison himself says in his work on Kierkegaard's discourses:

> The Christian communicator must be indirect in so far as he must meet his "audience" where they are, in the aesthetic and the babel of hermeneutic ambiguity. But it is never simply his intention to leave them there. His aim is rather to bring them to a point at which they will be appropriately receptive to the kerygmatic imperatives of the gospel.[34]

Evidently, Pattison does not want to minimize Kierkegaard's kerygmatic witness, even as he remains critical of the Reformational moorings in which it is often seen. But he primarily wants to stress the possibilities inherent in the hearer, as forming part of a revised view of the Kierkegaardian kerygma. Elsewhere Pattison points to the mode of the "subjunctive" in the discourses (lying somewhere between the "indicative" and the "imperative") as a way to guarantee the hearer's freedom in the midst of proclamation: "The ideality of the subjunctive . . . concerns what *may be* and, specifically, what may be a possibility for subjective appropriation . . . The subjunctive does not present its subject matter as simple fact, but makes the narrated facts available as ideal existential possibilities elicited from history."[35] This evokes an important distinction between the hearer of the Gospel and their sinfulness.

Between Sin and Redemption

In *Philosophical Fragments* the idea of "the Socratic" is distinguished against the decisive "moment" of Christian revelation.[36] For the Socratic hearer it is supposed that the truth must merely be "recalled" in order to be grasped. They are what Pattison might call "privileged." However, the hearer of the Gospel recognizes that they cannot recall anything whatsoever since they begin in a state of fundamental "error."[37] They are bound

---

33. Pyper, *Joy of Kierkegaard*, 1.

34. Pattison, "Theory and Practice," 86.

35. Pattison, *Kierkegaard's Upbuilding Discourses*, 157.

36. See Kierkegaard, *Philosophical Crumbs*, 88–110, 125–39.

37. "If the teacher is to be the occasion that reminds the learner, then he cannot contribute to the learner's remembering that he really knows the truth, because the learner is actually in a state of error." Kierkegaard, *Philosophical Crumbs*, 92.

within this error and must be radically "liberated" and "delivered" by a Savior.[38]

Kierkegaard often makes the key distinction between what we might call the *act* of sin and the *condition* of sin:

> Fundamentally, the relation between God and man is in this, that a man is a sinner, and God is the Holy One. Confronting God . . . a man is not a sinner in this or that regard, but in his being he is sinful, not guilty in this or that, but guilty essentially and absolutely.[39]

Pattison claims that although we are tempted *by* sin, we are "free to resist and free to orient ourselves towards the good, to will it, and to pray for it."[40] If indeed this "we" includes all human beings, it must be asked—in light of Kierkegaard's apparent definition of the *ontological* entrapments of sin in light of the Pauline imperative of Eph 2:1–5 (dead in sin, made alive in Christ)—on what grounds are we free to overcome the problem of sin by ourselves? For Kierkegaard, as for Calvin,[41] the raising of Lazarus was a perfect analogy of the sinner's redemption. Indeed, in an 1849 journal entry, Kierkegaard relates this stark difference to the suppression of the ideal in Christendom: "What it means actually to be Christian is seen here (John 12:10): the Jews wanted to kill Lazarus—because Christ had raised him from the dead. So dangerous it is to be raised from the dead—by Christ!"[42]

As Kierkegaard concludes his introduction to *Sickness unto Death*: "Only the *Christian* knows what is meant by the sickness unto death."[43]

---

38. Kierkegaard, *Philosophical Crumbs*, 95. For a nuanced account of Kierkegaard's christocentric hamartiology regarding the place of sin within the purposes of redemption, see Mahn, *Fortunate Fallibility: Kierkegaard and the Power of Sin*.

39. Kierkegaard, *Gospel of Sufferings*, 89. The effect of the sin-consciousness of the person before God is also mentioned in an 1850 journal entry: "Original sin as guilt is also an expression of God's using his standard; for God sees everything in uno; and therefore the merely human understanding finds it so difficult." *Søren Kierkegaard's Journals and Papers*, 1:525, 207. This refers to the notion that the more that God (the superior one) loves the sinner, the more unhappy the sinner becomes—even if God lays down his standard (i.e., who he is, in the sense of a "flag") in order to love us. The more he loves us, the more the difference (his superiority) is accentuated; and thus, the more "difficult" it is for us, the more we suffer as a result of God's love.

40. Pattison, "Kierkegaard, Freedom, Love," 2.

41. Calvin, *Commentaries*, 395.

42. *Søren Kierkegaard's Journals and Papers*, 3:2866, 268.

43. Kierkegaard, *Sickness unto Death*, 8.

This is because the Christian has learned to fear God in the confrontation—and forgiveness—of their sin. This also assumes, of course, the paradox Kierkegaard refers to frequently, that original sin and individual guilt are complexly conflated, and may only be engaged via faith.[44] For Kierkegaard, the fundamental difference between paganism and Christianity is that Christianity knows what sin actually is.[45] So clear is Kierkegaard on the radical doctrine of sin that he claims it would be a terrible slight on Christianity if paganism's definition of sin were shown to be in agreement with its own.[46] It is this radical disjunction between the Christian and non-Christian that is labeled by Pattison as the "extreme" Augustinian-Protestant view of sin.[47] Unsurprisingly, this also manifests in a de-radicalized account of redemption *from* this sinful condition too, whereby Pattison argues that Kierkegaard's doctrine inclines more toward "recreation" than "satisfaction" of sin per se.[48] On Kierkegaard's frequent use of the term "satisfaction," Pattison sees this as related to God's love, not his wrath.[49] This reflects something of a common view in Western academic theology today whereby divine wrath is often entirely ignored within theological discussions of redemption.[50] In Pattison's case,

44. "That 'Original Sin' is 'guilt' is the real paradox. How paradoxical is best seen as follows. The paradox is formed by a composite of qualitatively heterogeneous categories. To 'inherit' is a category of nature. 'Guilt' is an ethical category of spirit. How can it ever occur to anyone to put these two together, the understanding says—to say that something is inherited which by its very concept cannot be inherited. It must be believed. The paradox in Christian truth always involves the truth as before God. A superhuman goal and standard are used—and with regard to them there is only one relationship possible—that of faith." *Søren Kierkegaard's Journals and Papers*, 2:1530, 194.

45. See Kierkegaard, *Sickness unto Death*, 89.

46. Kierkegaard, *Sickness unto Death*, 89–90.

47. Pattison, *Kierkegaard and the Theology of the Nineteenth Century*, 124.

48. Pattison, *Kierkegaard and the Theology of the Nineteenth Century*, 81.

49. See Pattison, *Kierkegaard and the Theology of the Nineteenth Century*, 157–60; Pattison, *Kierkegaard and the Quest for Unambiguous Life*, 216. Pattison's argument here is not wrong in its illustration of the colorful variety within Kierkegaard's account, but rather in assuming that Kierkegaard's emphasis on love thereby necessarily excludes the category of God's judgment simultaneously.

50. At an academic theology conference I attended on the subject of eternity a few years ago, the final session involved an anonymous Q&A box which had been set out for the panel of plenary speakers to discuss. One of the questions slipped into the box was the cause of great amusement as it highlighted a topic which had, rather curiously, not been mentioned *at all* throughout the entirety of the conference. The question simply stated: "Eternal death and hell, anyone?" It is one thing for contemporary

he seems to have expressed a false dichotomy of divine love over against divine justice. In doing so, however, this would seem to render the "requirement" of satisfaction something of a farce. God might have simply chosen to love in spite of the sin of his beloved rather than requiring satisfaction of sin *in order that* he might be reconciled to his beloved.

For Kierkegaard, the sinful condition is so severe that even the conviction of human depravity itself is dependent upon radical revelation: "There must be a revelation from God to teach man what sin is and how deeply it is rooted."[51] And yet, perhaps like the Reformers and like Augustine, Kierkegaard's expression of redemption is equally as radical as his expression of depravity: "The Atonement wants to eliminate sin so completely as if it were drowned in the sea."[52] One is able to apprehend the gift of this atonement only by faith, referred to in *The Concept of Anxiety* as "the inner certainty that anticipates infinity."[53] For Kierkegaard, the inner certainty of faith anticipates and expects much from God in eternity because it has eschewed the false foundation of doubt.

Between Doubt and Radicality

The antithesis to Kierkegaard's radical proclamation of this Gospel is the attitude of deliberative doubt. This is a particularly urgent problem in modernity, wherein doubt has become the unquestioned foundation prior to faith. Kierkegaard calls out the sinner's subtle way of attempting to bypass their sinfulness by assuming a kind of neutral starting point by which they may judge God's revelation: "If the starting-point be doubt, then long, long before the end God is lost to us . . . If, on the other hand, a sense of sin be the starting-point, then the starting point of doubt is

---

academic theology to nuance the various unreflective expressions of divine wrath in previous eras of the Church, but another thing entirely to eliminate the concept of divine wrath from the theological conversation per se. This reflects the wider problem of the general embarrassment within the modern theological academy toward those attributes of God which simply cannot hope to gain a hearing in contemporary Western society. See Ziegler, *Eternal God, Eternal Life*.

51. Kierkegaard, *Sickness unto Death*, 96. See also Fremstahl and Jackson's neat summary: "Because of human guilt and sinfulness, Kierkegaard holds that we are neither capable of realizing moral virtue nor eternal happiness by our own unaided powers; we are only capable of realizing our incapability and of choosing whether or not to accept divine grace." Fremstedahl and Jackson, "Salvation/Eternal Happiness," 3.

52. Kierkegaard, *Sickness unto Death*, 100.

53. Kierkegaard, *Concept of Anxiety*, 157.

made impossible, and so there is joy."[54] Doubt, for Kierkegaard, becomes an attitude of presumptuousness before God.[55]

In the discourse "The Care of Indecisiveness, Vacillation, and Disconsolateness" (a reflection on Christ's call that we cannot serve two masters), Kierkegaard says, "The Christian, free from care is never *indecisive*—he has faith; never *vacillating*—he is eternally resolved."[56] This is put in stark contrast to the pagan, who epitomizes Kierkegaard's critique of endless deliberation: "Perhaps one thinks that the longer a person deliberates the more earnest his decision becomes. Perhaps—if it does not entirely fail to come."[57] To an extent, modern Christendom itself epitomized the choice to privilege doubt over decision, becoming what Kierkegaard called "the slave of indecisiveness."[58] Faith, on the other hand, chooses God and "refuses to hear about anything else."[59] One can see, of course, as Pattison aptly observes, how easy it was for Kierkegaard to become co-opted into the "decisionistic" thinking of the twentieth century via controversial thinkers such as Emanuel Hirsch.[60] Kierkegaard, though certainly responsible for some of his interpretative litter, can hardly be faulted for readings which are so neglectful of the grounds for which his strong emphases on the concept of "decision" were expressed (namely, Christ as the qualitative "content" of the Gospel). To see his reflections as "unnuanced" would itself seem to be an ironically simplistic approach. Kierkegaard is not ignorant of complexity amid decisive action; in fact, he offers a deep knowledge of its inner workings, tensions, and implications. He is also profoundly aware of the perils of calling for "complexity" when this becomes accepted simplistically as the guiding mantra.[61] Kierkegaard's emphases—particularly in the discourses—ever

---

54. Kierkegaard, *Gospel of Sufferings*, 82.

55. Presumptuousness, of course, is the very thing one might often assume to be the "problem" with radically decisive faith.

56. Kierkegaard, *Christian Discourses*, 85.

57. Kierkegaard, *Christian Discourses*, 88.

58. Kierkegaard, *Christian Discourses*, 89.

59. Kierkegaard, *Christian Discourses*, 88.

60. Pattison, *Kierkegaard and the Quest for Unambiguous Life*, 86–114; see also Wilke, "Emmanuel Hirsch," 155–84.

61. If Hirsch could read Kierkegaard as a Romantic who enabled him to see the decisive action of National Socialism as a theological good, one must counter this with interpreters like Bonhoeffer, a great reader of Kierkegaard who saw in him precisely the opposite dynamic and a means by which individual decision (not passive vacillation to the Zeitgeist) was precisely necessarily in resisting the same ethical evils, which

urge his reader toward critical reflection, but cognizant of the ideology of critical reflection itself, knowing that unchecked reflection more often leads to vacillating deliberation rather than transformational decision.

Commenting on the preacher in Ecclesiastes, a book which fascinated Kierkegaard and in many ways epitomized his own dialectical-but-decisive approach, he says,

> He speaks not as one who wishes, not as one who longs, not as one who swoons, but he speaks to the young with the power of conviction, with the authority of experience, with the trustworthiness of assured insight, with the joyful trust of bold confidence, with the emphasis of earnestness, with the concern of the admonition.[62]

Yet it might be tempting for some to imagine that Kierkegaard may have been speaking ironically here, especially given the hermeneutical complexity of Ecclesiastes itself, and knowing Kierkegaard's own critiques of the assuredness of Christendom's preachers. Will Williams, however, counters such indirect interpretations, observing,

> While Kierkegaard can undoubtedly make potent use of humor and irony, I believe it is a mistake to read him as a thoroughgoing ironist at every turn. Kierkegaard uses the Preacher [of Ecclesiastes] non-ironically as a genuine authority on wise living. If one attempts an inappropriately ironic reading of the Preacher in order to generate ambiguity and so to escape the moral earnestness of a passage, Kierkegaard locates the fault in the reader and not in the author.[63]

This riposte to the perpetual hermeneutic of jest chimes in well with Kierkegaard's view of doubt as the temptation for the sinner to circumvent their sinfulness, and indeed their need of the Gospel. This is precisely what also concerned "the preacher," who—as Kierkegaard notes—spoke not with mere wishfulness but with "bold confidence."

To speak with boldness is to echo the Apostle Paul's prayerful plea "that words may be given to me in opening my mouth boldly to proclaim the mystery of the gospel . . . that I may declare it boldly, as I ought to

---

had been so seductively veiled within the tidal wave of *Völkisch* cultural energy. For an account of Kierkegaard's influence on Bonhoeffer, see Tietz, "Dietrich Bonhoeffer." See also Kirkpatrick, *Attacks on Christendom in a World Come of Age*.

62. Kierkegaard, *Eighteen Upbuilding Discourses*, 238.

63. Williams, "Ecclesiastes," 181n11.

speak" (Eph 6:19–20). Kierkegaard's desire to heed the realities of "New Testament Christianity"[64] opens up possible rhetorical comparisons with "Pauline apocalyptic."[65] Paul is often seen as having been eclipsed by James in Kierkegaard's writings, but in fact Paul appears far more abundantly than James across the whole authorship.[66] His employment of Pauline themes is numerous, and it is evident from Kierkegaard's genius/apostle distinction that Paul has particular interest for him as a bringer of revelatory authority.[67] It is not unimportant that something *happened* to Paul; this affects how one ought to hear what he says. His encounter with Christ is truly dramatic, beginning as it does somewhat violently and ending in temporary blindness (Acts 9:3–9). Like Lazarus's resurrection, this event is also a picture of what happens when sin is confronted by liberating love in its most supreme form.[68] This is a supremely chastening liberation, and yet it is one that could lead Paul to "rejoice" in all things (Phil 4:4) despite the avalanche of suffering which would confront him in fulfilment of his revelatory calling (2 Cor 11:23–30).

It is the Pauline combination of radical revelation and the willingness to suffer rejoicingly that Kierkegaard finds so inspiring contra Christendom's insipidness.[69] Kierkegaard's task as a Christian author from beginning to end was indeed to follow Paul's lead as the herald of a Gospel that was both dialectical and also undilutable. The radicality of sin was precisely what Kierkegaard believed had been "diluted" out of Christendom:

> The consciousness of sin shuts my mouth so that in spite of the possibility of offense I choose to believe. The relationship has to be that penetrating. Christianity repels in order to attract. But Christianity has been diluted, the aspect of Christianity which, so to speak, turns a man upside down, has been diluted, and

---

64. See, for example, *Søren Kierkegaard's Journals and Papers*, 2:1807, 296; 3:2379, 31; 4:4499, 324.

65. For an example of a Kierkegaardian implementation within this emerging theological movement, see Ziegler, *Militant Grace*, 153–68.

66. See Brandt, "Paul," 189–208. See also O'Regan's comments on the influence of a Pauline vision on Kierkegaard in "The Rule of Chaos," 154.

67. See Kierkegaard, *Without Authority*, 91–106.

68. See again Calvin's connection between the raising of Lazarus and the radically activating power of the Gospel. Calvin, *Commentaries*, 395.

69. See Kierkegaard, *Upbuilding Discourses in Various Spirits*, 315.

therefore the impetus of sin-consciousness is not needed to
drive one into it—that is, it is all sentimentality.[70]

Indeed, try telling Paul that we may free ourselves from the bondage of
sin-consciousness! With Kierkegaard, he might have responded, paradoxically, that it is *for freedom* that Christ has set us free (Gal 5:1). To submit again to a yoke of slavery (to the self-contained ego *or* to the crowd)
is to step back into a life which is abundantly *less* than the life abundant
that Christ's sacrifice secured for us.

But it is not only "for freedom" that we are set free, but also "from
freedom," as Kierkegaard well knew—that is, from notions of freedom
which conform precisely to this world.[71] This is the questionably "radical"
freedom which refuses to bow the knee to Christ's lordship, and which
sees radical discipleship as giving oneself away in vain, as per Sartre.[72]
Such "freedom" might reject the transformation by the liberating love
and power of the Spirit (Rom 12:1–2) to insist on the fetishization of one's
individual existential rights above all.[73] All such moves render the preaching of the cross more "foolish" to the modern self-understanding (1 Cor
1:18), rendering Kierkegaard's voice all the more important in preaching
such apparent foolishness in Paul's footsteps. Indeed, it is only by *not*
removing the veil of Kierkegaard's Gospel radicality—in all its thoughtful
offensiveness—that we retain his most vital and most nuanced contribution to modern Christian thought, however alarming that may appear to
many proponents of modern Christian thought.

The Nuance of Radicality

Pattison certainly sees Kierkegaard's later period (beyond 1851) as offering "a much less dialectical and nuanced view."[74] To be sure, the period
that led to the "attack" literature had a very polemical slant, but it is not as
though we are left in ignorance as to why Kierkegaard's approach changed.

70. *Søren Kierkegaard's Journals and Papers*, 6:6261, 64.

71. See Kierkegaard's critique of the false deification of the concept of freedom
in light of the 1848 European revolutions. *Søren Kierkegaard's Journals and Papers*,
2:1261, 67–9.

72. See Sartre, *Being and Nothingness*, 636.

73. See Hauerwas's critique of "the unlimited scope of rights language" in contemporary political discourse. Hauerwas, *Work of Theology*, 196–98.

74. Pattison, *Kierkegaard and the Theology of the Nineteenth Century*, 105n3. See
also Walsh, *Living Christianly*, 159–60.

He offers reams of reflection not only in his various "total" interpretations of his authorship but also especially in his journals, whereby we see
the contemplative agony that lay behind his careful change in emphasis.[75]
To simply label his attack period "unnuanced" is almost to act as though
this other reflective material simply does not exist.

As is well known, Kierkegaard thought long and hard about how
and why he would choose to communicate in particular ways at particular times during his life, based on numerous factors.[76] Although his later
work took a decisive turn toward a more radical emphasis it is not as
though there was a substantial change in his fundamental understanding
of the efficacy of sin, the incapacity of humanity, and the human need for
divine deliverance. These elements were already present in his theology
during the earlier writings, albeit sometimes veiled. This radicality itself
need not be deemed "unreflective." Kierkegaard is potentially just as dialectical in the attack literature as in the pseudonymous literature; he has
merely chosen the one thing needful to the moment, at that particular
time and in that particular place, taking into account all the complexities
of Danish public life and what it would entail to challenge Christendom's
lethargy most effectively.

One must also say, of course, that Kierkegaard saw the gravitation to
reflective nuance as itself something of a temptation, precisely by impris-
oning the self in a myriad of perpetually dialectical options. His critique
of what we might call cultures of incessant reflection offers a sharp point
of contact with our own contemporary digital existence, as Sheridan
Hough aptly notes: "What Kierkegaard calls the 'prison' of reflection is
nothing more than the infinite availability of yet another point of view,
opinion, or aspect of the notion at hand. Consider the endless Web-pa-
rade of images and opinions, its torrential, quenchless, and indeed sense-
less variety."[77] In a world still coming to terms with what this culture does
to our thought, Kierkegaard's riposte to incessant reflection—particularly
on the note of theological decisiveness—risks being drowned out for its
uneasiness within contemporary academic modes of practice.

What is easily forgotten is just how thoroughly modern is the problem of conceiving of the "appropriate" tenor for theological discourse.

75. See the section "A Theology of (In)direct Communication" in chapter 6.

76. For one of many possible examples, see Kierkegaard, *Judge for Yourself!*, 215.

77. Hough, *Kierkegaard's Dancing Tax Collector*, 18.

This is a trait that was frequently challenged by the late John Webster, who began one memorable essay with the following unapologetic caveat:

> What follows is half-way between a theological essay and a homily; but we should not be particularly troubled by its homiletic tone. The clear distinctions which some members of the academic theological guild draw between proclamation and critical reflection are part of the pathology of modern theology; our forebears would have been distressed by the way in which theology has succumbed to the standardization of discourse in the academy and the consequent exclusion of certain modes of Christian speech, and we should probably worry more about what Bernard or Calvin might think of us than about the way in which our *wissenschaftlich* colleagues may shake their heads.[78]

We might certainly add Kierkegaard to the chorus of Bernard, Calvin, and Webster, that a homiletic tone does not mean an absence of reflective thought, not least when we consider that the content of theology is inseparable from its kerygma. As Kierkegaard well knew, "the Gospel" is not the kind of content that can be spoken of abstractly, devoid of a kerygmatic imperative. This does not necessitate a sacralization of "homiletic tone" per se. Anyone who has ever marked a first-year undergraduate essay knows of the need for an iconoclastic "stripping of the pulpits" too, wherever a bombastic or explosive rhetoric seeks to hide the absence of thoughtful argumentation.

In another sense, Kierkegaard was also the greatest critic of the pulpiteering voices of Christendom who sought to proclaim Christianity in words alone.[79] But such abuses do not change a single iota about the fundamental and inseparable connection between theology and proclamation. This is something all too easily forgotten in contemporary academic settings which may promote deliberatively hazier perspectives of the many bygone theological voices who sought to embody the Gospel in appropriately strong words. In the next chapter we will see such Gospel radicality in action via Kierkegaard's paradoxical theology of indirect communication alongside his exhortations for direct communication in the most "extreme" forms.

---

78. Webster, "Christ, Church, and Reconciliation," 211.

79. See Kierkegaard, *Practice in Christianity*, 233–37.

6

Socratic Street Preaching

The Paradox of (In)Direct Communication

As we mine our way through Kierkegaard's understanding of the Gospel, there is another aspect of the Gospel's implications which has not yet been discussed: the role of indirect communication. For all that can be said about Kierkegaard's relationship to preaching, it remains the case that Kierkegaard believed that the nature of the Gospel was of such a kind that it cannot be communicated "directly." However, just as the anti-kerygmatic readers of Kierkegaard begin to get excited at all the aesthetic—and manifestly less "extreme"-sounding—possibilities which may be opened up by such a conviction, Kierkegaard has a paradoxical surprise in store for them. For although he believed that the implications of the Gospel mean that it ought to be communicated indirectly, he also seemed to believe that the very same implications of the Gospel mean that it ought to be preached on the street.

At the heart of this paradox is one of the most enduring elements of Kierkegaard's theological legacy: his rigorously dialectical approach to Christian communication. For the reader of Kierkegaard, comprehending his (in)direct communication is typically as perplexing as it is inspiring. Traveling through his authorship we find the twin calls to the direct and the indirect appearing side by side, back to front, or sometimes one on top of the other! It is well noted that although Kierkegaard displays different stages of emphasis, he never totally relinquishes the importance of *either* method. Building on what we have seen in the preceding chapters, this chapter will reengage this dialectical quandary to show how this paradoxical juxtaposition might prove both directly and indirectly instructive to a theology of Christian proclamation. Although Kierkegaard's interpreters have always been aware of this dual communicative emphasis, the tendency has been to focus upon one in particular rather than attempting to investigate what it means to genuinely heed the paradox of both. Analyzing their complementary juxtaposition sheds further light on the theological and existential implications involved when attempting to do something as apparently straightforward and/or complicated as "proclaiming the Gospel."

It may indeed come as a surprise to many that the notion of "street preaching" could even find a place within the same sentence as "Kierkegaard." Yet it will be shown that his support for such a socially interruptive form of proclamation is entirely conducive to his theological vision we saw in chapters 2–3, of how the Gospel should directly impinge upon the life and actions of the speaker. However, in order to fully appreciate the force of this Kierkegaardian "surprise" we must see this in contrast with the indirect communication for which he is best known, and by which he critiqued many of the preachers of his day. Knowing Kierkegaard's complex use of both methods allows us to see his thinking upon street preaching in a more productive light than is usually imagined. But this first entails a brief introduction to Kierkegaard's indirect communication per se, connecting it back to Socrates, his maieutic mentor, whose method underpins Kierkegaard's pseudonymous approach.

Pseudonymity and Socratic Maieutics

Kierkegaard's indirect communication has been, undoubtedly, the most intriguing and scholarship-spinning subject of his entire authorship. It is one of the reasons he has been adopted by so many different schools of thought today. Where would Kierkegaard scholarship be, one wonders, without his indirect communication? What if all he had given us was a clear set of doctrinal assertions in place of the ironical labyrinth of hobbitholes that is his authorship, continually baffling and evading the eager interpreters who venture its depths? Indeed, Kierkegaard is often best known and best caricatured for his pseudonyms, the assorted character-authors he created. Some of these curious figures express his own views, some offer exaggerated versions of his views, and some outright contradict his views. Kierkegaard's contemporaries were forced to trawl through authors like Constantin Constantius, Nicolaus Notabene, and

Vigilius Haufniensis, to engage with his thought—and having read them, one could not be sure which parts Kierkegaard even meant, nor *how* he meant them.[1]

It was these pseudonyms, with their webs of erotic seduction, satirical verbosity, and poetic despair that caught the Copenhagen imagination far more acutely than Kierkegaard's religious discourses, which were published simultaneously, though separately, in Kierkegaard's own name. Although there are many ways in which Kierkegaard's own perceptions of his authorship are interpreted, we can say, at least, what he *says* the pseudonymous texts were there for: they were supposed to draw us into the world of the "aesthetic"—that is, the *un*religious—to catch us there, showing us the despair of such a life, and thereby to lead us away from it, drawing us closer to God. Although many have contested this notion of his "golden thread" of authorial intent,[2] this *is* how Kierkegaard believed much of his indirect communication functioned. That is, of course, if we dare to believe him.[3]

Indirect communication is often referred to as the "maieutic" method. This is the midwife-like process of subtly drawing the hearer *into* the truth rather than delivering the truth into them. The maieutic communicator is seen as a "midwife" because they are merely playing the facilitating role of enabling the truth to come to light within the hearer, and even taking things *away* from the hearer without them knowing.[4] The maieutic does not "cause" the truth to be known (just as the midwife cannot cause a baby to be born), they merely assist the process. Ultimately, the truth must come alive for the individual; they must grasp it for themselves. The concept of maieusis, as Kierkegaard knew it, originated with the subject of his master's thesis, Socrates. Kierkegaard's methodological relation

1. Hartshorne, for example, draws attention to what he perceives as a neglected interpretative approach to Kierkegaard's authorship: "What is not generally recognized is the ironic character of the pseudonymous authorship in form and purpose." Hartshorne, *Kierkegaard, Godly Deceiver*, 91.

2. See, for example, Soderquist, "Irony," 348–50.

3. See Kierkegaard, *Point of View*, 41–42. Of course, many today simply refuse to believe that his pseudonymous texts carried any such function within the wider authorship and that he projected such a meaning upon them in light of the more overt religiosity of the later authorship. Refreshingly, this dominant critical view of Kierkegaard's "view" has been increasingly challenged of late. See Tietjen, *Kierkegaard, Communication, and Virtue*, 61–85.

4. See Muench, "Indirect Communication and the Art of 'Taking Away.'"

to the Greek philosopher is well-noted,[5] even as we must remember, as Mjaaland holds, that Socrates's influence on him "cannot be limited to a [mere] 'theory' of communication."[6] That said, emphasizing methodological points of contact between the two gadflies remains inevitable and essential in any foray into Kierkegaardian indirect communication.

What, then, was Socrates's "method"? It was a kind of self-pseudonymity in which the overtness of the teacher's identity and authority fades into the background as they "teach." Socrates's philosophical endeavors did not involve taking students under his wing in order to transfer knowledge as a commodity. Rather, he spent his time teaching his students *about* knowledge, probing them to think (for themselves) about their very attitude toward attaining knowledge. Take, for example, the following instance of one of Socrates's engagements with his students, recorded in Plato's *Theaetetus*:

> SOCRATES: Well now, the point I have difficulty with, and can't find an adequate grasp of in myself, is just this: what, exactly, knowledge really is. So can we put it into words? What do you all say? Which of us is going to be first to speak? If he goes wrong, and if anyone goes wrong when it's his turn, he'll sit down and be a donkey, as the children say in their ball game; but if anyone survives without going wrong, he'll be our king, and set us to answer any question he likes.
>
> Why don't any of you say anything?[7]

It was such maieutic questioning that lay behind Socrates's persistent use of irony. It is evident—to us, if not always to his actual students (or so we may think)—that the way he sought to achieve the final "product" of a wise student could not always be quantified based on what he actually communicated to them. The hope, rather, is that they will come to realize the truth about knowledge for themselves in a far more profound way. Kierkegaard, of course, spoke admiringly of such an approach: "[Socrates] was not like a philosopher delivering his opinions in such a way that just the lecture itself is the presence of the idea, but what Socrates said meant

---

5. For some especially helpful contemporary work on this relationship, particularly regarding indirect communication, see Muench, "Kierkegaard's Socratic Point of View"; Possen, "Kierkegaard on Socratic Irony"; Mjaaland, "Kierkegaard's Socratic Maieutics."

6. Mjaaland, "Kierkegaard's Socratic Maieutics," 115.

7. Plato, *Theaetetus*, 146a, 6–7.

something different. The outer was not at all in harmony with the inner, but rather was its opposite."[8]

The "outer" refers to the words Socrates says, and the "inner" to what he actually means to communicate *via* the words—even if those words do not seem to pertain to what he seems to mean. It is no wonder then, with such maddening ambiguity, that Socrates was a great aggravator to the Sophists of the Athenian marketplace. As Mooney notes, "Socrates says with a wink, '*I know nothing!*' (yet speaks on)."[9] Unlike his contemporaries, he taught philosophy always as one appearing in complete ignorance of the subject in question, as one "without authority." It is here, of course, that we see the essential connection between Socrates and Kierkegaard.

Indeed, Kierkegaard evidently saw himself as something of a Socrates too,[10] with the bustling coffee shops, theaters, and literary columns of Copenhagen becoming his very own *agora*. During the first stage of his authorship Kierkegaard sought to amplify, to lure, to hide, and to manifest himself in different guises and poses in what he would later describe as his overall strategy of inducing Christianity into (and out of) Christendom. The use of the pseudonyms, representing apparently contrary or half-contrary versions of particular perspectives which Kierkegaard wanted to highlight, precisely mirrored Socrates's approach to knowledge. Something was being communicated which could not be found (directly) in the content of the words alone. In the same way that Socrates could feign ignorance in order to draw his students into the truth, so Kierkegaard expressed pseudonymous perspectives aiming to prod the reader in a particular direction without them knowing it.

Reflecting solely on Socrates's influence, however, may lead us to neglect the role of the Gospel itself on Kierkegaard's use of communication. As will be seen, Kierkegaard did not simply take up "Christianity" as one theme within a broader commitment to indirect communication. His use of maieutics was no mere repetition of Socratic irony, as Mjalland notes: "[Kierkegaard] sees the Socrates figure as an ideal for communication and self-knowledge in nineteenth-century Europe. Accordingly, his

---

8. Kierkegaard, *Concept of Irony*, 12.

9. Mooney, "Pseudonyms and Style," 206.

10. Hartshorne certainly exaggerates this connection when he says, playfully, "Had he not been a Christian, Kierkegaard would, I am persuaded, have found divinity in that Greek philosopher, whose use of irony evoked his highest admiration." Hartshorne, *Kierkegaard, Godly Deceiver*, 6.

maieutics is not a simple copy of the Socratic pattern, but a genuinely new application of the maieutic problem in a different historical and spiritual context."[11] As we will discuss, Kierkegaardian maieutics had a very particular *theological* purpose for the communication of Christianity in Christendom.

Before approaching this broader theological purpose, however, we should first ask a more specific question: What are the theological implications for the listener, as recipient of indirect communication?

Indirect Communication and Responsive Freedom?

What does Kierkegaard think is happening when somebody becomes the recipient of indirect communication? One way he seems to describe the process is that of the deliberate representation of a paradox to the listener. Confronted by an apparent incongruity, the listener is intrigued to the extent that they engage with the material in a unique way that may not have been possible had they been presented with the same material in a straightforward manner. This is because their own involvement in attaining the information would have been diminished. With indirect communication, however, listeners are drawn into the knowledge process on an existential level, as Kierkegaard defines it:

> For example, it is indirect communication to place jest and earnestness together in such a way that the composite is a dialectical knot—and then to be a nobody oneself. If anyone wants to have anything to do with this kind of communication, he will have to untie the knot himself.[12]

This "dialectical knot" is a summons for the hearer to step up and grasp the truth for themselves with no other compulsion than the intrigue of the "knot." In such an instance, the communicator may appear to have vanished, though actually they have orchestrated the entire didactic moment.

As noted, this approach has been well-supported in Kierkegaardian scholarship, particularly for its propensity to affirm individual choice. David Law, in *Kierkegaard as Negative Theologian*, suggests "this process of inculcating subjectivity in the individual cannot be carried out directly or objectively because this would override the autonomy and freedom

11. Mjaaland, "Kierkegaard's Socratic Maieutics," 116.
12. Kierkegaard, *Practice in Christianity*, 133.

to choose that is essential for genuine appropriation of the truth."[13] Benjamin Daise, in *Kierkegaard's Socratic Art*, makes a similar (though not identical) point regarding the importance of human autonomy: "Kierkegaardian indirect communication . . . aims at shaping the world in such a way that each recipient of the communication is fundamentally free to choose to shape the world as one sees fit."[14] Although it is true that the individual should not be forced down a cul de sac by perpetual direct communication, in the context of the entire authorship, it is clear that Kierkegaard's burden is not to induce a "general" concept of human freedom, but to provide a theological parameter for how one views the communication and reception of the Gospel.

We see this distinction borne out especially in *Philosophical Fragments*, where "the Socratic" is continually contrasted against the *sui generis* "moment" of Christian revelation.[15] Whereas the Socratic teacher believes the truth already exists *within* the learner—and thus the teacher need only call it to "recollection"—the Christian teacher or preacher aims to show that the learner is, in fact, "in error."[16] Although Kierkegaard (or, Johannes Climacus) adds that the learner's debilitated condition is their own doing, changing this condition cannot come from another "free" act because they are already "bound":

> To the extent that the learner is in error, but is there through his own fault . . . one might think he was free . . . And yet he is not free, but bound and exiled, because to be free of the truth is to be exiled from it, and to be exiled through one's own act is to be bound.[17]

Although the Socratic teacher may also highlight the erroneous condition within the learner, they cannot take them any further because, unlike Christ, they themselves are not "the teaching": "The Socratic lies precisely in this, that precisely because the learner is himself the truth and has the condition for understanding this, he can push the teacher away; yes, the Socratic art and heroism lay precisely in helping people to do this."[18] Kierkegaard then adds the key contrast between this kind of teaching

---

13. Law, *Kierkegaard as Negative Theologian*, 62.

14. Daise, *Kierkegaard's Socratic Art*, 26.

15. See Kierkegaard, *Philosophical Crumbs*, 88–110, 125–39.

16. Kierkegaard, *Philosophical Crumbs*, 92.

17. Kierkegaard, *Philosophical Crumbs*, 93.

18. Kierkegaard, *Philosophical Crumbs*, 131.

and distinctly Christian teaching. With Christianity, because it is not the learner but the teacher who is the truth, the learner cannot merely discard the teacher once they have "learned" the doctrine: they "must hold firmly onto the teacher."[19] Because the ultimate teacher in the reception of Christian truth is Christ himself, the learner paradox is transformed. The teacher no longer lies in the background of the learning event, he *is* the learning event, and is subsequently the only possible liberator of the learner's erroneous condition:

> What should we now call such a teacher who gives [the learner] the condition again and, with it, the truth? Let us call him a Saviour, because he liberates the learner from his bondage, saves him from himself; a deliverer, because he delivers from bondage one who had bound himself.[20]

For Kierkegaard, to accept Christian truth is not simply to accept a doctrine, but the teacher himself. This remains fundamental to how the preacher understands their own unique role in conveying the "teaching" of Christianity, which—unlike any other teaching—insists upon the unique inseparability of teaching and teacher.

Thus, for Kierkegaard, us learners are not the harbingers of choice and change, Christ is the one who confronts us and moves us to act in a particular way, liberated from our bondage. It is this conviction of being freed *by* and *for* Christ which shapes Kierkegaard's attraction to maieutic communication rather than an anxiety over human freedom per se. Indeed, as is evident in *Practice in Christianity*, it is Christ himself who becomes, as Mjalland says, "the master of maieutics and the final reason for using the maieutic method."[21] Kierkegaard's overall goal is to induce a particular *kind* of existential response conducive to the Gospel. As we have already seen, within Danish Christendom such existential response was almost entirely lost in a torrent of apathy by the numbing regularity of direct communication: "Since it has been demonstrated, and on an enormous scale, that Christianity is the truth, now there is no one, almost no one, who is willing to make any sacrifice for its sake."[22] This reveals the kernel of Kierkegaard's communicative concerns. If direct communication reigns indefinitely, no one need put their life on the line because the

---

19. Kierkegaard, *Philosophical Crumbs*, 131.

20. Kierkegaard, *Philosophical Crumbs*, 95.

21. Mjaaland, "Kierkegaard's Socratic Maieutics," 143.

22. Kierkegaard, *Practice in Christianity*, 144.

truth becomes *merely* true, or absentmindedly true, rather than true to the extent of radical personal cost.

Wherever the truth of the Gospel has become domesticated to the world's level, direct communication may no longer induce the hearers to stake their lives upon it; and when it comes to the Gospel, this ultimately means such truth has not actually been spoken (or heard) in its fullness. For Kierkegaard, therefore, the Christian is not "free to choose to shape the world as they see fit," as Daise suggests, but free to shape the world as Christ sees fit, now that they have been liberated from the bondage of sin. The Christian is existentially awakened to "practice" their Christian faith—to live as if it is real, true, and effectual. They do choose to act, but this choosing is a spiritual awakening to a particular *kind* of action which is inseparable from the holistic message of Christianity.[23]

What will now follow is a brief account of Kierkegaard's theological presuppositions behind his indirect communication, demonstrable particularly in his later work, *Practice in Christianity*. It is from this basis that we will begin to see the force of the dialectic between the indirect and the direct, particularly when seen at their most extreme.

A Theology of (In)Direct Communication

As noted, Kierkegaard's indirect communication was not the product of methodological application *to* the theological; it was a clear consequence *of* the theological. He did not find Socrates's method and seek a subject in which to experiment it; he found Christianity and realized its inseparable connection to the maieutic capabilities which Socrates had seen for existential truth in general. For Kierkegaard, of course, his theological approach to indirect communication always remained contextually angled. In *Practice in Christianity* the need for indirect communication of Christian truth is tied specifically to the situation of Danish Christendom, where an overabundance of direct communication had annihilated the necessary existential response to the Gospel:

> It became much easier to be a pastor—the one speaking did not preach anymore; he used those moments to make some *observations*. Some observations! One sees it on the speaker; his gaze is withdrawn; he resembles not so much a human being as one of

---

23. For more on the complexity of human freedom in relation to divine activity in the Christian life, see Torrance, *Freedom to Become a Christian*.

those sculptured stone figures that have no eyes. He thereby sets
a chasmic abyss between the listener and himself.[24]

For Kierkegaard, these chillingly statuesque preachers taught the most
paradoxically glorious Christian doctrines as though they were perfectly
uncontroversial and ordinary. Indeed, he says the incarnation is often
communicated as neatly and matter-of-factly (that is, "directly") as though
it were a mundane daily chore: "In the modern approach everything is
made as direct as putting one's foot in a sock."[25] There is something about
the doctrine itself that necessitates an appropriate mode of communication. For Kierkegaard, Jesus Christ is the "Sign of Contradiction,"[26] whose
incarnation cannot be assimilated into human categories of thought like
data. Rather, the incarnation really ought to offend us. Kierkegaardian
indirect communication is what Kierkegaard believes is the only appropriate response to Christology. Direct communication neutralizes the
scandal of the christological paradox by transforming it into a segment of
humanly tolerable information, emptying its faith-inducing power.[27] The
result is that Jesus becomes an object of our observation rather than the
living paradox in whom we strive to believe.

Kierkegaard's problems with direct communication often recur
throughout the authorship around the same point regarding the disconnection between the hearing and heeding of information. A notable line
in *Concluding Unscientific Postscript* captures this well: "In a Christian
country it is not information that is lacking; something else is lacking."[28]
Where all people think themselves already "Christian," where the preachers preach by rote, disconnected from the content of their message, this
"something else" refers to the existential appropriation of the truth for
genuine faith. It is not that information is unnecessary in itself, but that
its perpetual non-application renders its purpose absurdly self-defeating.
Kierkegaard ridicules the inherent irony which occurs when a direct
communicator subverts the very purpose of their communication as an

---

24. Kierkegaard, *Practice in Christianity*, 236.

25. Kierkegaard, *Practice in Christianity*, 126.

26. Kierkegaard, *Practice in Christianity*, 126.

27. For Kierkegaard, knowing that Jesus is God in an *entirely* direct sense is impossible because the very fact itself can only be accepted through faith: "The single
direct statement . . . can serve only to make aware in order that the person who has
been made aware, facing the offense of the contradiction, can choose whether he will
believe or not." Kierkegaard, *Practice in Christianity*, 136.

28. Kierkegaard, *Concluding Unscientific Postscript*, 614.

exact consequence of their communicative method. He tells the story of a man who—directly and passionately—announces his philosophy to the world that "one should *not* have any followers or disciples!" Such a man, Kierkegaard says, having been so convincing in his speech, would immediately gain ten followers who fall at his feet and begin to proclaim the very same doctrine—that "one should *not* have any followers or disciples!"—to others.[29] In being totally converted by the message, they totally contradict it, proving that the communicative form was wholly inappropriate to its content. For Kierkegaard, the enslavement to absolute directness in the Christendom pulpit usually ensured its sermons remained unheard, unapplied, and unfaithful to the theological message itself, thereby defeating the entire reason for their communication.

Kierkegaard's indirect communication, then, is a response to the misuse of direct communication. It relies not simply upon an appetite for witty irony but is determinatively based upon doctrinal presuppositions within the Christian message. This is often overlooked by those wishing to mine the Kierkegaard corpus for philosophical or literary gems divorced from Kierkegaard's theological intentions.[30] Where some delight in his use of the indirect method in isolation, Kierkegaard himself saw it as inseparable from other forms of direct communication.[31] To this end,

---

29. Kierkegaard, *Concluding Unscientific Postscript*, 75.

30. Poole, for example, sees no theologically didactic purpose in any of Kierkegaard's indirect communication beyond mere playfulness: "There is no unadorned instruction or doctrine or objective fact to be had, but only the mutually shared experience of perplexity." Poole, *Kierkegaard: The Indirect Communication*, 10. Tietjen helpfully critiques such an approach to Kierkegaard's authorship: "[Poole's] reasoning rests largely on a false dilemma: *either* take seriously Kierkegaard's use of indirect communication, commonly taken to include devices such as irony and pseudonymity, *or* read him 'on religious grounds.'" Tietjen thus offers a positive conception of Kierkegaard's indirect communication, highlighting its edifying facets: "The intention of the indirect communication—which is composed of both jest *and* earnestness—is not endless dialectical play with the knot . . . Rather, the intention is to work on the problem of the knot, to struggle with it, and eventually to untie it and, in accomplishing this, receive the message of indirect communication, albeit in a particular (playful) way." Tietjen, *Kierkegaard, Communication, and Virtue*, 19.

31. There are also complex personal reasons for Kierkegaard's cross-switching between methods, including a desire to protect his former fiancée Regine Olson's reputation by perpetuating his own scandalously "aesthetic" guise. Although the theological basis for indirect communication is evident, it is also clear that Kierkegaard was not always able to understand the holistic implications of his task until later: "For me indirect communication has been as if instinctive within me, because in being an author I no doubt have also developed myself, and consequently the whole movement is

he critiques his beloved maieutic mentor for his reluctance to move beyond the singular use of the indirect: "Socrates [plays] the ignorant one and remains that until the end," but "this tactic cannot and ought not to be maintained to the end."[32] Clearly, there is a dialectical relationship between the direct and the indirect here: the indirect is incomplete by itself, and is necessarily subordinate (in an undefined sense) to the direct. What Kierkegaard began to realize was that, although the listener may need indirect communication for existential response, the speaker may, ironically, use it to avoid their own existential response to the message, separating themselves from its life-changing implications and evading the potential persecution evoked by the Gospel: "The dubiousness of the indirect method in the proclamation of Christianity is that it could be an attempt to avoid suffering for the doctrine."[33] Indeed, it is often far easier to hide oneself in cleverly-devised pseudonyms and exaggerations than to stand up and be counted. An 1848 journal entry reveals Kierkegaard's intentions to overhaul his maieutic guise: "The thing to do now is to take over unambiguously the maieutic structure of the past, to step forth definitely and directly in character, as one who has wanted and wants to serve the cause of Christianity."[34] Of course, Kierkegaard had *always* sought to serve the cause of Christianity, but this change is significant in the way in which he chooses to do that.[35] As he does so, he does not dispense with the maieutic, he merely reallocates it.

---

backward, which is why from the very first I could not state my plan directly, although I certainly was aware that a lot was fermenting within me. Furthermore, consideration for 'her' required me to be careful. I could well have said right away: I am a religious author. But later how would I have dared to create the illusion that I was a scoundrel in order if possible to help her. Actually it was she—that is, my relationship to her—who taught me the indirect method. She could be helped only by an untruth about me; otherwise I believe she would have lost her mind. That the collision was a religious one would have completely deranged her, and therefore I have had to be so infinitely careful. And not until she became engaged again and married did I regard myself as somewhat free in this respect." *Søren Kierkegaard's Journals and Papers*, 2:1959, 384–85.

32. *Søren Kierkegaard's Journals and Papers*, 2:1962, 386–87.

33. *Søren Kierkegaard's Journals and Papers*, 6:6783, 427.

34. *Søren Kierkegaard's Journals and Papers*, 6:6231, 42. Prior to this journal entry, another factor in Kierkegaard's communicative shift involves his unpublished (and unfinished) lectures on communication, written a year earlier in 1847, though never actually delivered. See *Søren Kierkegaard's Journals and Papers*, 1:649–57, 267–308. These lectures "mark an important change in his reflections on the role of maieutics." Mjaaland, "Kierkegaard's Socratic Maieutics," 137.

35. The incident with *The Corsair*, in which he was publicly ridiculed before the

Just to confuse things further, Kierkegaard leaves various related comments in his journals which can seem even more baffling, such as: "When a person uses the indirect method, there is in one way or another something demonic [about it]—but not necessarily in the bad sense."[36] Whatever it can mean to have "good" or "bad" demons in one's communicative method,[37] it is evident that Kierkegaard sensed a residual tension between the direct and the indirect. He did not want to relinquish the indirect even as he sought to downplay it.[38] Rather, he saw that it was valuable in a particular context: "Christianity needed a maieutic and I understood how to be that, although no one understood how to appreciate it. The category 'proclaim Christianity, confess Christ' is not appropriate in Christendom—here the maieutic is exactly right."[39] Kierkegaard is fully aware that indirect communication served a particular function, "to shake up the illusions" of Christendom, but not at the expense of the fact that "Christianity, after all, has grace to proclaim."[40] Indeed, "proclaim" is the operative word for Kierkegaard. To "proclaim" something means the communicator must show an unambiguous link between what they say, what they mean, and what they do *as* they communicate. The tension between indirect and direct communication is certainly at its most complex wherever Kierkegaard considers the Christian necessity of preaching itself, which appears to stand in absolute contrast to the maieutic method.

Copenhagen media and public, also played a huge part in his resolute shift to direct communication: "He then became more occupied with the radical incommensurability of Christian thought and its call to represent a *scandalon* and provocation in society." Mjaaland, "Kierkegaard's Socratic Maieutics," 137.

36. *Søren Kierkegaard's Journals and Papers*, 2:1959, 384.

37. One possible explanation may be related to the alternate meaning of the classical mythological term *daimon*, connoting a spiritually mediating presence between heaven and earth, and one which certainly carried both Homeric and Socratic heritage. However, it is highly likely that—as always—Kierkegaard was aware of the negative connotations by drawing attention to their connection.

38. We also see direct communication referred to as a seemingly "transitional" mode too; for example, in the proclamation of the early Church: "The position of the apostle is something else, because he must proclaim an unknown truth, and therefore direct communication can always have its validity temporarily." Kierkegaard, *Concluding Unscientific Postscript*, 243. Both indirect and direct communication are "temporary" measures, dependent upon context, even though there are *objective* and unchanging doctrinal reasons for using both.

39. *Søren Kierkegaard's Journals and Papers*, 5:5987, 372.

40. *Søren Kierkegaard's Journals and Papers*, 6:6783, 427–28.

Direct Proclamation and Street Preaching

We saw in chapters 2–4 Kierkegaard's particular preoccupation with sermonic communication, which spanned the entirety of his writing life. Possen has even suggested that Kierkegaard was more preacher than scholar, given that "Kierkegaard's forays into scholarship are unscholarly by design." Indeed, in many instances, "he does not follow the standard scholarly procedure of articulating a hypothesis and demonstrating its truth. Rather, he simply *declares* that his hypothesis . . . 'simultaneously appears as the truth.' But this is not scholarship; it is dogma."[41] Depending upon your point of view, this could be read as either a virtue *or* a vice! Nonetheless, Kierkegaard's preacherly posture shines through especially in his discourses, of which he says, "All the upbuilding writing has been direct communication."[42]

Kierkegaard was aware that in order to preach directly, one's life must become a part of the communication itself. It is for this reason that he said, "It is a risk to preach!"[43] Preaching is "risky" because preachers themselves are (indirectly) communicating whether their sermon "works" or not by how much it has (or has not) affected their own life. No preacher is afforded the luxury of being a mere passive conveyor-belt of information. Indeed, for Kierkegaard, preaching is much more difficult, even, than acting. This is because, in the theater, the audience *knows* that an actor is acting, whereas the preachers of Christendom often had to pretend that they were *not* acting in their pulpit performance, to which Kierkegaard remained both unamused and unpersuaded:

> Alas, how many of those who go up into the holy place to proclaim Christianity have hearing keen enough to discover the displeasure of the holy place and its mockery of him because he proclaims so enthusiastically, movingly, and with tears in his eyes that of which his life expresses the very opposite![44]

When preachers are to preach directly, their life and their sermon are woven together intrinsically. Otherwise, for Kierkegaard, such an act ceases to be genuinely *Christian* preaching.

---

41. Possen, "Kierkegaard on Socratic Irony," 103.

42. *Søren Kierkegaard's Journals and Papers*, 6:6701, 361.

43. Kierkegaard, *Practice in Christianity*, 235.

44. Kierkegaard, *Practice in Christianity*, 235.

It is the conflation of the preacher's words and their existential actions that prompted Kierkegaard's imaginative thinking on the appropriate setting for the Christian sermon. He reflects that "there should be preaching every day," though it should take place in "small chapels" rather than "great churches."[45] He adds, "But an enormous auditorium, a mass of people, a scholar-orator, and then a roaring—it is appalling. It would be all right if it were a matter of market prices."[46] The aesthetic settings for such sermons negated the possibility of existential change in the hearers. The very setting limited the expectations for personal transformation. Regardless of whatever these grand Copenhagen orators spoke, the whole aesthetic atmosphere meant their hearers could too easily place them (and their sermons) "at an artistic distance from actuality."[47]

In response to what he saw as the statuesque preaching of Christendom, Kierkegaard wanted proclamation to become actualized for both speaker and hearer.[48] As we saw in the previous chapters, Kierkegaard believed that the Gospel message Luther had first preached was vital for humanity to heed given its radical consequences, but that the bourgeois inconsequentiality of sermons produced only waddling geese who admired and ignored the message. It was the very grandness of the pulpit in its context that had become detrimental to the existential demands of the Gospel message, leading both speaker and hearer into greater passivity: "It is this failure to demand or enable an active response on the part of the listener that Kierkegaard criticizes most strongly."[49] Copenhagen's purportedly "Lutheran" preachers no longer truly preached Luther's Gospel because their message had become aesthetically obscured and existentially debilitating, leading to "sermons that could more appropriately end with 'Hurrah' than 'Amen.'"[50] For Kierkegaard, such preaching does violence to the Gospel by pretending to proclaim its importance while subtly perpetuating the illusion of peaceful tranquility inherent to Christendom.

45. *Søren Kierkegaard's Journals and Papers*, 3:3521, 607.

46. *Søren Kierkegaard's Journals and Papers*, 3:3521, 608.

47. *Søren Kierkegaard's Journals and Papers*, 6:6957, 562.

48. For more on Kierkegaard's approach to preaching in Christendom, see Edwards, "Kierkegaard the Preacher"; Plekon, "Kierkegaard at the End"; Breuninger, "Søren Kierkegaard's Reformation of Expository Preaching"; and Burgess, "Kierkegaard on Homiletics."

49. Campbell-Nelson, "Kierkegaard's Christian Rhetoric," 30.

50. Kierkegaard, *Practice in Christianity*, 107.

Kierkegaard's alternative suggestion to this fatal condition, with some help from Luther, is somewhat surprising: "Luther was absolutely right in saying that preaching really should not be done in churches but on the street. The whole modern concept of a pastor who preaches in a church is pure hallucination."[51] Indeed, on the street the preacher is removed from the distanciation of the pulpit and is thereby propelled into existential reality: "A nobody who preaches *gratis* on the street—even if he makes observations that are ever so objective—remains a subjective and vivifying person."[52] Here we see one of Kierkegaard's key communicative insights: the form of the sermon must communicate something about its content precisely by how—and indeed, where—it is communicated. If the forgiveness of the atonement is really as astounding as the preacher says it is, then its effect upon them ought to be overtly demonstrable, not only in word and action but even in location. For Kierkegaard, in that context, there is little other reason for someone to muster up the courage to preach on the street than that their message has so gripped them that they want it to infiltrate everyday reality. So, Kierkegaard concludes, "preaching should not be done in churches but on the street, right in the middle of life, the actuality of ordinary, weekday life."[53]

Although Kierkegaard's thoughts on street preaching hardly saturate his authorship, where such references crop up in his journals, we can see they are not actually divorced from his primary existential-theological concerns. This means that, although such comments are indeed polemical, they are far from being flippant, and we may actually be forced to take them seriously if we want to understand what Kierkegaard is getting at regarding the heart of Christian communication. Indeed, the idea of the great philosopher, Søren Kierkegaard, standing on a box in the town square with a bullhorn, is an admittedly bizarre thought. However, such a scene would not be inconsistent with his existentialized view of proclamation. For Kierkegaard, although the paradox of preacherly authority always looms large,[54] the Gospel must be nonetheless preached with existential urgency and self-abandonment because it deals with life and death in such stark contrast.[55] Kierkegaard knew that street preaching, precisely

51. *Søren Kierkegaard's Journals and Papers*, 1:651, 287.

52. *Søren Kierkegaard's Journals and Papers*, 6:6687, 355.

53. *Søren Kierkegaard's Journals and Papers*, 6:6957, 562.

54. See Snowden, "Kierkegaard on Pastoral Authority and Authenticity."

55. Kierkegaard becomes progressively starker in how he presents the connection between the reality of the human need of the Gospel and the urgency of the minister's

in its inappropriate outrageousness, offered one of the most fertile opportunities for demonstrating one's subjective appropriation of the Gospel. What better way to show that the Gospel is real, that its eschatological and existential hope has so truly liberated the one proclaiming it, than to render oneself a social absurdity in the middle of the street for it? This is the place, after all, where one least expects to hear a sermon. In Kierkegaard's Copenhagen, where the impact of the average sermon normally ceased the very moment one left the church building, a sermon on the street could not be so easily escaped.

Within Kierkegaard's lifetime, his ideas about the (un)suitability of street preaching remained, somewhat ironically, "hidden" in the unpublished depths of his journals rather than making their way into the authorship proper. However, this does not mean that the idea was not seriously contemplated as a genuine possibility. One of the most sustained reflections appears in the midst of the attack literature period, where he was attempting to face Christendom's hypocrisy head-on, and bearing the full personal implications. The reflection occurs in a journal entry of April 8, 1855, as a draft for a piece in the secular *Fædrelandet* newspaper. In it, though he excuses himself from the task of street preaching due to his own physical fragility,[56] it is clear that he planned to activate his street preaching "theory" first through his attack literature,[57] gesturing

---

call to sacrificial proclamation. It is this calling, bearing great existential cost, from which Kierkegaard feels Christendom's pastors have conveniently escaped: "To believe that there is a hell, that others go to hell—and then get married, beget children, live in a parsonage, think about getting a bigger parish, etc.—that is frightful egotism. But the N.T. is not like that. Anyone who believes that there is a hell, that others go to hell, is eo ipso a missionary, that is the least he can do." *Søren Kierkegaard's Journals and Papers*, 6:6851, 490.

56. See *Søren Kierkegaard's Journals and Papers*, 6:6957, 563. Although this appears an ironically "convenient" excuse (the kind of excuse, perhaps, for which Kierkegaard might well have chastised the clergy), it should be remembered that Kierkegaard collapsed in the street later that same year, an event which led to his subsequent death. Although the particularities of his condition remain somewhat mysterious, it is known how much preaching affected him physically based upon previous experiences, as well as the fact that his voice was particularly weak for oratorical purposes. See Edwards, "Kierkegaard the Preacher," 155; *Søren Kierkegaard's Journals and Papers*, 6:6769, 416–17. It seems fair to give Kierkegaard the benefit of the doubt that if it was difficult to hear him in a church, this problem would have been even more difficult on the street. The mid-nineteenth century, of course, was before the age of the microphone, so a naturally strong voice was deemed essential to the preaching ministry. See for example, Spurgeon, *Lectures to My Students*, 117–35.

57. He recounts how he has attempted to make up for his inability to street-preach

that the way had to be "prepared" before street preaching could be truly unleashed in all earnestness: "Our age might not be ready for this and perhaps must first be prepared for it."[58] This possibly indicates a future strategy for initiating some kind of street preaching mission, whatever on earth that might have entailed! In one sense, the attack literature could well have been what he had in mind as this "preparation" for truly existentialized proclamation to begin, even if it were to be ultimately fulfilled by another.[59] It is even possible that had Kierkegaard lived through the aftermath of his stress-inducing "attack" period (1854–55), there would have been movements toward a more fleshed-out account of how Christian street preaching might become a possible and necessary means of Christian proclamation in Christendom.

What might we do with Kierkegaard's curious street preaching reflections today? Street preaching, of course, carries all sorts of negative connotations in the modern world. Ironically, Fred Craddock, who we discussed in chapter 3, uses Kierkegaard's indirect communication to critique street preaching precisely because its form does *not* appear to fit the content of the Gospel:

> I am sure all of us have had the experience of coming under the smiling attack of a sidewalk witness, overwhelming us with well-worn clichés and Scripture fragments. Perhaps we were left speechless—sputtering sounds of anger, confusion—with a sense of having been violated. Very likely the primary cause of our being so disturbed was not the content of what was said . . . [but] the method by which the message came, because we know almost instinctively that if the province of the gospel does not include manner as well as matter, music as well as words, then we are not interested . . . There is such a thing as a *Christian*

---

by writing columns within the nonreligious political newspaper *Fædrelandet*, viewing this as the closest equivalent of preaching on the street because of the stark juxtaposition between *what* he would be saying and the location of *where* he would be saying it. See *Søren Kierkegaard's Journals and Papers*, 6:6957, 563. Whether this absolves Kierkegaard of hypocrisy is still open to debate. It is clear that his struggle over his own calling was an intense one, and his chosen path was by no means lightly taken. On Kierkegaard's anguished reflections on his calling, see again chapter 2, and Benktson, "'The Ministry,'" 224–25.

58. *Søren Kierkegaard's Journals and Papers*, 6:6957, 563.

59. See Kierkegaard's reflections on being a kind of proto-reformer (but not an actual reformer) of the Church in Kierkegaard, *Judge for Yourself!*, 211.

style, a method of communicating congenial to the nature of the Christian faith.[60]

Here, Craddock asserts the impropriety of impassioned street proclamation because it does not fit the appropriate form for Christian witness. As noted already, his homiletical gravitation to more narratival and ambiguous preaching styles were intended to marry the Gospel's content to a congenial communicative form: to "induce" rather than to "assert." Craddock's emphasis on the indirect in a world of exclusively direct communication was a corrective perhaps akin to Kierkegaard's own corrective task. But it is the lack of simultaneity in the approach which most misrepresents Kierkegaard. Holding the indirect at the ultimate expense of the direct not only misinterprets the nuances within Kierkegaard's overall thought scheme, but entirely disregards Kierkegaard's reflections on street preaching itself, whereby its very form is seen as contextually congenial to the content of the Gospel.

For Kierkegaard, the Gospel must be an overt proclamation through the medium of an existentially-involved communicator whose very willingness to communicate in such a mode testifies to the content of the message. As Socratically playful as he is, Kierkegaard will not let us get away with hiding from that which may seem the appropriately inappropriate way to proclaim the Gospel in certain contexts, leading him to say things like: "What Christendom needs at every moment is someone who expresses Christianity uncalculatingly or with absolute recklessness."[61] Such uncouth expressions—the kind we discussed in the previous chapter, which many might wish to expunge from Kierkegaard's thought project—are a far cry from the cunning hiddenness of the pseudonyms. By calling for "recklessness" he is certainly not calling for the abstract rantings of a disconnected hell-preacher, for they may often appear existentially distanced as the grand pulpiteers. Kierkegaard is in fact calling for a kind of calculated uncalculatedness, whereby the preacher knows precisely why they ought to preach in such an apparently uncautious manner: their very message demands it.

It is in forgetting Kierkegaard's inherently dialectical approach that usually leads people to interpret Kierkegaard either as a direct *or* indirect communicator. Having sketched the nuances inherent in both of these primary conceptions within his communication, it remains to be seen

---

60. Craddock, *Overhearing the Gospel*, 19–20.
61. *Søren Kierkegaard's Journals and Papers*, 3:2642, 153.

how it may be possible to recall and incorporate the importance of both of them, and to do so without compromise.

Midwife Meets Madman

The image of such radically direct communication as street preaching seems very much at odds with the notion of the maieutic midwife. For, although the midwife remains essential for Kierkegaard, the street proclaimer is a truly existential demonstrator of Christianity. Ironically, because the street preacher demonstrates Christianity existentially, this means they do not "fit" within Christendom: "We are all Christians: and then if one is earnest about existentially expressing Christianity, all would laugh, would find it a ridiculous exaggeration, and the man would be regarded as mad."[62] The figure of the "madman" crops up a number of times in the authorship, often ironically. Kierkegaard knew that he himself was regarded within Copenhagen as "a half-mad eccentric,"[63] whereby "there are 1,000 preachers, approximately 2 million Christians, and they all flatly regard me as mad."[64] This seemed more than a little absurd to him because he felt that he was the one who was attempting to be a genuine witness of Christianity and yet was ostracized for it by a supposedly Christian society.

To stand up with such overt directness is to lay down the subtlety of the indirect. However, although Kierkegaard is content to be regarded as "mad" for the sake of the Gospel, nonetheless, he stands by the maieutic method as being uniquely necessary in Christendom. The maieutic is essential for invoking subjectivity in those who think they already know the truth, though it remains a mere instrument which is inadequate to proclaim the Gospel by itself. It is even possible to see street preaching as a "type" of maieutic communication. This is because something *more* is communicated than the mere spoken content of the words themselves: the very act conveys an existential truth which remains unspoken but nonetheless communicated in actuality.[65] Indeed, Kierkegaard says, "To teach in actuality that the truth is ridiculed, etc., means to teach it as

---

62. *Søren Kierkegaard's Journals and Papers*, 1:175, 69.

63. *Søren Kierkegaard's Journals and Papers*, 6:6168, 14.

64. *Søren Kierkegaard's Journals and Papers*, 6:6252, 57.

65. For a contemporary reflection on this idea within a secular context, see Edwards, "Secular Apathy and the Public Paradox of the Gospel."

one ridiculed and scoffed at himself."[66] As with Socrates's students, such doubly ironical communication may only be perceptible to those with ears to hear.

It is evident that both the direct and indirect methods are vital and indispensable from one other. Not long before his untimely death, as Kierkegaard reflected on all he had accomplished, he declared that his task from beginning to end had always been "Socratic."[67] This does not mean he was ever *non*-theological in this Socratic task, but it does mean that in a very real sense Kierkegaard should always be considered a maieutic communicator, albeit variously manifested.[68] The problem for the preacher, of course, is that one cannot be a good midwife and a good madman at the same time. To incorporate both methods inevitably dilutes the strength of each ("dilution" being one of those concepts Kierkegaard loathes most).[69] To speak of the indirect "to a certain extent" and the direct "to a certain extent" would be to speak of "neither/nor," not "both/and." Kierkegaard does not present his own solution to this problem, he merely hands it over to us: we must deal with both, and both truly. Kierkegaard has objective doctrinal reasons for holding to both methods and is reluctant to renege upon either of them. Incorporating both methods, though, need not be impossible in the sense of holding to their contingent contextual appropriateness. In other words, one need not say "yes" to both at the same time, but one might defiantly refuse to say "no" to both at *all* times. In this way, the indirect and the direct might have their appropriate place precisely when and where they *become* appropriate. Such dialectical awareness differs from outright rejections *or* outright syntheses of both.

It is noteworthy, in fact, that Kierkegaard justifies the most extreme forms of both methods because of his Christendom context. In the increasingly secular Western context today, one might find Kierkegaard's Christendomian polemics on communication of little use within Christian theology. However, as the remaining chapters will discuss, "Christendom" may also be seen as the incessant heart condition which afflicts all spheres of ecclesial life, wherever the content of the Gospel remains

66. *Søren Kierkegaard's Journals and Papers*, 1:646, 286.

67. See Kierkegaard, *The Moment*, 340–47.

68. "When talking about Kierkegaard, it is not a question of maieutics or not maieutics, but a question of *how* the maieutic communication takes place and to what extent it influences his thinking." Mjaaland, "Kierkegaard's Socratic Maieutics," 124.

69. See chapter 5.

assumed and quickly loses its appropriate forms of expression and application in the life of the believer. Preachers face the relentless challenge of communicating the Gospel to clusters of congregants who struggle to see the significance of the sermon for their daily life, where the sermon no longer carries its necessarily invasive force as Christian proclamation of the Word of God. In such contexts, mere direct communication cannot have the desired effect because it may simply bounce off the hardened hearts of those who already feel they "know" the Gospel but remain unmoved. Similarly, many outside the Church—perhaps those walking through shopping malls on Sunday afternoons with handfuls of superfluous shopping—already believe they "know" the Christianity they are rejecting by persisting in their "non-religious" life, when in fact they may have never truly heard the Gospel proclaimed because they have never *seen* it (that is, in the lives of those who have claimed to propagate it).

Although such dialectical communicative awareness may seem like an enslavement to contingency, we have seen that it is not necessarily doctrineless in its conception. Forms of indirect communication are uniquely able to catch those who think they have heard it all before. This is not due to it being an effective "technique," but due to its inseparable connection to the Gospel itself, which is always more than the sum of its parts. But Kierkegaard does not allow indirect communication to reign without the necessary caveats that allow for the urgent and direct proclamation of the Gospel. It is clear that different aspects of the Gospel fuel Kierkegaard's different approaches to the direct and the indirect. For the indirect, as noted earlier, it is the paradox of the incarnation and the notion of faith which induces the need for maieutic communication (because faith in the paradox cannot be communicated as though it were mere information). For the direct, this aspect of faith is also central, whereby the giving of the good news must be given existentially, demonstrating that one truly has received this gift for themselves.

It is also clear that the indirect method is not entirely divorced from the direct. The purpose of the indirect, in fact, is to lead us to the direct— to an existential revelation of the direct message. Indeed, if the "midwife" is not accompanied by the "madman" (at least occasionally), there may be something fundamentally missing from Christian proclamation. Again, this claim is not aesthetic but distinctly theological, since the Messiah did not remain a mystery indefinitely but became a revelation, calling his preachers as *witnesses* to that reality. It is for this reason that Kierkegaard considers the concept of "witnessing" to be "the form of communication which strikes the truest mean between direct and indirect communication." Indeed, he adds, "Witnessing is direct communication, but nevertheless it does not make one's contemporaries the authority. While the witness's 'communication' addresses itself to the contemporaries, the 'witness' himself addresses God and makes him the authority."[70] For Kierkegaard, all Christian communication is grounded in who God is and who he has called the communicator to be *as* they communicate: a witness. To be such a witness today might well mean rejecting street preaching as a real possibility. However, Kierkegaard's urgent call for such radical witness means not only that street preaching can never be off the table entirely (as most preachers would likely prefer) but that something similar must be enacted to communicate the required "recklessness" of the communicator who has been truly liberated by their message and seeks to have it proclaimed not only within the confines of a congregation but to the surrounding world. In duly Socratic style, Kierkegaard might well leave the specific application to the self-examination of the preacher, with the caveat that they remain alert to their tendency to avoid the cost of what an endeavor such as street preaching would mean for them personally. At the very least, Kierkegaard might say that one must be free *to* street-preach before they can truly choose *not* to street-preach. Only then can they be free to be the kind of witness that Christ has called them to be in and before the world.

If it is evident that both methods are necessary, how do we know when to use which? For Kierkegaard, this "dialectical knot" is something he himself wrestled with, and perhaps he never meant to untie it. The tension remains and seems to stare back at us. At times, there appear to be two Kierkegaards standing either side of us: the Kierkegaard on our left is ready to rap our knuckles for daring to preach directly the unpreachable paradox of the God-man; meanwhile the Kierkegaard on our right prepares to scold us for our cowardly reluctance to proclaim. Of which Kierkegaard are we most afraid? Which one haunts us most acutely, challenging us to change our ways, to fall in line, or perhaps more likely, to fall *out*-of-line? Kierkegaard might add, with Socrates—and, more pertinently, with Christ—that this decision may well depend upon where we are standing and to whom we are speaking.

70. *Søren Kierkegaard's Journals and Papers*, 1:670, 314.

7

The Image of Love
and the Ideal of Christendom

An Indirect Theological Engagement

IN LIGHT OF THE discussion of Kierkegaard's rigorously kerygmatic approach to Christianity, what are we to do now with his "aesthetic" works, especially the ones which don't seem to be about Christianity or "religious" life at all? As we saw in chapter 5, it is important to correct overly "aesthetic" interpretations of Kierkegaard's oeuvre given that his theological reflections on indirect communication govern how we should read them. Yet, as was gestured to in the conclusion of the last chapter, we might also be tempted to do away with his indirect reflections altogether and pretend as though the aesthetic works have no ongoing value given his overtly "direct" purposes for appropriating the Gospel within Christendom. Without wishing to move beyond the argument of the preceding chapters, then, this chapter takes a slightly different approach by offering a close textual engagement with one of Kierkegaard's more famously aesthetic works, *Either/or* (1843). I will do so in order to showcase not only how different such literary depictions were to some of the more overtly theological and philosophical texts that have been discussed thus far, but also to demonstrate how such a depiction might even be seen to contribute—indirectly—to Kierkegaard's theological critique of Christendom.

Kierkegaard's poetical-philosophical-theological masterpiece, *Either/Or* (1843) is simultaneously surprising, perplexing, and profound.

One doesn't know quite where to put it or what to do with it, nor whom to believe about what it all means. Historically, one way in which readers have saved themselves the trouble has been simply to read *Either/ Or*'s most scandalous segment, *The Seducer's Diary* as a stand-alone piece, however much such selective reading irked its enigmatic composer.[1] This chapter would, seemingly, further irk the great composer's wishes by offering a reading of this text in relation to one element in particular: its dialectical depiction of the pursuit of love between "the real" and "the ideal image." This manifests primarily in the protagonist, Johannes, whose fantastical pursuit of Cordelia deliberately perpetuates this tension in which objective reality is subsumed within the ideal of his own imagination. What will follow is an explication of what this dialectic may mean both within and beyond this well-traveled text.

Given that *The Seducer's Diary* has always been the best-known part of *Either/Or*, it has appeared frequently in the history of Kierkegaard scholarship. Many have noted the connotations of the mythic and the philosophical complexity involved in the depicted conception of "seduction" or "the erotic."[2] This particular reading of *The Seducer's Diary* is concerned primarily with the depicted dialectic itself, which serves to inform the connection between the literary and (latent) theological dimensions of this text. As mentioned, theological connections in *The Seducer's Diary* are often left unnoticed due to it being a pseudonymous text *within* a pseudonymous text, seemingly devoid of anything even covertly "Christian." This reading of the *Diary* is, therefore, a creative interpretation of Kierkegaard's depiction of the real-ideal dichotomy, mapping Kierkegaard's depiction back onto his wider perspective on the inherent idealism of Christendom.

The twin concepts of the "real" and "ideal" are frequently found in dialectical tension throughout Kierkegaard's authorship, particularly regarding the concept of image.[3] His perpetual awareness of this tension is evident especially in his personal writings, as Isak Winkel Holm notes: "It is striking that Kierkegaard, even in his early notebooks, is highly

---

1. See Garff, *Søren Kierkegaard*, 222.

2. See, for example, Dewey, "Erotic-Demonic," 1–24; Becker-Theye, *Seducer as Mythic Figure*; Downing, *Artificial I's*, 75–127; de Lacoste, "Dialectic of the *Real Erotic*," 125–38; Pattison, "Looks of Love," 182–97.

3. The real-ideal dichotomy, of course, is not "Kierkegaardian" per se, but may be located as a common conception within Romanticism, to which Kierkegaard was, no doubt, responding. See McDonald, "Kierkegaard and Romanticism," 94–111.

conscious of the stylistic problems caused by the conflict between invisible concepts and visible images."[4] In *The Seducer's Diary* we see a kind of dialectical "conquest" of the ideal image over the reality, despite the residual tension. This chapter will explore how this dialectic plays out in the text itself, considering crossovers with Kierkegaard's own "real-ideal" relationship to his former fiancée Regine Olson, as well as some formal and thematic comparisons with Goethe's *The Sorrows of Young Werther*, a similarly literary diary depicting a wilfully unobtainable romantic pursuit. Although connections have sometimes been made between Werther and Kierkegaard in general,[5] there is little written which has proposed any sustained comparison between Werther and Johannes,[6] nor of the connections between the "real" and "ideal image" in both texts.

As in Goethe's *Werther*, we are never supposed to actually *witness* love. What we witness, rather, is the idealized "idea" of the imagized beloved, through which the lover is ultimately conquered by his own *unreality*. Bringing Johannes's diary into conversation with Werther's diary, we see not only a literary forerunner which likely contributed to Kierkegaard's real-ideal conception, but we can also reevaluate Kierkegaard's depiction of the aforementioned dialectic (the deliberate pursuit of the unobtainable image) in a clearer light. It will be seen that this dialectic is not only a disconnected fragment, but an inadvertent theological pointer whereby Johannes becomes quasi-emblematic of Christendom's rejection of *real* encounter with God.[7]

---

4. Holm, "Monstrous Aesthetics," 53.

5. See, for example, Martinez, "Melancholy as a 'Romantic Passion.'"

6. Brandes, a literary critic and near-contemporary of Kierkegaard, did make a *general* connection between Johannes and Werther in among allusions to other literary characters, but nothing with any sustained analysis. See Ziolkowski, *Literary Kierkegaard*, 33.

7. Of course, it may well seem a venturesome stretch to highlight such theological implications in *The Seducer's Diary* given its aesthetic "place" within the authorship. However, building not only upon Kierkegaard's own—seldom-believed—reflections that he was *always* a "religious" author (see Kierkegaard, *Point of View*), we have at least some grounds for probing into what he might have been doing through such a deliberate depiction of the real-ideal dialectic (or perhaps even what we might glean from it without him knowing).

The Emergence of the Ideal "System"

Johannes's pursuit of Cordelia portrays a dialectic of the anticipatory drama of awaiting the "reality" of love with deliberate perpetuation. Johannes perpetuates his pursuit knowing, even *willing*, that the reality will never actually be "realized." This unceasing drama of anticipation leads to all-conquering reflection in the speculative realm of the "ideal." Johannes, like the *Diary* as a whole, draws us away from the real into the imaginary, the metaphysical. The task of introducing this drama falls to Victor Eremita, our faithful Dantean guide, who is deployed as the diary's "editor" within the framework of *Either/Or*. As he anxiously attempts to make sense of the scattered collection of letters and journal scraps belonging to this mysterious figure, Johannes the Seducer, he offers an apt reflection to set the stage:

> Behind the world we live in, in the distant background, lies another world standing in roughly the same relation to the former as the stage one sometimes sees in the theatre behind the real stage . . . Through a thin gauze one sees what looks like a world of gossamer, lighter, more ethereal, of a different quality from the real world. Many people who appear bodily in the real world do not belong there but to this other world.[8]

Eremita appears to be opening a door to a mythical world into which the reader will soon be taken. Indeed, the world of this diary is one in which the reality of the experience of mutual love is submerged behind an all-conquering ideal image. It is not, after all, the "experience" of true love that the Seducer seeks, but an unquenchable and impossible pursuit of the image of unattainability itself.

It is reasonable, perhaps, not to presume that Johannes's pursuit of Cordelia has anything to do with "love" at all. It is often seen merely as a conceited pursuit of power, or a form of emotional rape.[9] Brandt has noted Johannes's "ruthless cynicism" as a "vigorous man of pleasure," seemingly incapable of any inkling of actual love.[10] This is true, of course, to Kierkegaard's intended portrayal of the "aesthetic" stage. We are not

---

8. Kierkegaard, *Seducer's Diary*, 4.

9. Ferreira, though, notes that contrary to the apparent absence of love, the *Diary* "show[s] how jest can be in the service of earnestness, as superficial and deceptive forms of love are revealed as such." Ferreira, "Love," 329.

10. Brandt, *Søren Kierkegaard*, 39.

meant to be attracted to Johannes's psyche but "repulsed" by it.[11] Yet there is a particular dynamic within Johannes's view of love which we see at play here, not only in his pursuit of Cordelia but of his personal reflections within the pursuit itself. This is the dialectic of the ideal and the real in perpetual conflict, revealing perhaps more than a merely "systematic" plan of ruthless seduction. We see, rather, Johannes falling into his own web through the medium of an idealized Cordelia. This is Kierkegaard's portrayal of the inescapable tension experienced in the aesthetic pursuit of love.[12]

The theme of the failed idealist, of course, is an ever-present polemic in Kierkegaard's thought. Johannes is the systematician who is undone by finding no place for his own existence within his strategy of seduction.[13] In the language of the *Concluding Unscientific Postscript*, we might say that Johannes is the speculative Hegelian who fails to find a place for *himself* inside his vast system, thereby undoing the entire construction.[14]

The Imagined Image

Kierkegaard uses Johannes to depict the ideal-real dialectic through Johannes's conceptualizations of relationship as pure image, as Johannes himself notes: "Every erotic relationship should be lived out in such a way that one can easily conjure up an image which possesses all of its beauty."[15] One of Johannes's first sightings of Cordelia comes, aptly,

11. *Søren Kierkegaard's Journals and Papers*, 6:6472, 196.

12. Finding this dialectic within this "poetic" diary could be an example of what Winkel Holm calls the "implicit poetological layer in the text." Holm, *Tanken i billedet*, 12. This is particularly evident in Kierkegaard's perpetual contrasting of concept and reality throughout the pseudonymous writings.

13. The seductive "method" is precisely what Kierkegaard wanted readers to notice, as Garff notes: "In his own copy of *Either/Or* he underlined 'The' in 'The Seducer's Diary', and in the margin he added this comment: 'In a review in *Forposten* I see it quite properly pointed out that this tale is not called "A Seducer's Diary" but "*The* Seducer's Diary,"' which of course indicates that the main point is the method, not the portrayals of Johannes or Cordelia.'" Garff, *Søren Kierkegaard*, 221–22. This might appear to counteract what I have been arguing in this chapter regarding the dialectical portrayal. However, in speaking of the dialectic of the "real" and "ideal image" I am still primarily emphasizing the Seducer's method (or, "system"), which encompasses how he chooses to depict the pursuit and how he falls into the existential architecture of his method, becoming lost within his own system.

14. Kierkegaard, *Concluding Unscientific Postscript*, 209.

15. Kierkegaard, *Seducer's Diary*, 83.

through a mirror. This mirror soon becomes a kind of surrogate for his own perception: "That unhappy mirror, which can capture her image but not her."[16] This reflects his own dialectical frustration of wanting to see her at a distance but yearning to move *beyond* her mere image. As he begins to list Cordelia's physical features poetically, he speaks to this mirror as to a brother suffering the same torment: "How beautiful she is! Poor mirror, it must be agony!"[17] Johannes is also stuck in this agony, which he refers to continually as "the contradiction."[18] His plan of seduction, of course, requires him to remain in this contradiction, to keep this distance and linger as the "observer" until the right moment.

But he is not *entirely* systematic in this strategy. That is, he is not personally uninvolved or unaffected in the process itself; he has become existentially active.[19] His reflections continue to reveal that he cannot escape the effects of her image upon him as he finds himself continually remembering and forgetting the image from the mirror. This image is felt most strongly in its absence: "Have I gone blind? . . . I have seen her, but it's as if I'd seen a heavenly revelation, so completely has her image vanished from me again."[20] At this point it is clear that the "her" in question is really nothing more than an image; ontologically, her existence is bound *solely* to this image. Soon enough, he forgets the image almost entirely, remembering only her elusive "green cape."[21] This evokes the paradoxical experience of being drawn to the memory of an image that no longer exists beyond an incidental fragment. He refers to this paradox as "catching the cloud instead of Juno."[22] Yet one begins to wonder if Johannes had perhaps only wanted the "cloud" all along, since this keeps him in the safety of his system, away from the dangers of *actual* encounter. The Green Cape becomes the emblem by which he knows and yearns for her

---

16. Kierkegaard, *Seducer's Diary*, 13.

17. Kierkegaard, *Seducer's Diary*, 13.

18. Kierkegaard, *Seducer's Diary*, 17.

19. Marrs has noted that Johannes's seduction plot, in contrast to Don Giovanni, is fundamentally flawed because he must project reflective meaning and idealism upon his encounters: "The Seducer's efforts at seduction are marred, not only by the intricate orchestrations required to generate a suitably poetic encounter, but also by the need for subsequent reflection to further raise these encounters to a more idealised level." Marrs, "Love-as-Confession," 7.

20. Kierkegaard, *Seducer's Diary*, 20.

21. Kierkegaard, *Seducer's Diary*, 21.

22. Kierkegaard, *Seducer's Diary*, 21.

image again; he recalls it a number of times in the early diary entries.[23] The flash of the cape seems to haunt him as he continues to seek her image again and again: "Turkey cocks puff themselves up when they see red; it's the same with me when I see green, every time I see a green cape . . ."[24]

This recurrence of seeing "her" about town echoes Kierkegaard's memorable journal entry in May 1852 ("About Her") in which he recounts the experience of continually crossing paths with Regine Olson— his own "unrealized" beloved—through various sightings, nods, and glances.[25] Kierkegaard's own Cordelia had also become something of a haunting image to him on various walking routes through Copenhagen's parks and streets, or brief glimpses of her in the Sunday church pews. For Kierkegaard this existential torment seemed to continue at his own deliberation. Johannes, in his idealism, even passes up the opportunity to pursue a different girl, at which point it is not the thought of Cordelia herself that stops him, but the image of the green cape, which chastens his advances: "the green cape demands self-denial."[26] This cape has an immense power over his actions and emotions. Yet this flash of green is not *her*; it is not even her image; it is a mere symbol of an *imagined* image, far removed from the reality of Cordelia herself (of whom at that point he still knows virtually nothing). A similar depiction of this fragmentation between image and reality can be seen in another of Kierkegaard's better-known works, *Repetition* (1843). Rick Antony Furtak has noted, "It seems that the young man [in *Repetition*] replaces 'the girl' herself with an image formed in his own mind such that her actual existence becomes irrelevant."[27] This theme continues to pervade throughout the various textual layers and narratives of Kierkegaard's thought. It remains an essential dialectical construct in understanding the existential processes involved in the drama of idealized love.

The Perpetual Pursuit of the Image

Although the lack of actual connection with the owner of the mysterious green cape is the source of Johannes's torment, it is also the very entity on

23. Kierkegaard, *Seducer's Diary*, 22, 25, 27, 28.

24. Kierkegaard, *Seducer's Diary*, 22.

25. *Søren Kierkegaard's Journals and Papers*, 6:6800, 442–44.

26. Kierkegaard, *Seducer's Diary*, 27.

27. Furtak, "Insights of Love," 15.

which he thrives. The diary is fettered with poetic images that describe this condition of being infatuated but preferring the agony of distance to the reality of connection.[28] This ongoing dialectic of the veiling and unveiling of her image serves to perpetuate her ideality at the expense of her reality: "Her image floats by me like the moon's, indistinct, blinding me now with its light, now with its shadow . . . how enjoyable to be stirred in oneself."[29] The "stirring" that this veiling and unveiling reveals is itself the very *content* of Johannes's love. Although his infatuation draws him ever closer to her, he doesn't really want this stage to end: "The thought of her disappearing a second time can be irritating but in a sense it pleases me."[30] Bornedal calls this a state of "pre-lust" which Johannes perpetuates: "The point of realization of the seduction is pushed ahead to a vanishing point, which he maintains because otherwise the very notion of seduction would lose its meaning."[31]

This pursuit of the girl's image dominates the first quarter of the diary until it changes form as of the entry of May 19, at which point the mysterious girl of the infamous green cape is named as "Cordelia."[32] After this point the image is "filled in" as it were, as he begins to gain more information about her (address, family, preferences, and so forth). It had been the absence of information up until this point that had spurred his pursuit. Information becomes that which is desperately desired and simultaneously reviled as it further reveals her humanity and her uni-deality. This, of course, is a common theme in any love story, which Kierkegaard knows. Yet the real-ideal dialectic we see in Johannes's pursuit does not cease at this turning point. The image still prevails over the real as the pursuit continues and the concrete gives way to the conceptual: "I do not meet her, I merely touch tangentially upon the periphery of her existence."[33] Of course, this keeping of distance is also a tactic in the

---

28. Indirectly, we see this exemplified in Johannes's delighted "unrest" at sitting in a boat looking up to the "vault of heaven," "when the clouds scud before the strong wind . . . the moon vanishes for a moment and then reappears . . . The swift flight of the clouds, the shifting light and shadow, intoxicate me so that I am in a waking dream." Kierkegaard, *Seducer's Diary*, 23. As in his pursuit of love, Johannes actually seems to prefer this reverie-like in-between state to the prospect of "the moon" itself.

29. Kierkegaard, *Seducer's Diary*, 23.

30. Kierkegaard, *Seducer's Diary*, 31.

31. Bornedal, *Speech and System*, 113.

32. Kierkegaard, *Seducer's Diary*, 32.

33. Kierkegaard, *Seducer's Diary*, 37.

seduction process, to draw her toward him indirectly, through the very same process of enigma and mystery with which he sees her:

> I prefer arriving a little early at Mrs. Jansen's, and then if possible meeting her at the door as she is coming and I am leaving, or on the steps where I run unheedingly past her. This is the first net she must be spun into . . . She must certainly be struck by our continual encounter.[34]

However, it is evident that he is simultaneously caught up in the outcome of his own strategy, enticed by her ideality as he seeks to entice her in his own. As he and Cordelia become closer, this manifests itself once again in the prevalence of the image over *real* interaction or mutual relationship: "I can yearn for her, not to talk to her, but just to have her image float by me."[35] She need not even exist beyond his imagination, beyond his ideal "system."

The Absurdity of Engagement

Naturally, Johannes's conceptualization of Cordelia relegates engagement to a "foolish prank," after which "it's all over in the twinkling of an eye."[36] When he and Cordelia *are* eventually engaged he soon plans to break it off "so as to ensure a more beautiful and more significant relationship with Cordelia."[37] In his overall strategy, this means he wants her to love him in her "freedom" rather than in the supposed "binding" of an engagement.[38] Although Johannes stands by this maieutic strategy as though it were the more noble thing to do, it belies his own deep-rooted desire for dialectical uncertainty. This is ultimately where the relationship has meaning for him: "This anxiety is just what is most fascinating."[39] He wants the love to remain unrequited without being entirely nonexistent. He tells her, "I long for you even when I sit by your side."[40] On one level this is merely a romantic gesture, but in fact, this is a further reflection

34. Kierkegaard, *Seducer's Diary*, 37.

35. Kierkegaard, *Seducer's Diary*, 56.

36. Kierkegaard, *Seducer's Diary*, 31.

37. Kierkegaard, *Seducer's Diary*, 70.

38. Kierkegaard, *Seducer's Diary*, 78.

39. Kierkegaard, *Seducer's Diary*, 115.

40. Kierkegaard, *Seducer's Diary*, 88.

of his simultaneous desire and repulsion for reality. He longs for what he already has because what he has is mere image.

It is Johannes and Cordelia's engagement, of course, that conjures the strongest connotations of Kierkegaard and Regine. Kierkegaard's well-known journal entries about "Her" show this very same desire for disconnected connection: "But however much I loved her, it seems I continually wanted to conceal from myself how much she actually affected me."[41] We see also the desire to project an imaginative hermeneutic upon the state of their relationship: "My relationship to her was always kept so ambiguous that I had it in my power to give the interpretation I wanted to."[42] Kierkegaard shows the same desire as Johannes for a reconnection of relationship despite its impossibility: "Although it is unwise for my peace of mind to think about it, I nevertheless do think about the ineffable moment when I would go back to her."[43] He knows this "ineffable moment" is impossible because he himself could not allow it—yet he is still tempted to *imagine* it because its very ineffability is the very point of delight. We can see that Kierkegaard is attempting to depict something of this tension which he experienced in his own "existential" situation, even as he attempts to do so with a particular stratagem in mind in the context of the authorship.[44] His lifelong devotion to Regine—specifically *because* they can never actually be together—could be seen as an exemplification of Johannes's perpetual reluctance to truly *engage* Cordelia even when he is officially "engaged" to her: "True, I do possess her in a legal and petty bourgeois sense but, to me that means nothing at all."[45] Here we see a deeper layer in Johannes's view of what comprises the "actual." A legally-bound engagement, for many, would certainly constitute an "actual" engagement which is thoroughly real, unspeculative, and unimagined. But for Johannes, there is a deeper existential layer to the concept of "engagement" which renders the exterior officiality superfluous. In a deliberately paradoxical sense, Johannes has constructed a psychological situation for himself in which the "ideal" is more *real* to him than the "real."

Johannes's frequent disparagement of the social concept of engagement is a demonstration of this desperation to avoid actuality. As

41. *Søren Kierkegaard's Journals and Papers*, 6:6472, 193.

42. *Søren Kierkegaard's Journals and Papers*, 5:5521, 177.

43. *Søren Kierkegaard's Journals and Papers*, 5:5515, 175.

44. See Kierkegaard, *Point of View*, 41–42.

45. Kierkegaard, *Seducer's Diary*, 72.

de Lacoste has noted, "He is never able to abandon himself to Cordelia, and can never take the risk of real intimacy."[46] This is because his love can only exist in the pursuit of the ideal; it simply has no other content once the image has become reality. Engagement, which could be seen as the zenith of a loving courtship, here signifies its death, whereby "the erotic disappears."[47] Without the dialectic of the erotic, Johannes cannot *see* love, and thus he ends up seeing engagement as "tomfoolery,"[48] and "the most ridiculous thing of all."[49] Love, for Johannes, can be seen only in perpetual dialectical conflict, a warlike state which cannot know the peace that supposedly arrives through engagement: "When love stops fighting it has come to an end."[50] Thus, despite seeing engagement as fundamentally absurd—in that making love "official," love is thereby nullified—his own perspective of love-as-perpetual-conflict is even more absurd. This is because he supposes to pursue meaningfully what he never truly wants to grasp, like Sisyphus's supposed joy in the perpetual rolling and re-rolling of his rock.[51] This embrace of the absurd is seen further in Johannes's overtly anti-Hegelian thoughts on contradiction: "Let scholarly disputants take pride in avoiding all contradiction; a young girl's life is too rich for there not to be contradictions in it and so makes contradiction necessary."[52] This again points to Johannes's (and Kierkegaard's) incessant awareness of existential dialectical tension, and highlights his deliberate dependence upon such tension within the realm of human love.

The Mythical Chaste

In the midst of the ambiguous engagement period, Johannes continues to deconstruct the relationship which he is simultaneously building, with his view of Cordelia constantly regressing back to the image. In this psychological reenactment, it is as though she has become *un*known to him again, happily beyond his reach:

46. De Lacoste, "Dialectic of the *Real Erotic* and Eroticism," 132.
47. Kierkegaard, *Seducer's Diary*, 74.
48. Kierkegaard, *Seducer's Diary*, 71.
49. Kierkegaard, *Seducer's Diary*, 69.
50. Kierkegaard, *Seducer's Diary*, 72.
51. See Camus, *Myth of Sisyphus*, 78.
52. Kierkegaard, *Seducer's Diary*, 75.

> You have vanished from me in the forest. Behind every tree I see
> a womanly being that resembles you; when I get nearer, it hides
> behind the next tree . . . Everything is in confusion before me . . .
> I see everything as a sea fog, where womanly beings resembling
> you everywhere appear and disappear. But you I do not see, you
> are always moving on the waves of intuition.[53]

This is reminiscent of the earlier veiling and unveiling and the flashes
of green cape in which Cordelia is seen. Again, we see a delighting in
ambiguity, uncertainty and "lostness" which has characterized his love.
And having come so close to her, his view of her does not (as one might
expect) become more *real* but it does quite the opposite, ascending into
a hyperbolized mythology, as yet unforeseen. Reflections upon Cordelia
become increasingly poeticized and less concrete. Allusions to nymphs,
goddesses and fairy tales become commonplace, most strikingly in the
retelling of the ancient legend of a river that falls in love with a girl's
reflection:

> At one moment it is peaceful and allows your image to be re-
> flected in it deeply and undistorted; at another it fancies it has
> captured your image, and its waves foam to prevent you getting
> away; sometimes it softly ruffles its surface and plays with your
> reflection, sometimes it loses it, and then its waves become dark
> and despairing.[54]

It is, of course, the image, which holds the power and sway over Johannes
as he finds himself unable to grasp the "her" which he has essentially
invented. Soon enough, he finds himself lost in his own river of mythological allusion. Cordelia becomes "the image of Venus" and the "pure
virginity" of Diana.[55] She has become the transcendent deity, eternally
chaste and eternally chased. His pursuit of her imaginary image becomes
increasingly driven by this theme of chastity, which begins to dominate
his conception of her. The very ontology of femininity itself is sublated
into this ideal image of the chaste: "As being-for-another, woman is characterized by pure virginity"; "for the woman [innocence] is her whole
worth."[56]

53. Kierkegaard, *Seducer's Diary*, 91.

54. Kierkegaard, *Seducer's Diary*, 99–100.

55. Kierkegaard, *Seducer's Diary*, 125–26.

56. Kierkegaard, *Seducer's Diary*, 121, 135.

As he rides out to meet Cordelia on their last and only night together, his anticipations are again saturated in mythical grandeur.[57] So affected has Johannes become by his own game of ambiguous infatuation that he himself has collapsed into the very myth he tried to create: "Everything is image. I myself am a myth about myself, for is it not rather as a myth that I hasten to this meeting?"[58] His reflections *after* this evening with her are so *un*real that one has to reread the passage a number of times to check if there are any *actual* references to a sexual encounter.[59] We are left merely assuming, as Johannes moves on to a new conceptualization of Cordelia: "Why can't a night like that be longer? . . . Still, now it is over and I never want to see her again. Once a girl has given away everything, she is weak, she has lost everything."[60] Once they are together the power of the myth is broken and he must escape the reality immediately. She has become, for him, completely asexual: "If I were her I would do what Neptune did for a nymph: change her into a man."[61] The cold brutality of these latter reflections is almost difficult to believe, as if it really was just an erotic experiment in which Johannes had remained *entirely* existentially absent. But from the totality of his pursuit it is evident that he had become far more involved than even *he* could have planned. De Lacoste comments, "[Johannes] refuses to let himself experience 'the ambiguity of the erotic' which leads to the blurring of the separation of self and other."[62] This rejection of ambiguity and abandonment is not simply a part of the plan, but a necessary coping mechanism to retain a different kind of ambiguity. It is within the disconnection of the dialectic that he feels *most* connected to Cordelia and most "in love." As soon as the disconnection is "broken," as it were—through their *connection* [!]—Johannes must cut himself off entirely.

57. Kierkegaard, *Seducer's Diary*, 134–35.

58. Kierkegaard, *Seducer's Diary*, 134–35.

59. It could be a quite plausible reading, in fact, to say there was no sexual encounter at all, especially given the fact that Johannes may well have become so idealistic that the act of sex itself, and the vulnerability it brings even to a "seducer," is literally *beyond* him. However, I would argue that the starkness of the post-event reflections (albeit elusive) leads us to assume that it was their sexual encounter that led to his newfound disinterestedness in Cordelia, rather than simply her *willingness* to give herself up entirely.

60. Kierkegaard, *Seducer's Diary*, 135.

61. Kierkegaard, *Seducer's Diary*, 135.

62. De Lacoste, "Dialectic of the *Real Erotic* and Eroticism," 132.

It is impossible not make at least some further connections here between Johannes and Kierkegaard himself. Predominantly, we see this in the necessary withdrawal from the ensuing vulnerability that would incur from the actuality of marriage. Even though we may still respect Kierkegaard's original intention for the character of Johannes (as a character intended to "repel" and certainly not a reflection of his own "view") there is nonetheless a fair amount of Søren lurking in Johannes's idealizations of love and his preference for image over actuality, even as these appear to contradict Kierkegaard's more trenchant theological polemics in which *actuality* becomes his primary focus. This does not discount the validity of his anti-idealism, as we will see, but merely belies his own inescapability from that which he wants to critique.

The Sorrows of Young Johannes

Alongside these connections to Kierkegaard's autobiographical situation, Johannes's flights from reality also connote Goethe's forlorn and angst-ridden lover, Werther. The dialectic of "real" and "ideal image" is magnified even more clearly by comparison with Goethe's text, which may even have influenced both the form and style of Johannes's diary. The comparison with *Werther* provides a potential lens through which to see a similar dialectical depiction which may well have acted as a precursor to Kierkegaard's text, with regard to the "imagizing" of the beloved.

Although *The Seducer's Diary* has often been seen as loosely reliant upon Friedrich Schlegel's *Lucinde* (1799), Martin takes this to be a major misconception, noting that other Romantic works, including those of Goethe's, could have been just as influential.[63] Kierkegaard's debt to European Romantic literature in general, of course, has been widely noted.[64] *The Sorrows of Young Werther* (1774) was undoubtedly Goethe's most culturally influential work in terms of its imitational impact. In the wake of its unparalleled cultural success at the height of "Werther fever" in the late eighteenth century, stories abound of melancholic young Romantics flocking to purchase Werther-esque blue frock coats, embracing his reveries of unrequited love, and even glamorizing his "poetical"

---

63. Martin, "Common Mistake," 192. Gouwens also suggests, as have others, that *Werther* influenced Kierkegaard's very conception of "Either/Or" as a phraseological concept. Gouwens, "Kierkegaard's *Either/Or*," 14.

64. See Steiner, "Wound of Negativity," 106.

suicide.[65] It is almost impossible for Kierkegaard not to have been aware of its significance,[66] nor could he have avoided its depiction of Werther's tragically unrequited love. This is especially the case when we consider that Werther is often seen as a standard-bearer for the "excessive ideal-ism" of this period of German Romanticism, immersed in "the triumph of spirit over external reality."[67] Kierkegaard's depiction of incessant im-agistic idealism through Johannes cannot have been unaffected by this most emblematic of *Sturm und Drang* texts.

Although it has been noted that "Kierkegaard's relation to and use of Goethe is highly diverse and complex,"[68] Goethe's diary-and-letter-based tale is very likely to have influenced Kierkegaard in the writing and con-ception of *The Seducer's Diary*, both formally and philosophically, even as he reacts against it. Stewart and Nun have noted comparisons between Kierkegaard's and Goethe's personal circumstances regarding the angst of abandoning a loved one and working this out in their writings.[69] Others have noted a deliberate self-contrasting by Kierkegaard between himself and Goethe.[70] Purver has even suggested that Kierkegaard made allusions elsewhere in *Either/Or* as a negative "riposte to Werther" in overcoming the angst that had led Goethe's melancholic "hero" to commit suicide.[71] Indeed, we may even notice that Victor Eremita's quotation of Goethe in his introduction may well have been deeply intentional on Kierkegaard's part, offering a hermeneutical key to the directedness of the diary as a whole: "When [Cordelia] referred to her relationship to Johannes she usually cited a little verse, I believe by Goethe, which seemed to convey a different meaning according to her moods and the difference in delivery these occasioned: 'Gehe / Verschmähe / Die Treue, / Die Reue / Kommt nach.'"[72]

65. Johnson and Johnson, *Social Impact of the Novel*, 170. See also Atkins, *Testa-ment of Werther*.

66. J. L. Heiberg's essay, "Astronomical Year" (1844), which Kierkegaard both read and critiqued, actually referred to Werther in connection with Kierkegaard's *Repeti-tion* (1843). See Stewart and Nun, "Goethe," 76.

67. Johnson and Johnson, *Social Impact of the Novel*, 169.

68. Stewart and Nun, "Goethe," 51.

69. Stewart and Nun, "Goethe," 72.

70. Josipovici, "Kierkegaard and the Novel," 121.

71. Purver, "Eichendorff," 43–44.

72. Kierkegaard, *Seducer's Diary*, 9.

Whether the Goethean undertones in *The Seducer's Diary* are explicitly Werther-oriented or not, there are remarkable similarities between the idealism of Werther and Johannes, alongside the obvious contrasts.[73] The mythical divinization of Cordelia is also seen in Werther's references to Lotte: "She is sacred to me";[74] "I can no longer pray except to her";[75] "I am too close to her magic realm."[76] Werther's romantic connection to Lotte is largely the work of his own imagination. Although with Johannes there *is* a real relationship (of sorts), like Werther's it can never truly materialize; it remains imprisoned in the abstract. Lotte, like Cordelia, becomes enshrined in the distance of the image:

> How her figure haunts me! Waking or dreaming, she fills my entire soul! Here in my head, in my mind's eye, I see her dark eyes the moment I close my own . . . deep as an ocean or an abyss, and they are within me, filling the senses of my mind.[77]

Such a haunted reflection could well arise within any obsessed lover, of course. But the connection between Johannes and Werther remains tailored to their incessant *imagization* of their beloved as replacing the desire for the real. It is the image to which they are both primarily drawn and which they are continually reconstructing.

Fittingly, one of Werther's most distressing moments is when he is no longer able to cast an image to his beloved, in which the very ontology of his love for her was invested. Like Johannes's clutching for sights of the green cape having forgotten Cordelia's face, Werther too finds he cannot recall Lotte well enough to paint her portrait, and he settles instead for a silhouette: "I have started on a portrait of Lotte three times, and three times I have failed disgracefully; which depresses me all the more since I could take a very good likeness not so long ago. So then I cut a silhouette profile of her, and that will have to do."[78] The concept of the silhouette perhaps best summates Werther's and Johannes's ideals of their women.

---

73. One such contrast (other than the obvious difference in the main characters' romantic intentions and their radically different fates) is between the two "rivals," Edvard (Johannes's) and Albert (Werther's). Where Albert appears as flawless and impenetrable, Edvard is weak and easily manipulated; he is more of a tool in Johannes's plan than a true "rival."

74. Goethe, *Sorrows of Young Werther*, 53.

75. Goethe, *Sorrows of Young Werther*, 68.

76. Goethe, *Sorrows of Young Werther*, 56.

77. Goethe, *Sorrows of Young Werther*, 105.

78. Goethe, *Sorrows of Young Werther*, 55.

A silhouette majestically elevates the outline at the expense of the inner contours and details of the face, in which the ideal of an image triumphs over the depiction of reality. This "silhouettian" connection between Werther and Johannes serves to illustrate, most overtly, the contours of Kierkegaard's complex portrayal of love here, as the dialectic between the real and the ideal image.

In Werther we not only have a conceptual forerunner to Johannes, but we see the potential for viewing Johannes as an *inversion* of Werther, a literary strategy certainly plausible given Kierkegaard's noteworthy connection to Goethe. If Kierkegaard did indeed intend such an allusion in Johannes, the differences between them are, of course, channeled by their deliberate perpetuation of the anticipatory via the *un*real images of the object of their desire which they do not truly desire to attain. In Kierkegaard's Johannes, we not only see a typological Werther who is "empowered" in his control of the pursuit, but one who—even in the con- temptible use of such power—is ultimately powerless to prevent his own fall into the seductive trap of the imagined image, which ultimately con- sumes him. This not only highlights the perils of the aesthete's idealism (the kind Kierkegaard was so keen to criticize in bourgeois Copenhagen) but also the "religious" idealism that lurks within Christendom. With this reflection, we will conclude this penultimate chapter, offering a prepara- tion for the final chapter on Kierkegaard's deconstruction and potential reconstruction of the Church in light of the Gospel.

The "Ideal Image" of Christendom

The depicted tension between the real and the ideal for Johannes is in no way a full representation of Kierkegaard's own more comprehensive conception of love itself. Indeed, in his overtly Christian text, *Works of Love* (1847), Kierkegaard depicts a formulation of love that is almost en- tirely opposite to that which has been discussed thus far: "In loving the individual person it is important that one does not substitute an imagi- nary idea of how we think or could wish that this person should be. The one who does this does not love the person he sees but . . . something unseen, his own idea or something similar."[79] One imagines, indeed, that Kierkegaard may have had Johannes in mind as the antonym for what he was expressing here. In the same work, Kierkegaard critiques

79. Kierkegaard, *Works of Love*, 164.

the ambiguous, mythical conception of idealistic love: "The condition is to find the firm footing of actuality. Error is always vague; that is why it sometimes seems so easy and so spiritual—because it is so ethereal."[80] The necessity of "actuality" in love is vital for Kierkegaard, even where hints of "idealism" also arise with his references to loving the dead as the "most faithful" kind of love.[81] This emphasis, however, appears more as a "test" of faithfulness and unselfishness precisely because the dead person is *non*-actual and, therefore, requires an entire self-emptying on the part of the one who *is* "actual."[82] Actuality, it seems, remains Kierkegaard's key criterion for genuine love.

Even given Kierkegaard's unique biographical situation, with all its undertones, overtones and in-between-tones, it is clear that he and Johannes are in direct contrast with regard to the definition of what love *actually* is. *Works of Love*, of course, is certainly the theologically richer of the two works, harboring the immediacy to loving the other concretely in response to divine love in the Gospel.[83] Kierkegaard's distinctly *theological* trajectory for love cannot be ignored even when we are on the verge of letting the pseudonyms carry us away with them. Indeed, Laura Hall speaks of Kierkegaard's deliberate portrayal of inadequate types of love to lead us heavenward: "By revealing the many ways that merely human love may go awry [Kierkegaard's characters] give force to [his] call in *Works of Love* for us repeatedly to turn to God."[84] Yet even with this strategy in mind, like Johannes we might even postulate that Kierkegaard himself becomes existentially involved within his own plot. Like Milton's enthralling Devil in *Paradise Lost*, Kierkegaard may find himself drawn to the devil in Johannes, further propelling his ever-conscious need for

---

80. Kierkegaard, *Works of Love*, 163.

81. Kierkegaard, *Works of Love*, 354–58.

82. Kierkegaard, *Works of Love*, 358.

83. Dalferth even says that Kierkegaard does not want to make a "definition" of love at all, so to speak, but rather, a mode of orienting *all* human activity: "In *Works of Love* Kierkegaard does not describe what love *is* and how it is in fact experienced and practiced but explores what love *ought to be* and how it should be practiced." Dalferth, "Selfless Passion," 1.

84. Laura Hall, *Kierkegaard and the Treachery of Love*, 173. This strategy seems to be culminated in the "direct communication" of *Works of Love*, as noted by Wells: "In *Works of Love*, [Kierkegaard's] goal is to demonstrate how temporality fails in producing love and how the eternal is essential in living out the good." Wells, "Love as Humanizing Virtue," 4–5.

dependency upon God.[85] Johannes's preference for the image over the reality may be just a small depicted facet within Kierkegaard's overall conception, but the real vitality with which this "idealism" is presented in the work shows that even Kierkegaard is not somehow *beyond* the dialectical tension faced in the pursuit of "merely human love." By portraying the depths of the human condition with such uncomfortable familiarity, Johannes's flaws become our own springboard to receiving the transcendental love of God within the finite, dialectical realm of human existence.

Such existentialized speculations, of course, are not essential to the theological import of *The Seducer's Diary*. In a more significant sense, Johannes's flawed pursuit of the image points us not only to our *need* for God, but to our ongoing *rejection* of God. This rejection does not arise overtly, say, in the form of atheism or an exclusively "aesthetic" life, but rather in the comfortable religious existence of "Christendom." Indeed, it is possible to read the aforementioned discussion of this chapter as not being ultimately about Johannes and Cordelia, nor even of Kierkegaard and Regine, but of the (would-be/won't-be) Christian within Christendom. To make such a theological connection is not to relegate *The Seducer's Diary* into a full-blown allegory, but rather to point to a possible outworking of Kierkegaard's complex use of the real-ideal dialectic as it may be seen throughout his overall authorial approach.

In Kierkegaard's *Point of View*, of course, he mentions *The Seducer's Diary* several times, often in relation to the scandalous disappointment readers may feel upon finding out his true authorial purpose: "That what it means to become a Christian should actually be the fundamental idea in the whole authorship—how boring! And all this about 'The Seducer's Diary,' this tremendously intriguing book! Well, that also belongs."[86] Indeed, the concept of becoming a Christian within Christendom is the unavoidable point of all of Kierkegaard's works, however indirectly stated; thus, an overtly "aesthetic" text like *The Seducer's Diary* "also belongs" within this wider purpose for religious awakening.

---

85. It is often noted, most famously by Stanley Fish in *Surprised by Sin* (1967), that the fascinating character traits and heroic speeches which Milton imbued to Satan were a deliberate literary-theological tactic by which the reader would be enticed to Satan's personal magnetism, thereby revealing their own fallenness and sinful depravity. This is, so goes the argument, why Satan and his speeches are the more "interesting" so that as the reader is enticed they see their own connection to sin, revealing a deeper need for repentance in turning to God.

86. Kierkegaard, *Point of View*, 92.

In relation to the real-ideal dialectic at play in the *Diary*, we see in those same authorial reflections of Kierkegaard's another hint at the connection between the false imagization of the beloved and that of the idealistic system of Christendom: "A person does not reflect himself into being a Christian but out of something else in order to become a Christian, especially when the situation is Christendom, where one must reflect oneself out of the appearance of being a Christian."[87] Christendom, for Kierkegaard, was indeed a kind of mirage, an "appearance" of the reality of what it means to be a Christian. It is a different thing to outright unbelief. Christendom's religious platitudes served as imagistic customs which replaced the need for any *real* encounter with God, nor any heartfelt action *for* God. As Kierkegaard reflected in his journal, "the guilt of Christendom is actually this—instead of what the New Testament understands by Christianity, Christendom has hit upon—playing at Christianity, of course as boldly and inexhaustibly as the human imagination can be."[88] For Kierkegaard, Christendom itself is one of the boldest experiments in human imagination imaginable. Indeed, "Christendom is an enormous illusion."[89] In Kierkegaard's descriptions of Christendom we continually see the notion of the ideal image.

As we saw in chapter 3, Christendomians do not want to fully avail themselves of God, but neither do they want to apprehend God in any consequential sense, with all the apprehensiveness that such apprehension might entail for them! The Christendomian may not wish to "seduce" God as such, but perhaps he fools himself into thinking he truly *is* pursuing God, rather than a mere "image" constructed by the outward religious practices which Christendom so readily offers, concealing the absence of genuine "inwardness." Such practices are merely a part of the game ("playing at Christianity"), given that they actively perpetuate the *non*-practice of real faith.[90] Whether or not Kierkegaard intended quite such fully-fledged connections when he first wrote *The Seducer's Diary*, the question the theologian might yet venture to ask, is: Are *we* a "type" of Johannes too, seeking a God whom we do not—in *reality*—want to meet?

---

87. Kierkegaard, *Point of View*, 93.

88. *Søren Kierkegaard's Journals and Papers*, 1:561, 229.

89. Kierkegaard, *Point of View*, 41–44.

90. See, for example, Kierkegaard's reflections upon *merely* "observing" and "admiring" Christian truth, or Christ himself, thereby perpetuating the existential distance between oneself and the *actual* "object" of admiration or observation. Kierkegaard, *Practice in Christianity*, 233–57.

After all, think of all that might be asked of us if we truly *did* meet him (as Abraham well knows). Although God in his being may be "unobtainable" in his "infinite qualitative distinction" from humanity,[91] we may wish to keep him unobtainable forever, scorning his "becoming flesh" for all that it might entail for our ideal if he ever got too close. Indeed, our gnostic Christendomian spirits may well prefer a God who remains enshrined in ethereality, re-entombed in image, and de-carnated into the distant realm of the ideal. Such would be a God whom we might only allow to exist—like the Seducer's conception of Cordelia—on our own terms and in our own *image*. This, of course, is the Seducer's most ethereal of sins: he refuses to let the object of his affection make *actual* impression upon him, and thus be changed beyond his own imagination.

Where we have seen, in this chapter, a close engagement with a very indirect way of critiquing Christendom, the final chapter will engage with an approach that could not be more opposite: Kierkegaard's "attack upon Christendom." It is through such an engagement that we may also see the latent possibilities of a Kierkegaardian "ecclesiology," where Kierkegaard offers hope for a *real* Church beyond the seductive ideal. However, in Kierkegaard's time such a hope could be little more than a figment of the imagination unless the "enormous illusion" of Christendom could first be exposed in all its inglorious reality.

---

91. Kierkegaard, *Practice in Christianity*, 28–29.

8

Taking the Individual Back to Church

Toward a Kierkegaardian Ecclesiology for Post-Christendom

ON JULY 7, 1855, four months before his own death, Søren Kierkegaard wrote the following eerie passage:

> Think of a hospital. The patients are dying like flies. The methods are altered in one way and another. It's no use. What does it come from? It comes from the building, the whole building is full of poison. That the patients are registered as dead, one of this disease . . . one of another, is not true; for they are all dead from the poison that is in the building.[1]

It is one of many vivid and scornful depictions of the Lutheran Church in nineteenth-century Denmark. By this point, Kierkegaard believes that Christendom has so co-opted Christianity into a "tranquilizing" illusion that there is no salvageable remnant left.[2] He himself has long since stopped attending church and even called the Christian masses of Copenhagen to a full Church boycott.[3] As far as Kierkegaard is concerned, the Church has been infected with the disease of Christendom: "the whole building is full of poison" and nothing is clearer than that the entire system must come down. Pastors, as the perpetuating figureheads

---

1. Kierkegaard, *Attack upon Christendom*, 139.
2. Kierkegaard, *Attack upon Christendom*, 262.
3. Kierkegaard, *Attack upon Christendom*, 59–60.

of this condition, come in for special rebuke, and are to be avoided at all costs. In one particularly *un*edifying assault, Kierkegaard compares these pastors to cannibals who keep the bodies of Christian martyrs in brine tubs for winter provision, living off the fruits of the martyrs' sacrificial legacy without being prepared to follow it themselves.[4] (The cannibals, he adds, are the nobler of the two because at least they are honest about their business.)[5] For Kierkegaard, the pastors who epitomize the state of the Church not only fail to build up the individual believers' faith, they subtly siphon it away under the illusion of a false Christianity.

It is in part because of the excessive tone which characterized the final months of Kierkegaard's writing life that he is still—to this day—held somewhat at arms' length by the Church. In one sense, as Kierkegaard might happily accept himself, it's his own fault. One doesn't expect he is all that surprised that the established Church has not quite taken him into its home. However, as we have seen already, a somewhat muffled reception has also played its part.[6] It is well-known that the earliest Kierkegaard translations that reached mainland Europe focused upon this more incendiary period of his authorship and were soon co-opted into the radically secularist and anticlerical agendas of others.[7] Nonetheless, for all Kierkegaard's contribution to modern thought, for many the attack upon Christendom leaves a black mark against his enduring ecclesial value. How can somebody so apparently *anti*-Church possibly inform the Church about what it is, and what it ought to be doing? More specifically, how can a thinker who so regularly pitted the notion of "the individual" against "the congregation" possibly contribute to the life *of* the congregation when it is not even clear that he believes there is such a thing *as* a "congregation"?[8]

Contrary to such expectations, this final chapter invokes important aspects of Kierkegaard's ecclesial approach which make possible—at least, in theory—a tentative Kierkegaardian ecclesiology. I will do this by first "attacking" Kierkegaard's stance on the grounds of his portrayal of Church, his partial use of Scripture, and his individualistic emphasis.

4. Kierkegaard, *Attack upon Christendom*, 268.

5. Kierkegaard, *Attack upon Christendom*, 269.

6. See especially chapters 1 and 4.

7. See Schreiber, "Christoph Schrempf," 305–8.

8. As Holm notes, "If it is possible to talk about a concept of the congregation in Kierkegaard, this congregation does not exist until after the Holy Spirit has had its effect on the individual." Holm, "Kierkegaard and the Church," 127.

Following this foundational critique, I will then try "defending" Kierkegaard's stance on the grounds of his wider ecclesial conceptions, his thoughts on reform, and a more nuanced account of the individual *in* the congregation. Finally, this partially critiqued and partially defended approach will then be applied to a fresh understanding of the concept of Christendom as a perpetual "condition" which may afflict the Church in any given historical moment, not least within the oft-lauded conception of "post-Christendom." It will be argued that to see Kierkegaard's approach in this light—even with its rhetorical extremities—renders it potentially useful in future ecclesiological conversations, whenever it appears that the Church is refusing to live by the Gospel it purportedly proclaims.

Attacking Kierkegaard's Ecclesiology

We begin, then, by surveying three of the most prominent blind spots one might notice in Kierkegaard's "ecclesiological" approach: Ecclesial Negativity, Exegetical *Partiality*, and Essential Individuality.

Ecclesial Negativity

The first "sin" which any would-be Kierkegaardian ecclesiology must confess is that of Kierkegaard's intensive negativity toward what the Church is *not*, noticeably uncomplemented by positive expressions of what the Church ought to *be*. As Anders Holm notes, "It is easy to understand why Kierkegaard stopped going to church; in a way, he had to. It is harder to make sense of why Kierkegaard was an avid churchgoer most of his life and yet so critical of the Church."[9] Although negative critique is an essential part of any ecclesiology,[10] there is a marked difference between Kierkegaard and, say, the Reformers, in that—in the midst of Kierkegaard's attack—he deliberately refrains from describing an overtly positive vision of the Church's theological meaning. Compare this, for example, with a reformer such as Calvin, whose acerbic tongue in ecclesiological

9. Holm, "Kierkegaard and the Church," 127.

10. "That a proper diagnosis and prognosis of an illness is more than half the battle, every physician will admit, and likewise that no ability, no care and vigilance, is of any avail when the case has not been correctly diagnosed." Kierkegaard, *Attack upon Christendom*, 139.

dispute was more than a match for Kierkegaard's own. Calvin denounces the pope—often referred to more affectionately, of course, as "the Antichrist"—whose "abominable kingdom" has "afflicted [the churches] by cruel despotism, corrupted and almost terminated their existence by false and pernicious doctrines, like poisonous potions," where "Christ lies half buried, the gospel is suppressed, piety exterminated, and the worship of God almost abolished," exhibiting "a picture of Babylon rather than the city of the holy God."[11] However, unlike Kierkegaard, Calvin doesn't stop here. He is still able to present a vision of the Church as glorious and—crucially—*essential* to genuine faith. Although Calvin's use of the term "Church" is more specifically ontological than Kierkegaard's more porous expression,[12] one could never imagine Kierkegaard speaking this following phrase of Calvin's: "We are certain, as long as we continue in the bosom of the Church, that we shall remain in possession of the truth."[13] Where Calvin says that "it is altogether fatally dangerous to be separated from the Church," one could say that Kierkegaard's entire project in those final years was to campaign for the exact opposite: that to *remain* in the Church, to *not* be separated from the Church, was fatally dangerous to one's faith. This leads us onto Kierkegaard's second possible ecclesiological blind spot: exegetical partiality.

Exegetical Partiality

One reason Calvin is able to present a more holistic picture of the Church is that, in writing the *Institutes*, he is attempting to present a kind of aggregation of scriptural teaching. Kierkegaard, on the other hand, although a dedicated and multifarious interpreter of Scripture,[14] never sought to offer its systematic doctrinal coherence. This does not mean he doesn't believe in such coherence, but simply that he doesn't believe in systematic presentation, full stop. This, of course, leaves him open to a hermeneutics not only of contingency, but of convenience. Despite criticizing Luther

---

11. Calvin, *On the Christian Faith*, 104 (*Institutes*, IV/ii:12).

12. "Kierkegaard rarely distinguishes between the various meanings of the term (for example, the physical building, the community of believers, and the social and political institution)." Tilley, "The Church," 211.

13. Calvin, *On the Christian Faith*, 102 (*Institutes*, IV/i.3).

14. See chapter 3, and Polk, *Biblical Kierkegaard*.

for being "one-sided" in his emphasis on justification,[15] Kierkegaard is himself noticeably silent about those glaring passages of the New Testament which speak of the Church as the body of Christ (Rom 12:5; 1 Cor 12:12), as the manifestation of God's wisdom (Eph 3:10), or as the pillar and buttress of the truth (1 Tim 3:15). Given Kierkegaard's repetitive use of the phrase "New Testament Christianity" to fuel his ecclesial attacks, the Church might be amply justified in throwing the same grenade back at Kierkegaard. As Hugh Pyper notes, "Kierkegaard, in common with every other Christian writer, does manifest a personal canon within the canon, one made up of those biblical writings that emphasize his particular concerns."[16]

There is a valid Kierkegaardian response to this, of course, relating to the way in which he construes the Bible's consequential efficacy in the believer's life and, therefore, which passages one ought to obey as a first port of call for obedient faith.[17] As we saw in chapter 3, Kierkegaard has little interest in abstract presentations of biblical doctrine for their own sake—what he calls for is that biblical doctrine be both known and heeded. That said, of course, at the outset it should be recognized that Kierkegaard has not done justice to the positive ideal set out in Scripture by which the Church is instructed to see itself. Such ecclesiocentric passages *also* ought to be "obeyed" in one's personal life if we are to take the New Testament seriously. Again, this is inextricably linked to another possible Kierkegaardian oversight: the exclusive denial of a congregational vision.

Essential Individuality

Perhaps the most problematic and infamous snare to a Kierkegaardian ecclesiology lies in Kierkegaard's incessant focus upon "the single individual" as the primary perspective from which the life of faith is imagined. He wrote so enthusiastically against the inherent "untruth" of the crowd,[18] and of the essential vitality of the individual, that it becomes dif-

---

15. *Søren Kierkegaard's Journals and Papers*, 3:2521, 83–84.

16. Pyper, *Joy of Kierkegaard*, 22.

17. See again chapter 3; see also Rasmussen, "Kierkegaard's Biblical Hermeneutics."

18. See Kierkegaard, *Point of View*, 109–30. Kirmmse refers to this general attitude as Kierkegaard's "anti-majoritarianism" and his "egalitarian individualism." See Kirmmse, *Kierkegaard in Golden Age Denmark*, 416. Kierkegaard was not pro-elite/anti-commoner, but anti- *any* grouping which attempts to set the bar for other individuals and stop them becoming a true Christian "self."

ficult to see in his work where or how the single individual belongs *in* the Church, nor why they should even need the Church at all. Kierkegaard describes the category of the "single individual" as "the very principle of Christianity":[19] "Christianity does not join men together—no, it separates them—in order to unite every single individual with God."[20] In direct contrast to the individual stands "the crowd," which Kierkegaard can only see pejoratively as a kind of "tyrant" which subtly drains the individuality from its subjects.[21] What is most abominable to Kierkegaard is the notion of a *theological* justification for such crowd-consciousness. Opposing this, he insists, "God is no friend of the cosy human crowd."[22] In the crowd, the individual loses their individual ability to *be*; they become corrupted: "In truth, there is no place, not even one most disgustingly devoted to lust and vice, where a human being is so easily corrupted—as in the crowd."[23] This despising of the malforming effects of crowd-consciousness undergirds his ecclesial critiques.

Applied to the Church, the crowdly corruption lies in the possibility of mass insincerity in faith and discipleship, where all believe themselves to be Christians by rote. On Jesus' call to make his disciples "fishers of men," with customary sarcasm Kierkegaard reflects,

> During 1800 years, kingdoms, countries, nations, etc. have been caught, a continent became Christian and has been Christian through these many centuries—an enormous catch, enormous catch, a marvellous fulfilment of our Lord's prophecy! Suppose a fisherman . . . got an order to catch whales and then caught a million sardines—an enormous catch, an enormous catch! . . . We have lowered the standard for being a Christian and thus have caught all the more. Instead of whales, we caught sardines—but countless millions of them . . . How wonderfully our Lord's prophecies have been fulfilled.[24]

In response to Christendom's corruption of true faith through crowd-consciousness, Kierkegaard seems to undermine the role of sanctifying fellowship itself: "Only as an individual can a man ever relate himself most truly to God, for he [alone] can best have the perception of his own

---

19. *Søren Kierkegaard's Journals and Papers*, 2:1997, 398.

20. *Søren Kierkegaard's Journals and Papers*, 2:2052, 425.

21. *Søren Kierkegaard's Journals and Papers*, 3:2951, 317.

22. *Søren Kierkegaard's Journals and Papers*, 2:2078, 438.

23. *Søren Kierkegaard's Journals and Papers*, 3:2926, 306.

24. *Søren Kierkegaard's Journals and Papers*, 3:2979, 337–38.

unworthiness."[25] Here we see a deep problem in Kierkegaard's focus. Although the single individual has undeniably exclusive access to much of their hidden depravity, Kierkegaard seems to think the human heart is itself capable of accurate self-diagnosis without recourse to self-deception (cf. Jer 17:9). This is, of course, why the Church *is* vital to one's personal relationship with God, precisely because of our tendency to turn a blind eye to our many planks (cf. Matt 7:7). With such an unremitting belief in the virtue of individuality, then, the question remains: has Kierkegaard left *any* space for ecclesiology? Could we indeed invite him back to Church? And if we did, would he even turn up?

Defending Kierkegaard's Ecclesiology

Although the case against a Kierkegaardian ecclesiology may appear overwhelming, there are a number of reasons to show restraint from an outright rejection of Kierkegaard's positive ecclesial value. One must take into account that, contrary to how he is often portrayed, Kierkegaard's polemical stance in the attack literature is not the only available source of his ecclesial vision. Not only this, but the attack literature itself can hardly be said to be without value for ecclesiology, especially when it is interpreted as a contextual homiletical moment within a broader vision. Although a number of approaches might be taken in Kierkegaard's defence, there are four primary aspects to which our attention should be drawn: his positive conceptions of the Church; his reflections on ecclesial "reformation"; his nuanced conception of the individual; and his momentarily diagnostic (or deconstructive) emphasis.

Ecclesial Conceptions

The first thing that could be noted in Kierkegaard's ecclesiological defence is that, in his own life, he truly was committed to the church congregation: "Most of his life Kierkegaard had been one of the most regular churchgoers in Copenhagen."[26] Although there is more to the life of a congregation than Sunday attendance, it is evident throughout his everyday personal and social life that the Church played a major role.[27] This

25. *Søren Kierkegaard's Journals and Papers*, 2:2009, 405.

26. Holm, "Kierkegaard and the Church," 113.

27. See chapter 2.

would seem implausible if Kierkegaard had truly felt that the Church per se had no real value within the Christian life. Indeed, it is noteworthy that Kierkegaard only resorted to full "attack" once he realized that his prior corrective attempts through his other writings had failed. As for his *conception* of the Church, although we have noted an absence of positivity, there are glimmers of hope elsewhere in his writings.

Beyond the "attack" itself, Kierkegaard makes a number of references to the Church as a concept, and even refers to the Church as the "true mother" of the single individual,[28] a passage which Kirkpatrick takes to be evidence for a "positive ecclesiology."[29] Kierkegaard even makes the statement that he blames most of the heresies in Christianity not upon the Church per se, but upon a truncated "doctrine of 'the Church,'" which had resulted in national Christendom.[30] Furthermore, in *Practice in Christianity*, we find Kierkegaard's lucid account of the difference between the "Church militant" and the "Church triumphant,"[31] and—again in the journals—a particular engagement with the Augsburg confession in which he highlights the implicit existential dimension in the phrase "communion of saints" (emphasis, of course, upon the word "saints"— i.e., those who truly live out their faith in ardent sacrifice).[32] Kierkegaard is concerned about any definition of the Church which shortcuts the existential, where *merely* assenting to a particular doctrine or executing particular exterior practices renders the Church "the Church." Kierkegaard wants to define the Church not by its exteriority but by its interiority. In one sense, his approach merely mirrors Paul's focus in Romans 2:28–9 on the "circumcision of the heart" for Jews. Indeed, if we were to map Kierkegaard's emphases onto Paul's language in that passage, it would run something like this:

> For no one is a [Christian] who is merely one outwardly, nor is [Church membership] outward and physical. But a [Christian] is one inwardly, and [Church membership] is a matter of the

28. *Søren Kierkegaard's Journals and Papers*, 1:596, 242.

29. Kirkpatrick, *Attacks on Christendom in a World Come of Age*, 218.

30. *Søren Kierkegaard's Journals and Papers*, 2:2045, 420.

31. The "Church triumphant" purports to live out its full eschatological inheritance *now*, whereas the "Church militant" self-consciously embraces its call to suffering and sacrificial witness, awaiting its full consummation. Kierkegaard, *Practice in Christianity*, 211–32.

32. *Søren Kierkegaard's Journals and Papers*, 1:600, 240.

heart, by the Spirit, not by the letter. His praise is not from man
but from God. (cf. Rom 2:28–9)

Being a true member of the Church is not a matter of status in the eyes of
others, but is unconditionally "a matter of the heart" because it requires
faith. Indeed, for Kierkegaard the Church must "walk in the footsteps of
the faith that our father Abraham had" (Rom 4:12).

Although Kierkegaard's existential impetus continually underpins
his ecclesial conceptions, it cannot be doubted that he not only had a
fairly clear "doctrine" of the Church,[33] but that he believed *in* the Church
as a necessary aspect of Christian witness in the world.[34] Indeed, behind
Kierkegaard's stringent call for the overturning of the tables lies a true
zeal for the Father's house (cf. John 2:14–17). It is such zeal which leads to
Kierkegaard's nuanced thoughts on the concept of "reformation."

Reforming Impetus

Kierkegaard regularly reflected upon the complex task and implications
of "reforming" the Church. Somewhat ambiguously, he remained both
approving and skeptical of its prospects. His primary suspicion of reformational aspirations in his own day was that some might use the project
of reformation as another form of veiled Christendom:

> Dabblers in reforming are more corrupting than the most cor-
> rupt established order, because reforming is the highest and
> therefore dabbling in it is the most corrupting of all. Let the es-
> tablished order have faults, many of them, say what you wish—if
> you are not willing to walk *in the character* of being a reformer,
> then hold your tongue about reforming.[35]

It is evident that, for Kierkegaard, reformation is a truly noble enter-
prise ("the highest"), and for this reason it requires great existential

33. As Johnson notes, "To assert that his doctrine of the Church is defective is
different from asserting that he had no doctrine at all." Johnson, "Kierkegaard and the
Church," 64.

34. See Kirkpatrick's helpful summation: "Near the beginning of his life, Kierkegaard showed a far greater concern for both a formal ecclesiology but also for the church
itself . . . to impact the lives of its members," while adding the key caveat: "The question
that must remain open is whether Kierkegaard ultimately maintained these desires
into his later life." Kirkpatrick, *Attacks on Christendom*, 219. I believe it is possible that
he did, and that the attack literature "indirectly" served this purpose.

35. Kierkegaard, *Judge for Yourself!*, 212.

responsibility. It cannot, therefore, be something one merely "takes up" as a novel activity, as something one seeks to achieve without heeding the necessary personal toll. Indeed, the "trendiness" of both ecclesial and political reforming in mid-nineteenth-century Denmark proved, for Kierkegaard, that such pretensions were indeed "worldly" rather than God-ordained at heart: "'God's thoughts are not man's thoughts.' Once it was God's thought that a reformation was needed, and no one at that time wanted to be the reformer. Now everyone wants to be the reformer—thus it is certain that a reformation is not God's thought."[36] One does not merely "volunteer" for ecclesial reformation; they must be called to it in fear and trembling.

The other complication, of course, is that wide-scale "reformation" on Kierkegaardian terms, is inherently paradoxical. How does one stop reformation becoming yet another movement of the non-individuated crowd following the *Zeitgeist*? Kierkegaard's stringent category of the single individual means that Church-wide reformation is technically unquantifiable, and may only lead to another situation of the crowd assuming the transformations of others. What Kierkegaard wants is *personal* reformation, which can only occur on an individual basis: "It is not 'doctrine' which ought to be revised, and it is not 'the Church' which ought to be reformed . . . No, it is existences which should be revised."[37] Kierkegaard worries that even the call to "reform" the Church could become a sly Christendomian ploy to keep oneself preoccupied from existential reformation. Only from this foundation, then, can there be any change in the Church, because the Church cannot exist without the individuality of its members. Kierkegaard admired Luther's Reformation because it was led by a personally transformed witness, but he criticized the fact that Luther subsequently became an imitative prototype for the masses and, thus, another "papal" mediator to God: "Ironically enough, his reformation engendered the same evil he was fighting against—an exegetical spirit of bondage, a hyper-orthodox Lutheran coercion that was just as bad as the Pope's."[38]

Although Kierkegaard rejects the aspiration to be a "reformer" himself, he could perhaps be seen as hearkening back to what Luther and Calvin were initially attempting in their own contexts. Indeed,

36. *Søren Kierkegaard's Journals and Papers*, 3:3730, 730–31.
37. *Søren Kierkegaard's Journals and Papers*, 3:3731, 731.
38. *Søren Kierkegaard's Journals and Papers*, 4:3724, 727.

Kierkegaard's call to boycott the Church has been described as an act of "negative reformation."[39] The difference is that Kierkegaard never presented a more overtly constructive account, and certainly got nowhere near forming an ecclesial establishment of his own, even if—somewhat bizarrely—there were contemporary rumors that some within Denmark were preparing to leave the established Church and "form a new religious society in the Kierkegaardian spirit."[40] Despite the fact that Kierkegaard would have objected to something like this being founded in his name, it does at least indicate that "the Kierkegaardian spirit" was indeed capable of ecclesial inspiration. Regardless of his own legacy, the concept of "reforming" remained a live category for Kierkegaard, as something to be undertaken with the highest sense of responsibility. Furthermore, Kierkegaard's indirect commitment to reforming the Church belies an inescapable commitment to the existential *being* of the Church, something Kierkegaard clearly held in highest esteem. How, though, does such a view of the corporate faith relate to his category of the single individual?

Relational Individualism

As noted, Kierkegaard held individuality as being essential to Christian faith, in distinction from the corrosive impact of crowd-consciousness. However, Kierkegaard also makes an interesting distinction between a "crowd" and a "community," both of which the Church may *become* at any given time. In the crowd, the individual itself is abolished as one of the mere numbers; however, in a true "community" the individual becomes "qualitatively essential" as the "presupposition" and "guarantee" for the community's existence: "'Community' is certainly more than a sum, but yet it is truly a sum of ones."[41] As Kirmmse aptly notes, "In asserting [his] radical individualism, Kierkegaard does not want to rule out entirely the concept of the congregation . . . but wishes to qualify it."[42] This qualification points toward a complementary dialectic between congregation and individual in which neither may exist without the other.

---

39. Kirkpatrick, *Attacks on Christendom*, 184.

40. Croxall, *Glimpses and Impressions*, 86.

41. Contrastingly, he adds, "the public is nonsense—a sum of negative ones, of ones who are not ones, who become ones through the sum instead of the sum becoming a sum of the ones." *Søren Kierkegaard's Journals and Papers*, 3:2952, 318.

42. Kirmmse, *Kierkegaard in Golden Age Denmark*, 407.

It cannot be escaped, of course, that reading Kierkegaard's individualistic focus today can often be difficult to stomach, especially when the negative impact of individualism upon the modern self continues to run riot. Many might be tempted to see Kierkegaard's thinking as a gene pool for twentieth-century preoccupations with psychoanalysis, with Nietzschean nihilistic solitude, or Ayn Rand's *Virtue of Selfishness*, with all their potentially devastating social effects. However, it is patently obvious that Kierkegaard's use of the "single individual" is used in a very particular way,[43] with particular theological qualification. Kierkegaard never begins with oneself *in se*,[44] but with the self before God and *for* God. Indeed, the action of God to draw us to himself—a favorite motif of Kierkegaard's discourses—looms large over any attempt to construe the individual as self-interested or self-involved. It is precisely because of true worship and true discipleship that Kierkegaard believes one cannot play communitarian games with one's walk with God, nor be led into false certainties by the shifting movements of the crowd: "It is not the single individual's relationship to the community or congregation which determines his relationship to God, but his relationship to God which determines his relationship to the congregation."[45] Pattison notes that Kierkegaard is looking for "a way of saying that the individual's relation to the revelation of God in Jesus Christ must have a basis other than the mere fact of participation in the life of the Church."[46] Indeed, if the Church is to have any content at all, it requires the realization of the importance of the single individual *by* the single individual.

This is essentially why Kierkegaard's attack on Christendom—or something like it—cannot be ignored within any robust ecclesiological

43. Although the category of the single individual "always relates to inward deepening," Kierkegaard notes that it may be used differently at different times, to bring about either "awakening" or "composure." *Søren Kierkegaard's Journals and Papers*, 2:2013, 406–7.

44. Kierkegaard's earlier journal entries even reveal significant criticism of self-interested individualism: "There is nothing more dangerous for a man, nothing more paralyzing, than a certain isolating self-scrutiny." *Søren Kierkegaard's Journals and Papers*, 2:1971, 390. He even suggests that the answer to the problem (of both self-scrutiny *and* crowd-consciousness) lies in—of all things—a better ecclesiology: "Who will point to a middle course between this self-consuming while reflecting as if one were the only human being who has ever lived or ever will—and a foolish confidence in the ordinary human commune naufragium? This is what an authentic doctrine of a Church should bring about." *Søren Kierkegaard's Journals and Papers*, 2:1970, 390.

45. *Søren Kierkegaard's Journals and Papers*, 1:595, 241.

46. Pattison, "Christianity after the Church," 197.

focus. As Kirkpatrick notes, "Kierkegaard did not emphasize the individual at the expense of the church, but rather fought against the church for the sake of the individual."[47] Kierkegaard's battle with the Church is indeed for the sake of the Church, to save its individuals from what Holm calls "the triumphant self-celebration of the congregation," whereby the congregation becomes an unreliable mediator of God's Word for the individual.[48] Thus, a concept of "communitarianism," however manifested, is no more faithful to ecclesiology than a concept of "individuality" per se. If anything, communitarianism can become more harmful because it *seems* to possess closer kinship with the Church, and thus, may be prone to a subtler self-deception. For Kierkegaard, the Church and the individual cannot be separated by any Romanticized ideal of a collective people. This is not to reject the concept of community, but merely to hold the real and the ideal together so as to evade the perpetuation of the ideal at the expense of the real, as we saw in the previous chapter. If Kierkegaard's distinction between the Church militant and the Church triumphant is true, then it should always be at the forefront of the Church's self-understanding. Wherever triumph supersedes militancy entirely, Kierkegaard wonders whether this can truly be called the Church: "Only the Church militant is the truth, or the truth is that as long as the Church endures in this world it is the militant Church that is related to Christ in his abasement even if drawn to him from on high."[49]

Such depictions of the evident "tenets" of the Church, however, appear fleetingly. For the most part Kierkegaard refrains from focusing upon what the Church *ought* to be and focuses predominantly upon what it ought *not* to be based on the debased version before him in Christendom.

Deconstructive Emphasis

As noted above, diagnostic deconstruction of the Church is what Kierkegaard seems to major on, and his attack literature in particular stands out as the greatest evidence against his value for ecclesial upbuilding. However, deconstruction has always been seen as a vital task of the prophetic office, as even claimed by that ancient and awkward ecclesiologist of the Hebrews, Jeremiah: "See, I have set you this day over nations and

47. Kirkpatrick, *Attacks on Christendom in a World Come of Age*, 219.
48. Holm, "Kierkegaard and the Church," 126–27.
49. Kierkegaard, *Practice in Christianity*, 232.

over kingdoms, to pluck up and to break down, to destroy and to over-throw, to build and to plant" (Jer 1:10). One must see the state of the Church in its true reality before attempting to depict its ideality, and if necessary to "destroy" before attempting to "build."[50] These are not sepa-rate tasks, of course. How can you diagnose a problem without having some idea of why the problem is a problem in the first place (i.e., why the Church is not *acting* like it *is*)? This ontological question of what the Church "is," is bound up with any attack upon its practices. A clear sense of the "ideal" for the Church is the very grounds for the "real" critique of it.[51] Even though Kierkegaard may have wrongly separated the two tasks too abruptly, his deconstructive ecclesiology still poses the possibility of reconstruction,[52] especially when he calls the boycotters to leave the "magnificent buildings" of Christendom—not in order to go off and form sects, but to worship God once again "in simplicity."[53] In the aftermath of the demolition—indeed, in the very call to enact the demolition—the vociferous voice of the melancholy prophet is calling the Church back to its maker and maintainer, Jesus Christ, who sustains the Church by the power of the Spirit.[54]

By calling the individuals of the Church back to Christ, even back to their personal relationships to Christ, Kierkegaard beckons the possibil-ity of a truly re-formed Church. Kierkegaard calls for a Church whose basis is a true communion of saints, comprising those whose faith leads them to follow Jesus wherever he might call them, however much they may struggle along the way. To paint the glorious ideal of the Church, in the way that a Calvin or perhaps an Aquinas does, is indeed essential, but

50. Kierkegaard is aware that his approach "does not presuppose the definitions as given and understood" but seeks to "awaken," "provoke," and "sharpen thought," to be "a gadfly" who is deliberately "impatient," thus deliberately aggravating. *Søren Kierkegaard's Journals and Papers*, 1:641, 263.

51. As Holm summates, "One thing is certain: the impassioned attack on the Church found in Kierkegaard's writings would never have occurred if it had not been for the fact that Church was very important to him and a place he cared strongly about." Holm, "Kierkegaard and the Church," 127.

52. It is for this reason that no connection should be made here to Derridean de-construction, whereby there is no guarantee of reconstruction according to any fixed norm or "ideal." See the brief critique of deconstructive readings of Kierkegaard in chapter 1.

53. Kierkegaard, *Attack upon Christendom*, 140.

54. See Kierkegaard's account of the role of the Spirit as the "royal coachman" to the "team" of horses, the Church. Kierkegaard, *For Self-Examination*, 87, 107–9.

it is perhaps not always appropriate. It may certainly not be the appropriate thing to emphasize at a time where such a view could be co-opted to remain within the cosy confines of a Christendom. Even the most christologically profound ecclesiological emphases, depending on the moment, might be used to keep Christ himself well and truly buried away from the Church. As Kierkegaard observes in his incisive poetic analogy between Joseph of Arimathea and Christendom: both ask for the State's permission to bury Christ in their own tomb, and both are granted it.[55] As the Prophets and the Reformers knew, high views of "the Church" can just as easily be used to provide an intoxicating and illusory "peace" when there is "no peace" (cf. Jer 6:14), rendering the individuals of the Church anaemic to the cost of discipleship,[56] and rendering them powerless to challenge ecclesiastical authority when the time may come to do so.

The Ecclesial Individual in "Post-Christendom"

What, then, of today? How might we bring Kierkegaard's "anti-ecclesiology," as David Law called it,[57] to bear upon our own far-removed post-Christendom context? Perhaps it would be better not to call it an "anti-ecclesiology" but rather a "partial ecclesiology." It is partial in two senses: firstly, because it is incomplete and requires further construction and application (as this chapter has attempted to do); and secondly, because it is both biased and pointed toward a very particular situation.[58] In post-Christendom, of course, this situation is no longer present. It was Paul Tillich's student, Harvey Cox, who famously said, in *The Secular City*, "The process of secularisation [has] alleviated Kierkegaard's problem."[59] Does this mean that all Kierkegaard's regaling against the impossibility of Christianity within Christendom is simply past its use-by date, never to regain its relevance bar some unlikely re-Constantinization of the West?

---

55. See *Søren Kierkegaard's Journals and Papers*, 1:359, 149.

56. For Kierkegaard, "treating the current existing, temporal church as the church triumphant is an attempt to take hold of what can only be achieved through a lengthy process of discipleship, suffering, and sacrifice." Tilley, "The Church," 212.

57. Law, "Kierkegaard's Anti-Ecclesiology," 86–108.

58. This incompleteness is the cause of another critique by Law: "[Kierkegaard] gives us insufficient guidance on how to be Christians in the concrete situations in which we find ourselves in this troubled world of ours." Law, "Discipleship and Church," 18.

59. Cox, *Secular City*, 91.

Even if one considers the complexities of what "secularism" actually entails,[60] or indeed whether various forms of "neo-Christendom" may well still exist,[61] for many it remains difficult to see how a theological position so acutely targeted toward a pre-secular context could equally relate to its aftermath. However, this is only the case if one conceives of "Christendom" in a purely historical mode.

Redefining Christendom?

As has been hinted at variously throughout the chapters of this book,[62] Christendom—as Kierkegaard saw it—is not only a literal connection between Church, state, and nation. Rather, the same implications of such a situation may continually afflict the Church's life in any epoch.[63] What, after all, *was* Christendom? It was a historical situation lasting numerous centuries in which Christian faith—*through* the auspices of the Church— was seen to be at one with the power of the state. Kierkegaard is primarily concerned with the *implications* of this situation, with what this situation *does* to individual Christians when Christian faith is en vogue, when Christian faith is existentially enslaved to an external source which is not God. Indeed, well before the "attack" period, Kierkegaard was describing Christendom by its "gangrenous" effects.[64] If "Christendom" refers to any such situation in which Christian faith becomes axiomatic by appeal to social forces beyond the individual, then for Kierkegaard, the authenticity of such Christianity is corrupted. This means that Kierkegaard's conception of Christendom, though based on an actual historical situation, rests more determinatively upon the content of the Christian faith, and thus his lament over Christendom has more to do with a theological principle about the Church's "existential" mission than about one particular epoch of the Western Church.

Curiously, Oliver O'Donovan notes the eschatological possibilities of a post-Christendom situation which further curtail the notion of a

---

60. See Warner et al, *Varieties of Secularism.*

61. See Mahn, *Becoming a Christian in Christendom,* 3–27.

62. See especially chapters 3, 6, and 7.

63. See Tilley's fairly open-ended construal of Kierkegaard's view of Christendom: "a geographical and sociological construct that misunderstands the church, faith, and how a Christian ought to relate to the world." Tilley, "Christendom," 210.

64. See Kierkegaard, *Fear and Trembling* and *Repetition,* 263.

purely historical interpretation, relating its effects far more closely with the implications of mission:

> The conversion of Constantine, with all that followed from it, was only an intermediate frontier which developed from the effective mission of the church to society and led back to it . . . Christendom has ended, we say—but in what sense of the word "end"? Has it fulfilled itself in transition from the rule of the kings to the rule of the Christ, or has it simply been eclipsed by the vicissitudes of mission, perhaps to return in another form or, if not return, to provide a standing reminder of the political frontier which mission must always address?[65]

Within some forms of the "post-Christendom" narrative there can indeed be a kind of self-congratulation at the decline of the Church and a denigrating of Gospel proclamation, as though the Church's diminished public influence was wholly beneficial to the purposes of mission.[66] Such perspectives miss O'Donovan's qualified concession that, although imperfect, Christendom was simply the result of the kind of effectiveness in mission which we are no longer accustomed to seeing in the West. This is a perspective James K. A. Smith has also observed. Following O'Donovan's cautiously positive account, he argues that the impetus to influence society with the virtues inherent to the Gospel means that it must be possible, on some level, to see the project of Christendom as "a missional endeavour."[67] These are interesting alternatives to the usual narrative around the legacy and/or meaning of Christendom. Indeed, one wonders whether it might even be possible to construct a missional understanding of "Christendom" for our secular era which was somehow more congenial to Kierkegaard's existential concerns than the Danish manifestation with which he was primarily engaged. I expect it would be a difficult task to convince *Kierkegaard* that Christendom was redeemable, however it was understood. But given the very different situation of the Western Church in the twenty-first century, it is certainly worth considering the potential implications of his dictum that "times are different, and different times have different requirements."[68]

---

65. O'Donovan, *Desire of the Nations*, 243–44.

66. See, for example, Murray, *Post-Christendom*, 217–50.

67. Smith, *Awaiting the King*, 162–63.

68. Kierkegaard, *For Self-Examination*, 15.

Whether one views Christendom-as-epoch as having been either a good or a bad thing,[69] just as Christendom-as-mission can recur in other forms of the Church's "political frontier," so too can Christendom-as-sickness. It can do so at any time within various microcosmic forms in how the Church understands itself and its role within the world, even within a particular denomination or local church—not just within an explicitly "national" or "established" Church. Like the "poison" Kierkegaard describes in the attack literature, it may have cause to return in new forms, re-armed against the antibodies that first fought it off, with or without state powers. This may happen whenever the Church—local or universal—is content to rest in its crowds, in its comforts, in its finances, in its influence, or in its cultural affability, rather than resting in God's protection alone: "But woe to the Christian Church when it has been victorious in this world, for then it is not the Church that has been victorious but the world."[70] Such a condition can even occur for a Church that believes itself to be threatened by rampant secularity beyond its walls, or even for a Church in self-imposed retreat. The illusion of Christendom—as Kierkegaard saw it—allows the Church to trust in its comforts and numbers (however large *or* small) and to count upon its people as numerical resources rather than individuals in need of ongoing faith and formation. Beyond its walls, the issue of the Church's faithful witness before an increasingly apathetic Western religious climate renders Kierkegaard's voice all the more essential in spelling out what ecclesial faithfulness means at a time when the Church must be especially clear about what and whom it stands for.

The Church Interior

One of Kierkegaard's key foci to this end was, as has been seen, the importance of spiritual interiority (or "inwardness"). This is what is most

---

69. For a representative example of the negative view from a Kierkegaardian perspective, see Westphal: "Today's task is different. But not entirely. For after Christendom is not the same as before Christendom. Remnants or traces of that Christendom still exist, and . . . there is a strong nostalgia for a Christendom partly remembered and partly imagined. What Kierkegaard helps us see is that theology need not mourn the steady demise of Christendom. Whatever advantages it may have brought to the Christian churches came at a high price. Too high." Westphal, "Kierkegaard, Theology, and Post-Christendom," 507.

70. Kierkegaard, *Practice in Christianity*, 223.

lacking in those churches which appear to be most comfortable with their "exteriority," especially those focused upon evangelism, cultural engagement, and community action. Such emphases are indeed essential operations for the Church's witness to the Gospel and the kingdom at *all* times, yet in their modern instantiation there is a tendency for a perpetually external focus to come at the expense of the spiritual integrity of the interior. The spiritual impulses germane to the Pietistic traditions (which were hugely influential on Kierkegaard) such as contemplation, prayer, steadfastness, virtue, and others, are easily lost in the perpetual pursuit of public statements, marketing strategies, and reputational affiliations—whether political, societal, or denominational. Such outward-facing endeavors may often be called "missional" but too often resemble the reasons Kierkegaard criticized the perpetually "public" trajectory of Christendom.

He argued how this problem even manifested in the very architecture of church gatherings:

> Even our churches express how superficial and externalized everything becomes. When one enters one of the old churches with those closed pews, with the old gallery, one unconsciously gets an impression of how much can lie hidden in a man's deep inwardness—of which those closed pews were indeed a symbol. But now everything is a lounge; churches are also built this way nowadays. It is awkward and bad taste for someone to have an interior life of his own; it is an affectation—"Why should he have something like that for himself"—no, we are a public.[71]

Kierkegaard saw that even the trappings of ecclesial furniture can speak of formerly vital existential-ecclesial practices which have now become dormant, as though the older closed pews were a kind of shrine to that bygone existential fervor. This critique chimes in with the ways that interiority is more easily forgotten in the contemporary marketized Church, where indeed "everything is a lounge" in the effort to maximise attendance at the expense of existential participation. This problem has been accentuated with the dubious advent of "online worship," which potentially becomes, simultaneously, more individualistic and less congregational, and yet even *less* inclined to the devotional interiority Kierkegaard was emphasizing.[72] It is in this sense that we can see a clear difference

71. *Søren Kierkegaard's Journals and Papers*, 1:594, 241.

72. For an extensive approach to Kierkegaard's spiritual emphases, see Evans, *Kierkegaard and Spirituality*.

in the kind of "individuality" Kierkegaard advocates compared with the "individualism" which pervades modernity in general.

The Ecclesial Individual

Contrary to expectations, it may well be the recovery of the category of the "single individual" which might help the contemporary Church understand something core to its message and being. Although many movements to reform contemporary Church mission highlight individuality as a primary problem or even a *cause* of diminishing faith, for Kierkegaard it is precisely the opposite: a Church in which faith is diminishing actively illuminates the importance of individual response. A return to the ecclesial individual might even be a Gospel witness *to* a hyper-individualistic society like today's, by demonstrating—*through* the revitalized Church—that individualism itself will only bring death, not life. As Hauerwas and Willimon noted in their now-classic book, *Resident Aliens* (1989), "We serve the world by showing it something that it is not, namely, a place where God is forming a family out of strangers."[73] Indeed, the very self-understanding of the Church should rightly contradict individualistic emphases: "It is as isolated individuals that we lack the ethical and theological resources to be faithful disciples . . . The church enables us to be better people than we could have been if left to our own devices."[74] True though this is, critiques of individualism also miss the fact that to highlight the individual is not necessarily to welcome "the European Enlightenment's infatuation with the individual self."[75] Contrastingly, individual transformation can actually be a meaningful starting point for thinking of the *telos* of Church, which is formed not merely upon the abstract basis of "community" (whatever that may actually mean), but upon faith in Jesus Christ.

Such a view would have no qualms with a critique of individualism, but it would curtail the ever-present (often inadvertent) danger of a situation in which one's faith may not only be served by—but lived out by—*others*. Here, as van der Ven aptly notes, one must remember that "ecclesiological reflections sometimes lapse into a kind of group

73. Hauerwas and Willimon, *Resident Aliens*, 83.
74. Hauerwas and Willimon, *Resident Aliens*, 80–81.
75. Hauerwas and Willimon, *Resident Aliens*, 81.

romanticism."[76] In such cases, the ideal of the "crowd" becomes amorphous and impregnable to critique, and the individual within it is not only minimized, but abolished, with detrimental effects upon the authenticity of the "crowd" itself. Particularly in post-Christendom, with all the complexities which comprise the different levels of social belonging between various groups and individuals, Kierkegaard's "single individual" may be essential in any theological approach to ecclesiology which places a high value on the outworking of Christian faith within and between its members. To emphasize as strongly as Kierkegaard did that the individual's response must be defined as *prior* to any cultural conceptions of "crowd," "group," or "mass," may help to ensure the Church is not defined along purely sociological or anthropological lines.[77] Rather, its theological center, founded upon the true reception of the Gospel in believers, is prioritized and guarded against the theological and existential problems which can emerge from an emphatic sense of group-think. This foundation may also be the best way to approach the kinds of cultural individualism that the Church ought to defy, since *this* community is a community in the world like no other, a community of individuals who have become *more than* individuals in joint communion with Christ, who alone may be called their congregational cornerstone.

The Church lays claim to such alterity because it is grounded in a theological freedom which is characterized not in Enlightenment self-autonomy, but in the Gospel. As Lesslie Newbigin notes,

> The individualistic model of freedom which pervades our society and controls the way we approach every question has to be challenged by the gospel affirmation that we are not naturally free but that we may receive the gift of freedom when we are in Christ, and that in every area of life there is only one Lord to be obeyed, namely the Lord Jesus Christ.[78]

---

76. Van der Ven, *Ecclesiology in Context*, 250.

77. This is not to say that a typically "Hauerwasian" ecclesial view, for example, affirms a purely sociological ecclesiology (a high view of the Church as a "body" or "family" could hardly be deemed "untheological"), but it is to notice the possible anthropocentric emanations which may flow *from* this minimisation of the individual's role in the community of faith, whereby such a notion of the all-inclusivity of Church might dominate the individual's faith to the point of effective abolition (as Kierkegaard believed to be the case within Christendom).

78. Newbigin, *Truth to Tell*, 72.

Kierkegaard could (and should) have done far more to combat the problems of self-autonomy in light of the Gospel. However, he succeeds in highlighting—perhaps more clearly than any other thinker in the modern period—what can go awry, existentially *and* ecclesiologically, when the significance of individual decision is minimized by an assumed conception of the congregation. Kierkegaard shows that, by so emphasizing "congregation," we may not end up with a congregation at all—not a *Christian* one, at least. Notably, he himself even predicted the dawn of a post-Christendom era where, once the masses had realized precisely what Christianity entailed for them *as individuals*, a mass exodus from the Church was inevitable. It would be, he forewarned, "a dreadful Reformation . . . identified by people 'falling away' from Christianity by the millions."[79] In this, we can be sure that he was absolutely correct.

Kierkegaard as Proto-Ecclesiologist

Far from being an anti-ecclesiologist, then, Kierkegaard's reflections remain vital to ecclesiological discussions in the twenty-first century. Kierkegaard's "single individual" is actually not "single" at all but united to Christ, and—therewith—to his body. This body is individually membered, whose substance is built upon the genuine *individual* confessions of faith in Christ, upon which he builds his Church (cf. Matt 16:16–18). Such confessions of faith are, of course, proclamations of the Gospel, despite all social norms, tyrannies, or seductions—including both individualism and communitarianism. The Church faces the temptation to diminish the implications of this Gospel in different ways in every generation, from pride, from greed, or from fear. Whether faced by the ruthless threat of the Assyrian sword or the charming invitation to the Babylonian banquet, the Church—through its members—fights such temptations which ask them to forsake "the cost of discipleship" for something else.[80]

79. *Søren Kierkegaard's Journals and Papers*, 3:3737, 733.

80. It is well known, of course, that the famous reflections on discipleship by another modern Lutheran, Dietrich Bonhoeffer, were significantly influenced by Kierkegaard's own critique of Lutheran Christendom. As Tietz notes, "Bonhoeffer agrees with Kierkegaard's existential perspective but misses a strong concept of sociality. Kierkegaard has some helpful insight here, but does not develop a relational concept of personhood and church. Bonhoeffer objects that in Kierkegaard's approach the encounter with Christ only takes place in the inner world of a human being, not in a situation of real encounter with somebody else. Yet in Bonhoeffer's view only from here can a responsible existence be conceived." Tietz, "Dietrich Bonhoeffer," 60. Bonhoeffer

In this sense, "Christendom," if seen not merely as historical "period" but as perennial "poison," must be diagnosed and treated before its influence upon the body becomes too pervasive.[81] There are indeed other poisons which infect the Church, and one of these, to be sure, is individualism. But there is a time for everything under the sun (Eccl 3:1), as Kierkegaard well knew, and there is always a time in which Kierkegaard's inconvenient voice must enter the ecclesiological party, whenever we forget what is truly at stake when we speak the name "Jesus Christ" in unison. As Kierkegaard says, "The situation is this. If everyone around defines himself as being a Christian just like 'the others,' then no one, if it is looked at this way, is really confessing Christ."[82] Awkward questions like this are those from which we, the Church, should never presume to graduate.

---

could even be seen as having constructed a kind of Kierkegaardian ecclesiology, given that he evidently built on many of Kierkegaard's fundamental existential emphases, referring to "Kierkegaard, who spoke like no other about the individuality of human beings" (*Sanctorum Communio*, 249) while branching out into more overtly ecclesiological conceptions which Kierkegaard could never have emphasized within his own context, such as the idea of "Christ existing as church-community." See Bonhoeffer, *Sanctorum Communio*, 189–211.

81. See Kierkegaard, *Judge for Yourself!*, 202.

82. Kierkegaard, *Practice in Christianity*, 219.

Bibliography

Allen, David L. "A Tale of Two Roads: Homiletics and Biblical Authority." *Journal of the Evangelical Theological Society* 43 (2000) 489–515.

Atkins, Stuart Pratt. *The Testament of Werther in Poetry and Drama*. Cambridge: Harvard University Press, 1949.

Backhouse, Stephen. *Kierkegaard: A Single Life*. Grand Rapids: Zondervan, 2016.

———. *Kierkegaard's Critique of Christian Nationalism*. Oxford: Oxford University Press, 2011.

Barrett, Lee C. "Faith, Works, and the Uses of the Law: Kierkegaard's Appropriation of Lutheran Doctrine." In *For Self Examination and Judge for Yourself!*, edited by Robert Perkins, 77–109. International Kierkegaard Commentary 21. Macon, GA: Mercer University Press, 2002.

———. "Karl Barth: The Dialectic of Attraction and Repulsion." In *Kierkegaard's Influence on Theology*, vol. 1, *German Protestant Theology*, edited by Jon Stewart, 1–42. Farnham, UK: Ashgate, 2012.

———. "Kierkegaard's Theological Legacy." In *T&T Clark Companion to the Theology of Kierkegaard*, edited by Aaron P. Edwards and David J. Gouwens, 159–74. London: T. & T. Clark, 2020.

Barth, Karl. "April 8, 1917." In *The Early Preaching of Karl Barth: Fourteen Sermons with Commentary by William H. Willimon*. Translated by John E. Wilson. Louisville: Westminster John Knox, 2009.

———. "Barth, 24. Juni 1920." In *Karl Barth—Eduard Thurneysen Briefwechsel*, pt. 1, *1913–1921, Gesamtausgabe*, vol. 3. Zurich: TVZ, 1973.

———. "But Take Heart—24 December 1963." In *Call for God: New Sermons from Basel Prison*, translated by A. T. Mackay. London: SCM, 1967.

———. *Church Dogmatics*. Edited and translated by G. W. Bromiley and T. F. Torrance. 4 vols. in 13 pts. Edinburgh: T. & T. Clark, 1956–75.

———. *The Epistle to the Romans*. Translated by E. C. Hoskyns. 6th ed. London: Oxford University Press, 1968.

———. *The Göttingen Dogmatics: Instruction in the Christian Religion*. Vol. 1. Translated by G. W. Bromiley. Grand Rapids: Eerdmans, 1991.

———. *Homiletics*. Translated by Geoffrey W. Bromiley and Donald E. Daniels. Louisville: Westminster John Knox, 1991.

———. "The Lord Who Has Mercy on You—27 December 1959." In *Call for God: New Sermons from Basel Prison*, translated by A. T. Mackay. London: SCM, 1967.

———. "Mozart's Freedom." In *Wolfgang Amadeus Mozart*, translated by Clarence K. Pott, 40–63. Grand Rapids: Eerdmans, 1986.

————. "On the Sinking of the Titanic." In *The Word in This World: Two Sermons*, translated by Christopher Asprey, edited by Kurt I. Johanson, 31–42. Vancouver: Regent College Publishing, 2007.

————. *Prayer and Preaching*. Translated by Sara Frantz Terrien. London: SCM, 1964.

————. "A Thank You and a Bow—Kierkegaard's Reveille." In *Fragments Grave and Gay*, translated by M. Rumscheidt. London: Fontana, 1971.

————. *The Theology of Schleiermacher: Lectures at Göttingen, Winter Semester of 1923/24*. Translated by G. W. Bromiley. Grand Rapids: Eerdmans, 1982.

————. "To Dr. Martin Rumscheidt, Toronto—1 November, 1967." In *Letters 1961–1968*, translated by G. W. Bromiley, 272–73. Grand Rapids: Eerdmans, 1981.

————. "To Hermann Diem—9 March 1964." In *Letters 1961–1968*, translated by G. W. Bromiley, 154. Grand Rapids: Eerdmans, 1981.

————. "What Is Enough—31 December 1962." In *Call for God: New Sermons from Basel Prison*, translated by A. T. Mackay. London: SCM, 1967.

————. *The Word of God and the Word of Man*. Translated by Douglas Horton. London: Hodder & Stoughton, 1928.

Bauckham, Richard. *James: Wisdom of James, Disciple of Jesus the Sage*. London: Routledge, 1999.

Bearden, Ronald. "To Tell or not to Tell: Theological Implications in Open-Ended Narrative Preaching." *Asbury Theological Journal* 55 (2000) 5–15.

Bebbington, D. W. *Evangelicalism in Modern Britain: A History from the 1730s to the 1980s*. New York: Routledge, 1989.

Becker-Theye, Betty. *The Seducer as Mythic Figure in Richardson, Laclos and Kierkegaard*. New York: Garland, 1988.

Benktson, B. E. "The Ministry." In *Theological Concepts in Kierkegaard*, edited by Niels Thulstrup and Marie Mikulová Thulstrup, 218–27. Bibliotheca Kierkegaardiana 5. Copenhagen: Reitzels, 1980.

Bonhoeffer, Dietrich. *Sanctorum Communio: A Theological Study of the Sociology of the Church*. Edited by Clifford J. Green. Translated by Reinhard Krauss and Nancy Lukens. Dietrich Bonhoeffer Works 1. Minneapolis: Fortress, 2009.

Bornedal, Peter. *Speech and System*. Copenhagen: Museum Tusculanum, 1997.

Brandt, Frithiof. *Søren Kierkegaard: His Life—His Works*. Translated by Ann R. Born. Copenhagen: Det Danske Selskab, 1963.

Brandt, Lori Unger. "Paul: Herald of Grace and Paradigm of Christian Living." In *Kierkegaard and the Bible*. Vol. 2, *The New Testament*, edited by Lee C. Barrett and Jon Stewart, 189–208. Farnham, UK: Ashgate, 2010.

Breuninger, Christian. "Søren Kierkegaard's Reformation of Expository Preaching." *Covenant Quarterly* 51 (1993) 21–36.

Brian, Rustin E. *Covering Up Luther: How Barth's Christology Challenged the Deus Absconditus That Haunts Modernity*. Eugene, OR: Cascade, 2013.

Brøchner, Hans. "The Recollections." In *Glimpses and Impressions of Kierkegaard*, edited by T. H. Croxall, 7–44. London: Nisbet, 1959.

Brown, Cynthia Bennett. *Believing Thinking, Bounded Theology: The Theological Methodology of Emil Brunner*. Cambridge: James Clarke, 2015.

Brown, James. *Kierkegaard, Heidegger, Buber and Barth: A Study of Subjectivity and Objectivity in Existentialist Thought*. New York: Collier, 1967.

————. *Subject and Object in Modern Theology*. New York: Collier, 1955.

Bukdahl, Jørgen. *Søren Kierkegaard and the Common Man*. Translated by Bruce H. Kirmmse. Grand Rapids: Eerdmans, 2001.

Bultmann, Rudolf. "Bultmann: Marburg, 10 December 1935." In *Karl Barth—Rudolf Bultmann: Letters 1922–1966*, translated by G. W. Bromiley, 82–83. Grand Rapids: Eerdmans, 1981.

Burgess, Andrew J. "Kierkegaard on Homiletics and the Genre of the Sermon." *Journal of Communication and Religion* 17 (1994) 17–31.

Busch, Eberhard. *Karl Barth & the Pietists: The Young Karl Barth's Critique of Pietism and Its Response*. Downers Grove: InterVarsity, 2004.

Calvin, John. *Commentaries*. Translated by Joseph Haroutunian. Philadelphia: Westminster, 1958.

———. *On the Christian Faith: Selections from the Institutes, Commentaries, and Tracts*. Translated by John T. McNeill. Indianapolis: Bobbs-Merrill, 1957.

Campbell-Nelson, John. "Kierkegaard's Christian Rhetoric." PhD diss., The School of Theology at Claremont, 1982.

Camus, Albert. *The Myth of Sisyphus and Other Essays*. Translated by Justin O' Brien. London: Penguin, 1988.

Carlyle, Thomas. *On Great Men*. London: Penguin, 1996.

Carson, D. A. *Becoming Conversant with the Emerging Church: Understanding a Movement and Its Implications*. Grand Rapids: Zondervan, 2005.

Chadwick, Owen. *The Reformation*. London: Penguin, 1979.

Coe, David L. "Kierkegaard's Forking for Extracts from Extracts of Luther's Sermons: Reviewing Kierkegaard's Laud and Lance of Luther." *Kierkegaard Studies Yearbook* (2011) 3–18.

———. "Preaching a Sigh: Søren Kierkegaard's Discourse on Martin Luther's Sermons." PhD diss., Concordia Seminary, St. Louis, 2011.

Collette, Jacques. *Kierkegaard: The Difficulty of Being Christian*. Notre Dame: University of Notre Dame Press, 1968.

Collins, James. *The Mind of Kierkegaard*. Princeton: Princeton University Press, 1983.

Come, Arnold B. *Kierkegaard as Theologian: Recovering My Self*. Montreal: McGill-Queen's University Press, 1997.

Cox, Harvey. *The Secular City: Secularization and Urbanization in Theological Perspective*. London: SCM, 1965.

Craddock, Fred B. *As One Without Authority*. Nashville: Parthenon, 1971.

———. *Overhearing the Gospel: Preaching and Teaching the Faith to Those Who Have Heard It All Before*. St. Louis: Chalice, 2002.

———. *Preaching*. Nashville: Abingdon, 1985.

Croxall, T. H., ed. *Glimpses and Impressions of Kierkegaard*. London: Nisbet, 1959.

Daise, Benjamin. *Kierkegaard's Socratic Art*. Macon, GA: Mercer University Press, 1999.

Dalferth, Ingolf U. "Selfless Passion: Kierkegaard on True Love." Paper presented at the Søren Kierkegaard Research Centre International Conference, Copenhagen, August 2012.

Dalrymple, Timothy. "Abraham: Framing Fear and Trembling." In *Kierkegaard and the Bible*, vol. 1, *The Old Testament*, edited by Lee C. Barrett and Jon Stewart, 43–88. Farnham, UK: Ashgate, 2009.

Damgaard, Iben. "Kierkegaard's Rewriting of Biblical Narratives: The Mirror of the Text." In *Kierkegaard and the Bible*, vol. 1, *The Old Testament*, edited by Lee C. Barrett and Jon Stewart, 207–30. Farnham, UK: Ashgate, 2009.

De Lacoste, Guillermine. "The Dialectic of the *Real Erotic* and Eroticism in Kierkegaard's *Seducer's Diary*." *Kierkegaardiana* 22 (2002) 125–38.

Dewey, Bradley R. "The Erotic-Demonic in Kierkegaard's 'Diary of the Seducer.'" *Scandinavica* 10 (1971) 1–24.

———. "Kierkegaard and the Blue Testament." *Harvard Theological Review* 60 (1967) 391–409.

DeYoung, Kevin, and Ted Kluck. *Why We're Not Emergent (By Two Guys Who Should Be)*. Chicago: Moody, 2008.

Downing, Eric. *Artificial I's: The Self as Artwork in Ovid, Kierkegaard and Thomas Mann*. Tübingen: Niemeyer, 1993.

Edwards, Aaron P. "Kierkegaard as Socratic Street Preacher? Reimagining the Dialectic of Direct and Indirect Communication for Christian Proclamation." *Harvard Theological Review* 110 (2017) 280–300.

———. "Kierkegaard the Preacher." In *T&T Clark Companion to the Theology of Kierkegaard*, edited by Aaron P. Edwards and David J. Gouwens, 139–58. London: T. & T. Clark, 2020.

———. "Life in Kierkegaard's Imaginary Rural Parish: Preaching, Correctivity, and the Gospel." *Toronto Journal of Theology* 30 (2014) 235–46.

———. "Secular Apathy and the Public Paradox of the Gospel: Towards Radical Inculturated Proclamation." *International Journal of Public Theology* 13 (2019) 413–31.

———. *A Theology of Preaching and Dialectic: Scriptural Tension, Heraldic Proclamation, and the Pneumatological Moment*. London: T. & T. Clark, 2020.

———. "Waddling Geese in the Pulpit: Kierkegaard, Hermeneutics and Preaching." *Theology* 115 (2012) 180–89.

Edwards, Aaron P., and David J. Gouwens, eds. *T&T Clark Companion to the Theology of Kierkegaard*. London: T. & T. Clark, 2020.

Engelke, Matthias. "David and Solomon: Models of Repentance and Evasion of Guilt." In *Kierkegaard and the Bible*, vol. 1, *The Old Testament*, edited by Lee C. Barrett and Jon Stewart, 101–14. Farnham, UK: Ashgate, 2009.

Evans, C. Stephen. *Kierkegaard and Spirituality: Accountability as the Meaning of Human Existence*. Grand Rapids: Eerdmans, 2019.

———. "A Misunderstood Reformer." *Christianity Today*, September 21, 1984.

Fremstedahl, Roe, and Timothy P. Jackson. "Salvation/Eternal Happiness." In *Kierkegaard's Concepts*, vol. 6, *Salvation to Writing*, edited by Steven Emmanuel et al., 1–8. Farnham, UK: Ashgate, 2015.

Furtak, Rick Anthony. "The Insights of Love: Kierkegaard on Passion and Truthfulness; or, The Reasons of the Heart." Paper presented at the Søren Kierkegaard Research Centre International Conference, Copenhagen, August 2012.

Garff, Joakim. *Søren Kierkegaard: A Biography*. Translated by Bruce H. Kirmmse. Princeton: Princeton University Press, 2005.

Gibbs, Eddie, and Ryan K. Bolger. *Emerging Churches: Creating Christian Community in Postmodern Cultures*. Grand Rapids: Baker Academic, 2005.

Goethe, Johann Wolfgang. *The Sorrows of Young Werther*. Translated by Michael Hulse. London: Penguin, 1989.

Gouwens, David J. *Kierkegaard as Religious Thinker*. Cambridge: Cambridge University Press, 1996.

———. *Kierkegaard's Dialectic of the Imagination*. New York: Lang, 1991.

———. "Kierkegaard's *Either/Or*, Part One: Patterns of Interpretation." In *Either/Or, I*, edited by Robert Perkins, 5–50. International Kierkegaard Commentary 3. Macon, GA: Mercer University Press, 1995.

Hannay, Alastair. "Something on Hermeneutics and Communication in Kierkegaard after All." Paper delivered at the Søren Kierkegaard Research Centre International Conference, Copenhagen, June 2001.

Hartshorne, M. Holmes. *Kierkegaard, Godly Deceiver: The Nature and Meaning of His Pseudonymous Writings.* New York: Columbia University Press, 1990.

Hauerwas, Stanley. *The Work of Theology.* Grand Rapids: Eerdmans, 2015.

Hauerwas, Stanley, and William H. Willimon. *Resident Aliens: Life in the Christian Colony.* Nashville: Abingdon, 1989.

Hinkson, Craig. "Luther and Kierkegaard: Theologians of the Cross." *International Journal of Systematic Theology* 3 (2001) 27–45.

———. "Will the Real Martin Luther Please Stand Up! Kierkegaard's View of Luther versus the Evolving Perceptions of the Tradition." In *For Self Examination and Judge for Yourself,* edited by Robert Perkins, 37–76. International Kierkegaard Commentary 21. Macon, GA: Mercer University Press, 2002.

Holm, Anders. "Kierkegaard and the Church." In *The Oxford Handbook of Kierkegaard,* edited by John Lippitt and George Pattison, 112–28. Oxford: Oxford University Press, 2013.

Holm, Isak Winkel. "Monstrous Aesthetics: Literature and Philosophy in Søren Kierkegaard." *Nineteenth-Century Prose* 32 (2005) 52–74.

———. *Tanken i billedet. Kierkegaards poetic.* Copenhagen: Gyldendal, 1998.

Holmer, Paul L. "Kierkegaard and the Sermon." *Journal of Religion* 37 (1957) 1–9.

Hough, Sheridan. *Kierkegaard's Dancing Tax Collector: Faith, Finitude, and Silence.* Oxford: Oxford University Press, 2015.

Johnson, Claudia Durst, and Vernon Johnson. *The Social Impact of the Novel: A Reference Guide.* Westport, CT: Greenwood, 2002.

Johnson, Howard A. "Kierkegaard and the Church." *Kierkegaardiana* 8 (1971) 64–79.

Josipovici, Gabriel. "Kierkegaard and the Novel." In *Kierkegaard: A Critical Reader,* edited by Jonathan Rée and Jane Chamberlain, 114–28. Oxford: Blackwell, 1998.

Jung-Kim, David Yoon, and Joel D. S. Rasmussen. "Martin Luther: Reform, Secularization, and the Question of His 'True Successor.'" In *Kierkegaard and the Renaissance and Modern Traditions,* vol. 2, *Theology,* edited by Jon Stewart, 173–217. Farnham, UK: Ashgate, 2009.

Kierkegaard, Søren. *Attack upon "Christendom," 1854–1855.* Translated by Walter Lowrie. Oxford: Oxford University Press, 1944.

———. *The Book on Adler.* Translated by Howard V. Hong and Edna H. Hong. Princeton: Princeton University Press, 1998.

———. *Christian Discourses* and *The Crisis in the Life of an Actress.* Translated by Howard V. Hong and Edna H. Hong. Princeton: Princeton University Press, 2009.

———. *The Concept of Anxiety.* Edited and translated by Reidar Thomte, with Albert B. Anderson. Princeton: Princeton University Press, 1980.

———. *The Concept of Irony with Continual Reference to Socrates.* Translated by Howard V. Hong and Edna H. Hong. Princeton: Princeton University Press, 1992.

———. *Concluding Unscientific Postscript.* Vol. 1. Translated by Howard V. Hong and Edna H. Hong. Princeton: Princeton University Press, 1992.

———. *Eighteen Upbuilding Discourses.* Translated by Howard V. Hong and Edna H. Hong. Princeton: Princeton University Press, 1990.

———. *Fear and Trembling and Repetition.* Translated by Howard V. Hong and Edna H. Hong. Princeton: Princeton University Press, 1983.

———. *Fear and Trembling*. Translated by Alastair Hannay. London: Penguin, 2005.

———. *For Self-Examination* and *Judge for Yourself!* Translated by Howard V. Hong and Edna H. Hong. Princeton: Princeton University Press, 1991.

———. *Gospel of Sufferings*. Translated by A. S. Aldworth and W. S. Ferries. Cambridge: Clarke, 2015.

———. *Letters and Documents*. Translated by Henrik Rosenmeier. Princeton: Princeton University Press, 1978.

———. *"The Moment" and Late Writings*. Translated by Howard V. Hong and Edna H. Hong. Princeton: Princeton University Press, 1998.

———. *Philosophical Crumbs*. Translated by M. G. Piety. Oxford: Oxford University Press, 2009.

———. *The Point of View*. Translated by Howard V. Hong and Edna H. Hong. Princeton: Princeton University Press, 1998.

———. *Practice in Christianity*. Translated by Howard V. Hong and Edna H. Hong. Princeton: Princeton University Press, 1992.

———. *The Present Age*. Translated by Alexander Dru. London: Collins, 1962.

———. *Provocations: Spiritual Writings of Kierkegaard*. Edited by C. E. Moore. New York: Orbis, 2003.

———. *The Seducer's Diary*. Translated by Alastair Hannay. London: Penguin, 2007.

———. *The Sickness unto Death*. Translated by Howard V. Hong and Edna H. Hong. Princeton: Princeton University Press, 1980.

———. *Søren Kierkegaard's Journals and Papers*. Vols. 1–6. Edited and translated by Howard V. Hong and Edna H. Hong. Bloomington: Indiana University Press, 1967–78.

———. *Stages on Life's Way*. Translated by Howard V. Hong and Edna H. Hong. Princeton: Princeton University Press, 1988.

———. *Upbuilding Discourses in Various Spirits*. Translated by Howard V. Hong and Edna H. Hong. Princeton: Princeton University Press, 1993.

———. *Without Authority*. Translated by Howard V. Hong and Edna H. Hong. Princeton: Princeton University Press, 1997.

———. *Works of Love*. Translated by Howard V. Hong and Edna H. Hong. Princeton: Princeton University Press, 1998.

Kimball, Dan. *The Emerging Church: Vintage Christianity for New Generations*. Grand Rapids: Zondervan, 2003.

Kirkpatrick, Matthew D. *Attacks on Christendom in a World Come of Age: Kierkegaard, Bonhoeffer, and the Question of "Religionless" Christianity*. Eugene, OR: Pickwick, 2011.

Kirmmse, Bruce H. *Kierkegaard in Golden Age Denmark*. Bloomington: Indiana University Press, 1990.

Kline, Peter. *Passion for Nothing: Kierkegaard's Apophatic Theology*. Minneapolis: Fortress, 2017.

Kolb, Robert. *Martin Luther and the Enduring Word of God: The Wittenberg School and Its Scripture-Centred Proclamation*. Grand Rapids: Baker, 2016.

Laura Hall, Amy. *Kierkegaard and the Treachery of Love*. Cambridge: Cambridge University Press, 2002.

Law, David R. *Kierkegaard as Negative Theologian*. Oxford: Oxford University Press, 1993.

———. "Kierkegaard's Anti-Ecclesiology: The Attack on Christendom, 1854–1855." *International Journal for the Study of the Christian Church* 7 (2007) 86–108.

———. "Redeeming the Penultimate: Discipleship and Church in the Thought of Søren Kierkegaard and Dietrich Bonhoeffer." *International Journal for the Study of the Christian Church* 11 (2011) 14–26.

Lowrie, Walter. *Kierkegaard.* Vol. 1. New York: Harper Torchbooks, 1962.

Luther, Martin. *The Bondage of the Will.* Translated by J. I. Packer and O. R. Johnston. Grand Rapids: Revell, 1997.

Mahn, Jason A. *Becoming a Christian in Christendom: Radical Discipleship and the Way of the Cross in America's "Christian" Culture.* Minneapolis: Fortress, 2016.

———. *Fortunate Fallibility: Kierkegaard and the Power of Sin.* New York: Oxford University Press, 2011.

Marrs, Daniel. "Love-as-Confession in 'The Woman Who Was a Sinner.'" Paper presented at the Søren Kierkegaard Research Centre International Conference, Copenhagen, August 2012.

Martin, Clancy W. "A Common Mistake about Kierkegaard's *The Seducer's Diary.*" In *Søren Kierkegaard and the Word(s): Essays on Hermeneutics and Communication,* edited by Paul Houe and Gordon D. Marino, 192–203. Copenhagen: Reitzel, 2003.

Martinez, Luis Guerrero. "Melancholy as a 'Romantic Passion': Werther and Kierkegaard." In *La melancolía entre la psicología, la filosofía y la cultura: Lecturas de Sileno,* edited by Valerie Martija et al. Mexico City: Universidad Iberoamericana Ciudad de México, 2010.

Matulštík, Martin J., and Merold Westphal, eds. *Kierkegaard and Postmodernity.* Bloomington: Indiana University Press, 1995.

McBride, William L. "Sartre's Debts to Kierkegaard: A Partial Reckoning." In *Kierkegaard and Postmodernity,* edited by Martin J. Matulštík and Merold Westphal, 18–42. Bloomington: Indiana University Press, 1995.

McCormack, Bruce. *Karl Barth's Critically Realistic Dialectical Theology: Its Genesis and Development, 1910–1936.* Oxford: Clarendon, 1995.

McDonald, William. "Kierkegaard and Romanticism." In *The Oxford Handbook of Kierkegaard,* edited by John Lippitt and George Pattison, 94–111. Oxford: Oxford University Press, 2013.

McKinnon, Alastair. "Barth's Relation to Kierkegaard: Some Further Light." *Canadian Journal of Theology* 13 (1967) 31–41.

McKnight, Scot. "Five Streams of the Emerging Church." *Christianity Today,* January 19, 2007. https://www.christianitytoday.com/ct/2007/february/11.35.html.

McLaren, Brian. *A New Kind of Christianity: Ten questions That Are Transforming the Faith.* London: Hodder & Stoughton, 2011.

Mjaaland, Marius Timmann. "Postmodernism and Deconstruction: Paradox, Sacrifice, and the Future of Writing." In *A Companion to Kierkegaard,* edited by Jon Stewart, 96–109. Chichester, UK: Wiley-Blackwell, 2015.

———. "*Theaetetus:* Giving Birth, or Kierkegaard's Socratic Maieutics." In *Kierkegaard and the Greek World,* vol. 1, *Socrates and Plato,* edited by Jon Stewart and Katalin Nun, 115–46. Farnham, UK: Ashgate, 2010.

Mooney, Edward F. "Pseudonyms and Style." In *The Oxford Handbook of Kierkegaard,* edited by John Lippitt and George Pattison, 191–210. Oxford: Oxford University Press, 2013.

Morgan, Jeffrey. "Grace and Christianity's Requirement: Moral Striving in Kierkegaard's *Judge For Yourself!*" *Heythrop Journal* 55 (2014) 916–26.

Muench, Paul. "*Apology*: Kierkegaard's Socratic Point of View." In *Kierkegaard and the Greek World*, vol. 1, *Socrates and Plato*, edited by Jon Stewart and Katalin Nun, 3–25. Farnham, UK: Ashgate, 2010.

———. "The Socratic Method of Kierkegaard's Pseudonym Johannes Climacus: Indirect Communication and the Art of 'Taking Away.'" In *Søren Kierkegaard and the Word(s): Essays on Hermeneutics and Communication*, edited by Paul Houe and Gordon D. Marino, 139–50. Copenhagen: Reitzel, 2003.

Mulder, Jack, Jr. "Grace and Rigor in Kierkegaard's Reception of the Church Fathers." In *A Companion to Kierkegaard*, edited by Jon Stewart, 155–66. Chichester, UK: Wiley-Blackwell, 2015.

Murray, Stuart. *Post-Christendom: Church and Mission in a Strange New World*. Milton Keynes, UK: Paternoster, 2004.

Newbigin, Lesslie. *Truth to Tell: The Gospel as Public Truth*. London: SPCK, 1991.

Nietzsche, Friedrich. *The Twilight of the Idols* and *The Anti-Christ*. Translated by R. J. Hollingdale. London: Penguin, 1969.

Noll, Mark, et al. *Evangelicals: Who They Have Been, Are Now, and Could Be*. Grand Rapids: Eerdmans, 2019.

Nowachek, Matthew T. "Living within the Sacred Tension: Kierkegaard's Climacean Works as a Guide for Christian Existence." *Heythrop Journal* 55 (2014) 883–902.

Oakes, Kenneth. *Reading Karl Barth: A Guide to the "Epistle to the Romans."* Eugene, OR: Cascade, 2011.

O'Donovan, Oliver. *The Desire of the Nations: Rediscovering the Roots of Political Theology*. Cambridge: Cambridge University Press, 1996.

O'Regan, Cyril. "The Rule of Chaos and the Perturbation of Love." In *Kierkegaard and Christian Faith*, edited by Paul Martens and C. Stephen Evans, 131–56. Waco, TX: Baylor University Press, 2016.

Olson, Roger, E. "Was Kierkegaard an Evangelical? Part 1." *Patheos*, August 29, 2011. https://www.patheos.com/blogs/rogereolson/2011/08/was-kierkegaard-an-evangelical-part-1/.

Pattison, George. *Kierkegaard and the Quest for Unambiguous Life: Between Romanticism and Modernism*. Oxford: Oxford University Press, 2013.

———. *Kierkegaard and the Theology of the Nineteenth Century: The Paradox and the "Point of Contact."* Cambridge: Cambridge University Press, 2012.

———. "Kierkegaard, Freedom, Love." Paper presented at the UK Søren Kierkegaard Society Conference, University of Glasgow, May 2016.

———. "Kierkegaard the Theology Student." In *T&T Clark Companion to the Theology of Kierkegaard*, edited by Aaron P. Edwards and David J. Gouwens, 89–109. London: T. & T. Clark, 2020.

———. *Kierkegaard's Upbuilding Discourses: Philosophy, Theology, Literature*. London: Routledge, 2002.

———. "Looks of Love: The Seducer and the Christ." *Kierkegaardiana* 24 (2007) 182–97.

———. "The Theory and Practice of Language and Communication in Kierkegaard's *Upbuilding Discourses*." *Kierkegaardiana* 19 (1998) 81–94.

———. "'Who' Is the Discourse? A Study in Kierkegaard's Religious Literature." *Kierkegaardiana* 16 (1993) 28–45.

Pattison, George, and Helle Mølle Jensen. *Kierkegaard's Pastoral Dialogues.* Eugene, OR: Cascade, 2012.

Perez-Alvarez, Eliseo. *A Vexing Gadfly: The Late Kierkegaard on Economic Matters.* Cambridge: Clarke, 2011.

Plato. *Theaetetus.* Translated by John McDowell. Oxford: Clarendon, 1978.

Plekon, Michael. "Kierkegaard at the End: His 'Last' Sermon, Eschatology and the Attack on the Church." *Faith and Philosophy* 17 (2000) 68–86.

Podmore, Simon D. "The Lightning and the Earthquake: Kierkegaard on the *Anfechtung* of Luther." *Heythrop Journal* 47 (2006) 562–78.

———. *Struggling with God: Kierkegaard and the Temptation of Spiritual Trial.* Cambridge: Clarke, 2013.

Polk, Timothy H. *The Biblical Kierkegaard: Reading by the Rule of Faith.* Macon, GA: Mercer University Press, 1997.

———. "Kierkegaard's Use of the New Testament: Intratextuality, Indirect Communication, and Appropriation." In *Kierkegaard and the Bible,* vol. 2, *The New Testament,* edited by Lee C. Barrett and Jon Stewart, 237–48. Farnham, UK: Ashgate, 2010.

Pons, Jolita. *Stealing a Gift: Kierkegaard's Pseudonyms and the Bible.* New York: Fordham University Press, 2004.

Poole, Roger. *Kierkegaard: The Indirect Communication.* Charlottesville: University Press of Virginia, 1993.

———. "The Unknown Kierkegaard: Twentieth Century Receptions." In *The Cambridge Companion to Kierkegaard,* edited by Alastair Hannay and Gordon Marino, 48–75. Cambridge: Cambridge University Press, 1998.

Possen, David D. "*Protagoras* and *Republic*: Kierkegaard on Socratic Irony." In *Kierkegaard and the Greek World,* vol. 1, *Socrates and Plato,* edited by Jon Stewart and Katalin Nun, 87–104. Farnham, UK: Ashgate, 2010.

Prenter, Regin. "Luther and Lutheranism." In *Kierkegaard and Great Traditions,* edited by Niels Thulstrup and Marie Mikulova Thulstrup, 121–72. Bibliotheca Kierkegaardiana 6. Copenhagen: Reitzels Boghandel, 1981.

Purver, Judith. "Eichendorff: Kierkegaard's Reception of a German Romantic." In *Kierkegaard and His German Contemporaries,* vol. 3, *Literature and Aesthetics,* edited by Jon Stewart, 25–49. Aldershot, UK: Ashgate, 2008.

Pyper, Hugh S. *The Joy of Kierkegaard: Essays on Kierkegaard as a Biblical Reader.* Sheffield: Equinox, 2011.

Rasmussen, Joel D. S. "Kierkegaard's Biblical Hermeneutics: Imitation, Imaginative Freedom, and Paradoxical Fixation." In *Kierkegaard and the Bible,* vol. 2, *The New Testament,* edited by Lee C. Barrett and Jon Stewart, 249–84. Farnham, UK: Ashgate, 2010.

Roberts, Kyle A. *Emerging Prophet: Kierkegaard and the Postmodern People of God.* Eugene, OR: Cascade Books, 2013.

———. "Francis Schaeffer: How Not to Read Kierkegaard." In *Kierkegaard's Influence on Theology,* vol. 2, *Anglophone and Scandinavian Protestant Theology,* edited by Jon Stewart, 173–87. Farnham, UK: Ashgate, 2012.

———. "James: Putting Faith to Action." In *Kierkegaard and the Bible,* vol. 2, *The New Testament,* edited by Lee C. Barrett and Jon Stewart, 209–20. Farnham, UK: Ashgate, 2010.

Rollins, Peter. *Insurrection: To Believe Is Human, to Doubt, Divine.* London: Hodder & Stoughton, 2011.

———. "Pyrotheology: From Unraveling to Raveling." https://peterrollins.com/pyrotheology.

———. "Ripping the Curtain: A Conversation with Peter Rollins, PhD." *Stance* 12 (April 2019) 127–45.

Roper, Lyndal. *Martin Luther: Renegade and Prophet.* London: Vintage, 2017.

Ryrie, Alec. *Protestants: The Radicals Who Made the Modern World.* London: Collins, 2017.

Salter, William Mackintire. "Schopenhauer's Contact with Theology." *Harvard Theological Review* 4 (July 1911) 271–310.

Sartre, Jean-Paul. *Being and Nothingness: An Essay on Phenomenological Ontology.* Translated by Paris Gallimard. London: Routledge, 2003.

Schaeffer, Francis. *Escape from Reason.* Downers Grove, IL: InterVarsity, 1968.

———. *The God Who Is There.* Downers Grove, IL: InterVarsity, 1968.

Schreiber, Gerhard. "Christoph Schrempf: The 'Swabian Socrates' as Translator of Kierkegaard." In *Kierkegaard's Influence on Theology*, vol. 1, *German Protestant Theology*, edited by Jon Stewart, 275–320. Farnham, UK: Ashgate, 2012.

Shakespeare, Steven. "Kierkegaard and Postmodernism." In *The Oxford Handbook of Kierkegaard*, edited by John Lippitt and George Pattison, 464–83. Oxford: Oxford University Press, 2013.

Slemmons, Timothy Matthew. "Toward a Penitential Homiletic: Authority and Direct Communication in Christian Proclamation." PhD diss., Princeton Theological Seminary, 2004.

Smith, James K. A. *Awaiting the King: Reforming Public Theology.* Grand Rapids: Baker Academic, 2017.

———. *Who's Afraid of Postmodernism? Taking Derrida, Foucault, and Lyotard to Church.* Grand Rapids: Baker Academic, 2006.

Snowden, Barry L. "By What Authority? Kierkegaard on Pastoral Authority and Authenticity." *Methodist Quarterly Review* 5 (Winter 1985) 43–57.

Soderquist, K. Brian. "Irony." In *The Oxford Handbook of Kierkegaard*, edited by John Lippitt and George Pattison, 344–64. Oxford: Oxford University Press, 2013.

Søe, N. H. "Karl Barth." In *The Legacy and Interpretation of Kierkegaard*, edited by Niels Thulstrup and M. Mikulvá Thulstrup, 224–37. Bibliotheca Kierkegaardiana 8. Copenhagen: Reitzel, 1981.

Søltoft, Pia. "The Power of Eloquence: On the Relation between Ethics and Rhetoric in Preaching." In *Søren Kierkegaard and the Word(s): Essays on Hermeneutics and Communication*, edited by Paul Houe and Gordon D. Marino, 240–47. Copenhagen: Reitzel, 2003.

Sponheim, Paul R. "God's Changelessness: The Triumph of Grace in Law and Gospel as 'Archimedean Point.'" In *"The Moment" and Late Writings*, edited by Robert L. Perkins, 101–28. International Kierkegaard Commentary 23. Macon, GA: Mercer University Press, 2009.

Spurgeon, C. H. *Lectures to My Students.* London: Passmore & Alabaster, 1875.

Stan, Leo. "The Lily in the Field and the Bird in the Air: An Endless Liturgy in Kierkegaard's Authorship." In *Kierkegaard and the Bible*, vol. 2, *The New Testament*, edited by Lee C. Barrett and Jon Stewart, 55–78. Farnham, UK: Ashgate, 2010.

Steiner, George. "The Wound of Negativity: Two Kierkegaard Texts." In *Kierkegaard: A Critical Reader*, edited by Jonathan Rée and Jane Chamberlain, 103–13. Oxford: Blackwell, 1998.

Stewart, Jon. *Kierkegaard's Relation to Hegel Reconsidered.* Cambridge: Cambridge University Press, 2003.

Stewart, Jon, and Katalin Nun. "Goethe: A German Classic through the Filter of the Danish Golden Age." In *Kierkegaard and His German Contemporaries*, vol. 3, *Literature and Aesthetics*, edited by Jon Stewart, 52–96. Aldershot, UK: Ashgate, 2008.

Storer, Kevin M. "Multiplying Meaning, Becoming an Individual: Kierkegaard's Upbuilding Hermeneutic of Scripture in the Discourses." PhD diss., University of Manchester, 2019.

Taylor, Justin. "Rob Bell Revisited: 5 Years Later." *Gospel Coalition*, June 2, 2016. https://www.thegospelcoalition.org/blogs/justin-taylor/rob-bell-revisited-5-years-later/.

Thompson, Curtis L. "Hans Latten Martensen: A Speculative Theologian Determining the Agenda of the Day." In *Kierkegaard and His Danish Contemporaries*, vol. 2, *Theology*, edited by Jon Stewart, 229–66. London: Routledge, 2009.

Thompson, Josiah. *Kierkegaard.* London: Gollancz, 1974.

Thulstrup, Niels. *Kierkegaard and the Church in Denmark.* Edited by Niels Thulstrup and Marie Mikulová Thulstrup. Bibliotheca Kierkegaardiana 13. Copenhagen: Reitzels Forlag, 1984.

Tiemeyer, Nathan. "Donald Miller: I Don't Connect with God at Church." *Every Square Inch*, February 4, 2014. https://www.everysquareinch.net/donald-miller-i-dont-connect-with-god-at-church/.

Tietjen, Mark A. *Kierkegaard: A Christian Missionary to Christians.* Downers Grove: IVP Academic, 2016.

———. *Kierkegaard, Communication, and Virtue: Authorship as Edification.* Bloomington: Indiana University Press, 2013.

Tietz, Christiane. "Dietrich Bonhoeffer: Standing 'in the Tradition of Paul, Luther, Kierkegaard, in the Tradition of Genuine Christian Thinking.'" In *Kierkegaard's Influence on Theology*, vol. 1, *German Protestant Theology*, edited by Jon Stewart, 43–64. Farnham, UK: Ashgate, 2012.

Tilley, J. Michael. "Christendom." In *Kierkegaard's Concepts*, vol. 1, *Absolute to Church*, edited by Steven M. Emmanuel et al., 207–10. Farnham, UK: Ashgate, 2014.

———. "Church." In *Kierkegaard's Concepts*, vol. 1, *Absolute to Church*, edited by Steven M. Emmanuel et al, 211–14. Farnham, UK: Ashgate, 2014.

———. "Corrective." In *Kierkegaard's Concepts*, vol. 2, *Classicism to Enthusiasm*, edited by Steven M. Emmanuel et al, 81–86. Farnham, UK: Ashgate, 2014.

Tolstrup, Christian Fink. "Jakob Peter Mynster: A Guiding Thread in Kierkegaard's Authorship?" In *Kierkegaard and his Danish Contemporaries*, vol. 2, *Theology*, edited by Jon Stewart, 267–82. Farnham, UK: Ashgate, 2009.

———. "'Playing a Profane Game with Holy Things': Understanding Kierkegaard's Critical Encounter with Bishop Mynster." In *Practice in Christianity*, edited by Robert Perkins, 245–74. International Kierkegaard Commentary 20. Macon, GA: Mercer University Press, 2004.

Torrance, Andrew. *The Freedom to Become a Christian: A Kierkegaardian Account of Human Transformation in Relationship with God.* London: T. & T. Clark, 2016.

Vainio, Olli-Pekka. "Kierkegaard's Eucharistic Spirituality." *Theology Today* 67 (2010) 15–23.

Van der Ven, Johannes A. *Ecclesiology in Context*. Grand Rapids: Eerdmans, 1996.

Van Til, Cornelius. "A Letter from Cornelius Van Til to Francis Schaeffer (11 Mar 1969)." *Ordained Servant* 6 (October 1997). https://www.opc.org/OS/html/V6/4d.html.

Vanhoozer, Kevin. "Pilgrim's Digress: Christian Thinking on and about the Post/Modern Way." In *Christianity and the Postmodern Turn: Six Views*, edited by Myron B. Penner, 71–104. Grand Rapids: Brazos, 2005.

Walsh, Sylvia. *Living Christianly: Kierkegaard's Dialectic of Christian Existence*. Philadelphia: University of Pennsylvania Press, 2006.

———. *Thinking Christianly in an Existential Mode*. Oxford: Oxford University Press, 2009.

Warner, Michael, et al., eds. *Varieties of Secularism in a Secular Age*. Cambridge: Harvard University Press, 2010.

Webster, John. "Christ, Church, and Reconciliation." In *Word and Church: Essays in Christian Dogmatics*, 211–30. London: T. & T. Clark, 2016.

Wells, Mark A. "Love as Humanizing Virtue in Kierkegaard's Thought." Paper presented at the Søren Kierkegaard Research Centre International Conference, Copenhagen, August 2012.

Wells, William, III. "The Influence of Kierkegaard on the Theology of Karl Barth." PhD diss., University of Syracuse, 1970.

Westphal, Merold. "Kierkegaard, Theology, and Post-Christendom." In *T. & T. Clark Companion to the Theology of Kierkegaard*, edited by Aaron P. Edwards and David J. Gouwens, 493–510. London: T. & T. Clark, 2020.

Weyel, Birgit. "Practical Theology as a Hermeneutical Science of Lived Religion." *Practical Theology* 18 (2014) 150–59.

Wilke, Matthias. "Emmanuel Hirsch: A German Dialogue with 'Saint Søren.'" In *Kierkegaard's Influence on Theology*, vol. 1, *German Protestant Theology*, edited by Jon Stewart, 155–84. Farnham, UK: Ashgate, 2012.

Williams, Will. "Ecclesiastes: Vanity, Grief, and the Distinctions of Wisdom." In *Kierkegaard and the Bible*, vol. 1, *The Old Testament*, edited by Lee C. Barrett and Jon Stewart, 179–94. Farnham, UK: Ashgate, 2010.

Willimon, William H. *Conversations with Barth on Preaching*. Nashville: Abingdon, 2006.

———. "Preaching with Karl Barth." In *The Word in This World: Two Sermons*, translated by Christopher Asprey, edited by Kurt I. Johanson, 10–22. Vancouver, BC: Regent College Publishing, 2007.

Wood, Arthur Skevington. *Captive to the Word: Martin Luther, Doctor of Sacred Scripture*. Exeter: Paternoster, 1969.

Ziegler, Philip G. "Barth's Criticisms of Kierkegaard—a Striking Out at Phantoms?" *International Journal of Systematic Theology* 9 (2007) 434–51.

———., ed. *Eternal God, Eternal Life: Theological Investigations into the Concept of Immortality*. London: T. & T. Clark, 2016.

———. *Militant Grace: The Apocalyptic Turn and the Future of Christian Theology*. Grand Rapids: Baker Academic, 2018.

Ziolkowski, Eric. *The Literary Kierkegaard*. Evanston: Northwestern University Press, 2011.

Index

Ingram Content Group UK Ltd.
Milton Keynes UK
UKHW041540070323
418182UK00004B/251

9 781725 259584